A Short History of
MALAYSIA, SINGAPORE and BRUNEI

C. Mary Turnbull

GRAHAM BRASH SINGAPORE

©C. Mary Turnbull 1980
First published by Cassell Australia Ltd. 1980
Asian Edition published by Graham Brash (Pte.) Ltd. 1981

Reprinted 1987
ISBN 9971-947-06-4

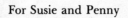For Susie and Penny

Contents

Illustrations

Tables

Maps

Foreword

Tradition persists into the present, and long-established patterns of ancient society are reflected in contemporary behaviour. In this book, therefore, 'modern' history is regarded in the context of the longer history of the country, and reference is made to early Asian trade and the rivalry of maritime and land-based kingdoms.

The history of Malaysia poses special problems. The national boundaries of modern Southeast Asia are a comparatively new creation. For the most part they are artificial products of European empires. But, though recent, they help to determine the way we look at the past, leading us to think in terms of a series of national histories — histories of Burma, Indonesia, Vietnam, Kampuchea. These national histories may serve to strengthen a sense of national identity in the countries of Southeast Asia, but they are nonetheless a distortion of the past. For the greater part of the history of Southeast Asian societies it would be more correct to think in terms, not of nations, with clear territorial claims, but rather of political centres, with power radiating out from a series of royal capitals — Pagan, Ayuthia, Angkor — or from smaller principalities, until in the nineteenth century external pressures re-shaped Southeast Asian politics and created new national frameworks. Malaysia may appear especially as an artificial creation. Only the accidents of British and Dutch empire determined that an international boundary should run through the Straits of Melaka, or that one part of the island of Borneo should be Indonesian territory and another part Malaysian territory.

This book sets the three countries studied in a long-term context. If history must have a utilitarian purpose, it is hoped that an emphasis on the more distant past will lead students to a more subtle and sympathetic understanding of the character of modern Malaysia, Singapore and Brunei.

J. D. LEGGE,
Monash University.

Author's Note

My connection with Southeast Asia began in 1952 when I was appointed to the Malayan Civil Service at a time when the Federation of Malaya was battling to overcome the Communist Emergency and at the same time striving for political independence from colonial rule. This kindled an interest in the country's past history and induced me in 1955 to return to academic life, where for nearly a quarter of a century I have been researching into the history of Malaysia and Singapore. The first sixteen of those years were spent teaching history at the Universities of Singapore and Malaya, where I was privileged to witness at first hand the dramatic events leading to the formation of Malaysia and the separation of Singapore to become an independent state.

I am grateful to the Centre of Asian Studies, University of Hong Kong, which made it possible for me to undertake research in Singapore and Malaysia during the long vacation in 1975 and to spend some time at the Public Record Office in London in the summer of 1976.

In acquiring and reproducing the illustrations I am indebted to the Arkib Negara Malaysia, the Muzium Negara in Kuala Lumpur, the Muzium Brunei, the Information Department of Sabah, and the National Portrait Gallery, London. I am particularly grateful for help given in collecting photographs to Tan Sri Datuk Mubin Sheppard, Hon. Secretary of the Malaysian Branch of the Royal Asiatic Society, and to Mr David McCredie, Curator of the Sabah Museum.

The maps were prepared by the Geography Department, University of Hong Kong, and I am grateful for their assistance.

Over the years I have benefited from the advice of people too numerous to mention here, but I owe a constant debt to my husband, Leonard Rayner, who has a longer experience of the region than my own. Dr Ron Hill kindly read the early sections of the book and made valuable suggestions.

As General Editor, Professor John Legge has been a source of sustained but gentle encouragement, and I am grateful for his patience and guidance which have seen the manuscript through a long period of gestation.

C. Mary Turnbull
University of Hong Kong

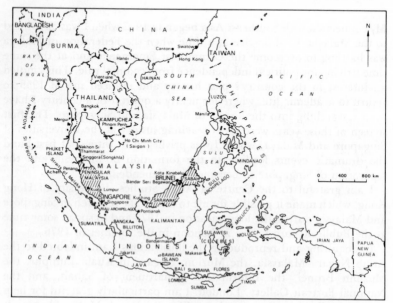

Southeast Asia

Introduction

Present day Malaysia, Singapore and Brunei are the successor states to the former British colonies and protectorates in Southeast Asia. The Malaysian federation is a constitutional kingdom, formed in 1963 and comprising eleven states in the Malay pensinsula, namely Penang, Melaka, Perak, Selangor, Negri Sembilan, Pahang, Kedah, Perlis, Kelantan, Trengganu and Johor, together with the two states of Sarawak and Sabah in northern Borneo. Singapore is a separate republic, which from 1963 to 1965 formed part of Malaysia, while Brunei remains a sultanate under British protection, but due to acquire independent sovereignty in 1983.

These distinct units emerged by historical accident rather than geographical or ethnic unity, since colonial rule cut across former links with parts of the Indonesian archipelago and with southern Thailand. At their closest points the Malay peninsula and the Borneo states are separated by 650 kilometres of the South China Sea, which represents more than a mere physical gulf and has meant major historical, cultural, social and economic differences. Yet, in some ways, the sea links more than it divides and the connections between these states transcend the temporary past subjection to British colonial rule and continued membership of the Commonwealth. While the Malay peninsula is physically part of mainland Southeast Asia, it is closer to maritime Southeast Asia in its climate, vegetation, ethnic and linguistic background, its social organization and economy.

The term 'Malaysia' acquired its current precise political connotation only in 1963. The word was apparently first coined in the 1830s and by the end of the nineteenth century was in general usage to describe a geographic-zoological-botanical region comprising the Malay peninsula, Singapore, Borneo, Sumatra and Java. In the twentieth century the term was sometimes employed to denote the indigenous people of the region, including some from the more easterly islands of the archipelago, and in 1937 Rupert Emerson used it to cover Malaya and the Netherlands Indies.[1]

Though small in size and in population, Malaysia, Singapore and Brunei are significant and complex in their heterogeneous racial composition, their long exposure to outside influences and cultures, and their place in the modern international economy.

The study of the region's history presents considerable difficulties. Little is known of the period before the fifteenth century when

1

geographical factors inhibited the growth of large centres of population. There are few stone inscriptions, a dearth of physical remains, and the climate did not favour the survival of tangible evidence, either in the form of buildings or written records. The oldest extant indigenous historical work, the *Sejarah Melayu,* or *Malay Annals,* dates at the earliest from the sixteenth century.

Historical evidence in more modern times is uneven and heavily weighted in favour of official and Western activities. A number of Malay histories described the glory of fifteenth century Melaka and the period of confused politics which followed. Of the immigrants who flooded into the Malay peninsula and to a lesser extent into Borneo in the British colonial period, the Europeans wrote prolifically of their experiences, the Chinese, Indians and Indonesians very little.

From the early twentieth century a small group of colonial scholar/administrators used some of the Malay texts to reconstruct the history of the individual Malay states, but most Western 'professional' historians, joined after the Second World War by increasing numbers of Western-trained local historians, tended at first to concentrate on official European activities in the nineteenth and first half of the twentieth centuries, a time of dramatic and rapid change, supported by comprehensive authoritative documentation.

Since the creation of the Malaysian federation in 1963 and the independence of Singapore two years later, history writing has been in a state of flux. In Singapore energies were devoted to the present and future rather than looking at the past, particularly a past which was so closely associated with colonialism. In Malaysia the special difficulties in creating a sense of nationhood in a plural society, where the nationalist movement in peninsular Malaysia had been based so much on a sense of *Malay* nationalism, introduced an element of sensitivity into many broad historical issues.

A new generation of historians reacted against the over absorption of past studies with government activities and came to realize that many of the most significant historical developments took place outside of official circles. They paid more attention to neglected Malay sources, to local and oral history, and to the story of economic, agricultural and commercial processes. The result has been somewhat fragmented, but the disparate evidence from a variety of sources, together with studies in geography, anthropology and archaeology, are combining to change our views and understanding of the history of the region, to affect our understanding of the nature of its society and why it evolved in this particular way. There are still enormous gaps in our knowledge, but perhaps the time has come to pull up the history of the region and examine the roots.

.. Emerson, R. *Malaysia: A Study in Direct and Indirect Rule.* Macmillian, New York, 1937; reprinted Oxford University Press, Kuala Lumpur, 1964.

CHAPTER 1

Land and People

Land

Lying between latitudes 1° and 7° north of the equator, the Malay peninsula and northern Borneo enjoy a uniformly hot, wet climate. The southwest monsoon, prevailing from May to September, and the northeast monsoon, blowing from October to April, bring some seasonal differences in rainfall but little in temperatures, which are high but not excessive, rarely rising much above 33° Celsius by day and sometimes falling by as much as 11°C at night. Nearly everywhere rainfall exceeds 2000 mm a year, and there is no marked dry season, but some regional variation. Northern Borneo and the east coast of the peninsula receive their heaviest rainfall at the height of the northeast monsoon in November–December, but the west coast and interior of the peninsula are wettest in the transition inter-monsoon periods.

Some 40 per cent of peninsular Malaysia is rugged mountain terrain and nearly three-quarters of the country is more than 330 metres above sea level. The main range stretches from the Thai border to inland Melaka parallel with the west coast, a formidable barrier with many 1700 metre peaks. The northern part of the country comprises a complex mountain mass, covering much of Kelantan, Trengganu and north Pahang, not so high as the main mountain range but including Gunong Tahan, peninsular Malaysia's highest peak, which is over 2400 metres. The west coast plain stretches unbroken for 900 kilometres from Perlis to Singapore, reaching a maximum width of sixty kilometres in Perak. East coast plains are narrow and not continuous, but the southern portion of the peninsula consists of low undulating hills and plains.

Sarawak, Sabah and Brunei are separated from Kalimantan (Indonesian Borneo) by a mountain divide, which reaches its peak in Mount Kinabalu in Sabah, at 4500 metres, the highest mountain in Southeast Asia outside of West Irian. While most of Sarawak consists of lowlying plain, Sabah is more mountainous, with a very narrow western coastal strip and disconnected if larger plains in the north and east.

People

Of Malaysia's 350 000 square kilometres of territory, east Malaysia, comprising some 200 000 square kilometres, forms the largest part but

3

carries a minority of the population. According to the last census taken in 1970 nearly 9 000 000 of Malaysia's ten-and-a-half million people lived in the peninsula, mainly in the west coast states, compared with a little under a million in Sarawak and 650 000 in Sabah. These proportions remain today, although the total Malaysian population has probably risen to about twelve million. More than two million people are concentrated on the 560 square kilometres of Singapore island, whereas Brunei with a land area ten times as great supports only 145 000 inhabitants.

The region is one of longstanding and widespread migration and immigration, which have produced a very mixed population. Apart from small minorities of Chinese, Indian and Arab traders, up to the early-nineteenth century most settlers were of Malayo–Polynesian stock. But in the period from the mid-nineteenth century until the Second World War the composition of the population changed dramatically, with a flood of immigrants from China, the Indian sub-continent and Ceylon, most of whom came to work in the tin mines or on the gambier, pepper, sugar, coffee and rubber plantations. While most intended to remain only a few years before returning to their homelands, many put down permanent roots in the Malay peninsula and northern Borneo, but they continued to remain distinct from the Malays and other peoples indigenous to the peninsula and the archipelago, the *bumiputras* of post-independence times.

Of the oldest indigenous groups, about 35 000 Negrito–Semang, Senoi–Temiar, Semai and Jakun aborigines remain in peninsular Malaya, and a few hundred Punan aborigines in Sarawak. Apart from those Jakuns who live in proximity with Malay peasants and have adopted a sedentary farming life, the aborigines keep to the forests of the main peninsular range and the far interior of Sarawak outside of the mainstream of modern life.

In peninsular Malaysia and Brunei the largest community are the Malays. But they constitute little more than half of the population of the peninsular states, and elsewhere Malays are in a minority, making up only 19 per cent of the inhabitants in Sarawak, 15 per cent in Singapore and less than 3 per cent in Sabah. The Malays are of mixed ethnic background, some having lived in the peninsula and on the northern Borneo coast for more than a millennium, others migrating in more recent times from Sumatra, Java, Sulawesi and other Indonesian islands, but they have adopted the Malay language, have assimilated to similar customs and subscribe to the Muslim faith.

The indigenous peoples of the northern Borneo territories belong to a diversity of linguistic, cultural and ethnic groups. In Sarawak the Sea Dyaks, or Ibans, and Land Dyaks together form the largest community, comprising nearly 40 per cent of the inhabitants, and in Sabah the biggest group are the Kadazans or Dusuns, who make up 28 per cent of the population. There are a number of other indigenous communities: coastal people such as the Bajau of Sabah, or the Kedayans, to be found in all three territories but mainly in Brunei; inland people such as the Kelabit and Murut, mainly of Sabah, or the Kenyah and Kayan of Sarawak; or the more widely dispersed Melanau of Sarawak and Bisaya of Sabah and Brunei.

The Chinese make up nearly four-fifths of Singapore's population and are the second largest community in all the other territories: 35 per cent in peninsular Malaysia, 30 per cent in Sarawak, 26 per cent in Brunei and 21 per cent in Sabah, with the greatest concentration in the former Straits Settlements of Singapore, Penang and Melaka and in the west coast peninsular states of Perak, Selangor, Negri Sembilan and Johor. The majority hailed originally from the southern Chinese provinces of Kwangtung and Fukien but belong to different dialect groups: Hokkiens, who predominate in Singapore, Melaka and Penang; Hakkas, who are the largest group in the Borneo territories and the tin mining and agricultural districts of peninsular Malaysia; Teochews, Cantonese and Hainanese.

The Indian minority is settled mainly in Singapore and the west coast Malay states, forming 11 per cent of the population of peninsular Malaysia and 7 per cent of Singaporeans. Pakistanis and Ceylonese are included in the 'Indian' community, which is very mixed. The majority come from south India and speak Tamil, Telugu or Malayalam, with an important minority of northerners made up of Gujaratis, Punjabis and Bengalis.

Much less numerous are the Eurasian population, chiefly living in the former Straits Settlements and tracing their European blood to Portuguese, Dutch and British ancestors; Arabs and Middle Eastern Jews, tiny but significant minorities based mainly in Singapore; Siamese in the northern Malay states; Filipinos in Sabah; and more widely scattered Indonesians.

The peoples of these territories are mixed not only in ethnic and linguistic origin but in customs and religion. The Malays, Arabs, some south Indians, Pakistanis and coastal Borneo people, such as the Bajau and Kedayans, are Muslims. Most Indians and Ceylonese are Hindus. Many Chinese are Buddhists or Taoists, while the Eurasians and many long settled Chinese and Indians hold the Christian faith. Most of the indigenous peoples of Borneo are animists, and Islam has only made headway in the interior in very recent years.

Chinese predominate in nearly all the larger towns in the Malay peninsula and northern Borneo, whereas the bulk of the Malay and indigenous Borneo people live in rural areas. A fair proportion of Indians are urban dwellers but many live on rubber plantations.

Livelihood

Much of the land area is difficult to develop economically, so that more
than 70 per cent of peninsular Malaysia and a larger proportion of the
Borneo states remain under dense rain forest. Despite this, Malaysia's
most important economic activity is agriculture. Singapore is intensely
urbanized with the vast majority of its population deriving their living
from commerce and manufacturing, while Brunei obtains the bulk of
its income from oil production.

Economic development in agriculture, mining, manufacturing and
commerce is concentrated in the western region of the Malay peninsula,
with outlets at the major ports of Singapore and Penang and rapidly
expanding Port Klang. Singapore launched an ambitious industrialization programme in the early-1960s, beginning with labour-
intensive production, such as textiles, which was appropriate to a small
island with no natural resources and a surplus labour force, but later
developing more highly skilled and capital-intensive industries, such as
electronics and oil refining.

In peninsular Malaysia more than four-fifths of the population is
rural based, and export-oriented agriculture remains the backbone of
the economy.

Rubber is by far the most important product: Malaysia's main foreign
exchange earner, its chief source of income and employment. Most rubber is grown west of the main mountain range in estates in the undulating foothill region or in small holdings on the coastal plain, and
also in areas of Kelantan and central Pahang within easy reach of the
railway.

Compared with rubber, other crops are of minor importance. Rice
comes second and is grown mainly on the fairly fertile alluvial plains of
Kedah and Kelantan, but even so Malaysia imports more rice than it exports. Coconuts are produced chiefly in Malay small holdings in the
coastal areas. Oil palm constitutes the second biggest estate crop but is
less important in terms of area under cultivation and employment than
coconuts and rice. First grown in well-drained coastal and riverine
alluvial areas of Perak, Selangor and Johor, oil palm production now
extends to a wider area of laterite soils in these states and in Trengganu,
and is almost entirely an estate crop. Pineapples, the most important
export fruit, support an important canning industry and are grown
mainly in the lowlying peaty soils of Johor. Small quantities of sugar-
cane, tea and coffee are produced, and cocoa farming is in the experi-
mental stage. Fisheries are important but mostly for domestic consump-
tion.

After rubber Malaysia's second most important product is tin, of
which it is the leading producer, accounting for 40 per cent of the
world's supply. 'Straits tin' is very pure and easily worked. Most is

surface-mined from alluvial sources by dredging or gravel pumping, and nearly three-quarters of production comes from the Perak and Selangor foothills region. Compared with tin, Malaysia's other minerals are negligible, and former mines for bauxite in Johor, low-grade iron in Pahang and Trengganu, and coal in Selangor have all been closed down.

The timber industry is important and Malaysia produces 13 per cent of the world's hardwoods. Of this, peninsular Malaysia accounts for almost half, and the balance comes from the Borneo states.

Concentration on export-oriented agriculture has inhibited the growth of manufacturing, and most of peninsular Malaysia's industries derive from its agriculture and mining: rubber and palm oil processing, tin smelting, saw milling, pineapple canning and pewter craft, although the discovery of oil off the east coast in the mid-1970s may make a radical change by providing a source of energy for local industry.

The small state of Brunei contains the bulk of the known oil and natural gas deposits of northern Borneo, and petroleum accounts for more than 99 per cent of its exports, although new deposits have recently been discovered off the coasts of Sarawak and Sabah.

Sabah accounts for nearly one-third of Malaysia's timber exports and the lumber trade forms the backbone of the state's economy. It also produces increasing quantities of rubber, copra and palm oil, mainly in the plains and undulating hill country in the north and east. But inadequate communications and lack of labour have held back the full exploitation of Sabah's resources.

Sarawak's resources have proved disappointing. Estates are confined to the swampy coastal plains, while inland agriculture still takes the form of shifting, primitive swidden (slash and burn) farming. Sarawak's main crop is rice, but even in this the state is not self sufficient. Antimony, bauxite and oil deposits are worked out, although new off-shore oil finds may prove to be rich.

Economic and population imbalances between the peninsula and the Borneo states are reflected in a contrast in communications. The peninsula has perhaps the best transport system in Southeast Asia, particularly in the western sector. An excellent network of well-surfaced roads is based upon a north-south trunk road, with an east coastal road running from Kota Bharu to Singapore, east-west highways from Selangor to Pahang and across Johor, and a planned northern cross-peninsular route from Kedah to Kelantan. A main trunk railway runs from Singapore to Thailand, with a branch line from north Johor to Kelantan. Shipping facilities are first rate, based upon the three important ports of Singapore, which is the world's fourth largest port, Penang and Port Klang.

In the Borneo states the inhospitable terrain, sparse population and lack of indigenous road-building materials inhibited highway construction, so that these states still rely mainly on coastal and river shipping, although they have no big port. In recent years an ambitious all-weather road-building programme has linked Sandakan with Kota Kinabalu and Kuching with Sibu, but a trunk road connecting Sarawak, Brunei and Sabah remains a planner's dream, beset with as yet insurmountable physical and political problems.

CHAPTER 2

Early History

Early Migrations

The early history of the region is obscure. There is no dated stone inscription in the Malay peninsula or the Borneo states earlier than the fourteenth century and very little written evidence. Scattered fragments of information can be gleaned from the descriptions of Chinese travellers and Arab geographers, but the earliest coherent narratives are the *Malay Annals* and early Portuguese writings of the sixteenth century.

Yet the rain forests of Southeast Asia, with their abundant food supplies of plants, animals and fish were probably one of the earliest habitats in which human life evolved. Java Man, one of man's ancestors, dates back 230 000 years, and Paleolithic tools found widely dispersed in South China, Indochina, Burma, Thailand, the Philippines, Borneo and Java show habitation going back over 50 000 years or more. The

Niah Caves, Sarawak *(By courtesy of Muzium Negara, Kuala Lumpur).*

earliest relics found in the Malay peninsula date back no more than 10 000 years, but excavations in the Niah caves in north Sarawak in 1958 revealed fragments of a *homo sapiens* skull estimated to be 40 000 years old. At that time, at the height of the last ice age, the present day Gulf of Siam and Sunda shelf were dry ground, and a land bridge linked the Philippine islands and Borneo.

As the ice began to thaw about 16 000 years ago, the seas rose, reaching approximately the present levels by about 8000 B.C. Meanwhile the earth grew warmer and the human race multiplied, although as the rising seas separated them, the peoples of the islands and the mainland began to develop in different ways.

The oldest known inhabitants in the Malay peninsula are the Negritos or Semang, small dark people, probably of Melanesian origin and possibly from the same stock as Australian Aborigines. At the end of the last ice age they probably roamed over a wide area but today are confined to the hill forests of northern Malaya, northeast India, north Sumatra, the Andaman islands and the Philippines.

Relics of human habitation going back thousands of years have been found in limestone caves and rock shelters of the northern Malay peninsular foothill region in Kelantan, Kedah, Perak and Pahang. Crude stone implements and rough pottery fragments indicate that these cave dwellers were part of the Mesolithic Hoabinhian culture of the region, but little is known of their ethnic origin.

The invention of the outrigger canoe and use of the simple sail about the beginning of the second millennium B.C. encouraged widespread migration of people from the present-day southern China into the Philippines and Indonesian islands. It used to be supposed that these migrants came in a succession of waves of different people, each more advanced than their predecessors: the Temiars and Semai of northern and central inland Malay peninsula; the Land Dyaks, Iban or Sea Dyaks, and other tribes of Borneo; the Jakuns of southern Malaya; and the so-called Deutero-Malays or Malays proper of the coastal regions. In fact the pattern of migration was slower, more continuous and complicated. All these immigrants were of similar ethnic Malayo/Polynesian/Mongoloid stock, belonging to the same Austronesian language group, acquiring differences in speech, culture and techniques from their various backgrounds, differences which were further accentuated by the pattern of settlement, occupation and lifestyle in their new home. It was not a simple outward migration from the mainland to the islands but cross migration within the region which continued until the Second World War: from Sumatra, Sulawesi and Java into the Malay peninsula; from Sumatra, Kalimantan and the Malay peninsula to northern Borneo.

In face of the influx of Malayo-Polynesian immigrants, the Semang of the Malay peninsula, who were timid, gentle and shy people, retreated to the hill forests, where they continued their traditional isolated nomadic life, living in makeshift shelters of branches and leaves, using bows and arrows to hunt birds and animals, catching fish and gathering jungle fruits and plants.

Immigrants such as the Temiar, Semai, Land Dyaks, Iban, Jakuns, Kadazans and Muruts, settling in the middle and upper reaches of the rivers, developed swidden agriculture to supplement hunting and fishing. In swidden agriculture they burned off the jungle to form clearings in which they grew mainly root crops, such as yams or taro, and domesticated some indigenous wild grains such as millet. Since the nutrients in the soil were rapidly used up, the community had to move after two or three years, but they were not nomadic, moving only short distances and returning to their old sites after these had lain fallow for a decade or so.

Swidden agriculture was well adapted to the equatorial rain forest, allowing the return of fertility within a cycle of years. Root crops required no storage and could be gathered when needed, and there was little risk in a mixed economy which was based on a food supply from tubers, grains, fruit, fish and wild game and was not heavily dependent on weather conditions. Nor did it require complicated social organization. Small groups of families, sharing the work of clearing, plant tending and hunting, and often living together in communal, wooden longhouses, formed the ideal unit for such pioneering and semi-mobile enterprise.

In the last millennium of the pre-Christian era improvements in boat building techniques using iron, coupled with political upheaval in south China and north Vietnam, induced increasing numbers of Malayo-Polynesian people to migrate to the South Seas. About 1000 B.C. migrants were moving along the northern coasts of the Malay peninsula, as evidenced by remnants of pottery of the type then common in south China.

Immigrants in the second half of the first millennium B.C. knew the use of bronze and iron. Metal implements dating from about 500 B.C. have been found in northern Borneo and others dating from about 300 B.C. in north Malaya. Bronze drums found at Klang (in Selangor) and Tembeling (in Pahang) date from the second century B.C., but these were probably imported, not locally made, since there were no nearby copper deposits.

These immigrants brought their knowledge of iron tools to improve farming techniques and formed settled coastal or riverine communities, living partly by fishing and partly by agriculture. They probably continued to grow tubers, supplemented by indigenous millet, and only took to rice planting in the first millennium A.D. Wild rice was not native to the Malay peninsula or northern Borneo, and although it was probably cultivated in north Thailand as early as the fifth millennium B.C., rice was a minor crop in Southeast Asia until the early years of the Christian era, when it was developed as a lowland crop in Tonkin and Funan.

Malay settlers sometimes intermarried with earlier Malayo-Polynesian people living in the lower reaches of the rivers, particularly with the Jakun in the less mountainous southern Malay peninsula, who sometimes traded jungle produce for cloth. But most swidden farmers of the middle and upper parts of the river valleys shunned contact with the outside world. Their economy was almost self sufficient, they produced little surplus, and although some of them bartered jungle products for salt or cloth from their downriver neighbours, they did not mix, intermarry or adopt either the customs or the sedentary farming lifestyle of the lowland peasants.

Whereas swidden farming did not call for large-scale community organization, the settled farmers in the lower parts of the river began to develop a village structure, looking to the leadership of *penghulus* or headmen. Permanent agriculture produced some surplus and division of labour, and trade grew between coastal and riverine villages.

Towards the end of the first millennium A.D. new bands of Malay immigrants appeared who did not settle on the land but kept to the sea as their main livelihood. Roaming the coastal waters of the Malay peninsula, the Riau archipelago and eastern Sumatra, and spreading from there along the northern coast of Borneo, these *orang laut*, or boat people, were daring sailors, enterprising rovers, tough and often violent, living on their wits by fishing, petty trading and pirating.

The Malay peninsula and northern Borneo being free from spectacular natural or climatic disasters (it was known as the 'land below the wind'), was a comparatively easy area for early man to eke out a living, but provided little opportunity for the production of food on a scale large enough to support big urban populations. Apart from small areas of volcanic soil in Sabah and the fairly rich alluvial soils of Kedah and Kelantan, most of the region was infertile: mountains and waterlogged plains. The hot, wet climate encouraged a luxuriant evergreen rain forest, but the constant humidity of the earth increased the soil's natural acidity, and nutrients were quickly leached away once the forest was felled. The coastal regions were inhospitable. The plains on the east coast of the peninsula were narrow and infertile, while in Borneo much of Sarawak and Brunei were peat swamps, most of which accumulated in the last 5000 years and was unsuited to any subsistence crop. The west peninsular coast was fringed by mud and mangrove belt. Even the alluvial plains of north Malaya needed considerable drainage schemes, so that settlement came first of all in the foothills and middle reaches of rivers, and the coastal plains defied agricultural exploitation until modern times.

On the island of Java and in certain parts of the mainland centralized states emerged, with control over manpower and resources on a scale which enabled them to leave great temple remains as evidence of their former greatness: Pagan, Angkor, Mataram, Majapahit. No part of the Malay peninsula offered the potential for supporting comparable states. Difficulties in communications also impeded the growth of centralized societies. The impenetrable rain forest meant that rivers and the sea were the only highways, but the northeast monsoon closed the east coast of Malaya and northern Borneo for months on end. Consequently most settlements were small villages, confined to their own river basin.

Throughout the region people followed complicated but similar animistic beliefs, placating nature through the spirits of trees and animals, of the sea, the forest and the mountains. But whereas the peoples of the interior tended to remain homogeneous groups, retaining their traditional way of life in relative isolation, those who lived near the coast were more mixed and mobile, more open to new external influences.

Indian Influence

Since the Malay peninsula lay across the sea route between China and the Indian Ocean, the region came into contact from prehistoric times with traders from more highly developed states. In the early days most traders probably transported their merchandise across the narrow northern isthmus, but as navigation improved the sea route through the Melaka Straits became more popular, particularly in settled times when big maritime interests could keep piracy in check. To take advantage of the trade winds, merchants had to tranship their goods in the Melaka Straits region and await the changing monsoon. This favoured the growth of a number of ports and trading settlements along the east Sumatran and west Malay peninsula coasts. Although the Malay peninsula was fabled in ancient times as a land of gold, initially the region's ports were probably more important in the international entrepot trade than as outlets for produce from the peninsula itself.

The earliest traders were probably Indonesians, the most skilled navigators of their age who penetrated far into the Indian Ocean before the Christian era, and may have been the first to bring Indian influence back to Southeast Asia. From the first century A.D. Indian traders also began to come, some from Bengal, others from southern India, probably impelled by the search for gold and helped by recent improvements in Indian navigation. There is no indication that Indians migrated in appreciable numbers to Southeast Asia in ancient times, but individual traders were highly respected and influential. Some helped to found trading settlements or married into the ruling families of existing communities, bringing with them Indian political and religious practices and the Sanskrit language.

The earliest recorded Indianized kingdom was Funan, founded in the lower Mekong in the first century A.D., which reached the peak of its power in the fifth century, when China called the king of Funan, General of the Pacified South, and Funan's suzerainty extended over a large part of the eastern coast of the Malay peninsula. A number of small trading states grew up on the isthmus and northern peninsula: on the west coast Takkola, the modern Takuapa; Kadaram, which was probably Kedah; and Kalah, probably near the present day Mergui; on the east coast, Langkasuka, perhaps near Singora; Pan-pan in the Bay of Bandon; Tambralinga, the modern Ligor (Nakhon Si Thammarat); Chih-tu, which perhaps was Kelantan; Tan-tan, which may have been Trengganu.

Very few archaeological remains date from these early centuries. Indians themselves left little in the way of written records and our knowledge comes mainly from the accounts given by Southeast Asian embassies to China, which appear in the Chinese dynastic annals. Chinese ambassadors occasionally visited the southern kingdoms but Chinese merchants probably had little influence in the region in the first millennium A.D., leaving trade to the Indians and later to Arabs. Nor did Chinese cultural influence extend into Southeast Asia beyond the then Chinese province of Tonkin.

Indian influence made some impact from the beginning of the Christian era but became widespread in the coastal regions by the fourth and fifth centuries and continued to be the dominant civilizing force in Southeast Asia for the next 1000 years. It was from India that the emerging states took their religion, their political structure, their forms of law and their writing. The oldest relics are small Buddhist statues, reflecting the personal religion of the early Indian traders, such as the sixth century Gupta-style statue found at Kuala Selinsing in Perak. But as the small commercial settlements expanded, Hinduism became the dominant Indian influence, based upon the worship of Vishnu and Siva.

Penghulus became rajas, setting up hereditary rule, surrounding themselves with elaborate Indian court ceremonial and often engaging Indian Brahmans as advisers and ministers. They adopted Indian ideas of kingship, particularly the concept of Sivaite royalty, in which the royal *linga* or phallus was worshipped as a symbol of strength and fertility. While Indian concepts permeated only the upper crust of society, the process of Indianization affected ordinary people to some degree. Perhaps because traditional Southeast Asia resembled pre-Aryan India so closely, Buddhist and Hindu beliefs blended easily with the older animist practices. Society became more stratified according to class, although Hinduism brought only a modified caste system and the status of women remained higher in Southeast Asia than in India. In farming methods Kelantan and Trengganu seem to have adopted Funan practices, while Kedah imported the plough from India. The metal and weaving crafts of Kelantan and Trengganu and the *wayang kulit* shadow plays, which are unique to that region of the peninsula, may have also been adopted from contacts with Funan or Langkasuka, or may be a legacy of later Khmer and Majapahit contacts.

Srivijaya

The decline and break up of Funan in the sixth century led to the rise of many new states, including the shadow Mon kingdom of Dvaravati, an Indianized state which probably centred in the lower Chao Phraya basin and claimed sway over the isthmian states. Malayu, the east Sumatran state based near Jambi,from which the Malay peninsula took its name and its language, is mentioned for the first time in the seventh century when it sent an embassy to China. But the most important state to emerge was the Indianized maritime empire of Srivijaya, centred near Palembang, which was a convenient transhipment port for ships from the west to catch the southwest monsoon for China. Srivijaya rose rapidly to power in the latter part of the seventh century, and by the eighth century extended its control over the coasts of the Malay peninsula and isthmus as far north as Takuapa in the west and Ligor in the east, over southern and east Sumatra, west Java and western Borneo, commanding both the Melaka and Sunda Straits, the keys to the route between the China Sea and the Indian Ocean.

Kadaram, in southern Kedah, centred on the Merbok estuary, was a key point in Srivijaya's empire, as the northern port of the Melaka Straits, where ships coming from Srivijaya and Malayu on southwesterly winds waited for the monsoon to change and carry them west to India. Kedah was a natural landfall for shipping from India, with Kedah Peak, or Gunong Jerai, towering behind, forming an outstanding landmark for shipping. A settlement of considerable wealth and luxurious living, described by an Indian writer of the eleventh century as 'the seat of all felicities', Kedah's relatively fertile hinterland may have made it a prosperous agricultural area. Numerous Hindu and Buddhist temples, particularly in the Bujang river valley, show that it continued to be an important trading centre for many centuries. The remains of Indian temples are more numerous in south Kedah than anywhere else in the Malay peninsula and include one of the most impressive of ancient Malayan temples, which was reconstructed in the late-1950s, on the southern slopes of Kedah Peak.*

Most of Kedah's trade travelled by the Melaka Straits route. It was possible to cross the peninsula from Kedah to Singora but the northern route from Takuapa to the Bay of Bandon was shorter and easier, and

* Chandi Bukit Batu Pahat

Chandi Bukit Batu Pahat, Kedah Peak *(By courtesy of Muzium Negara, Kuala Lumpur).*

from the seventh to the eleventh centuries Takuapa overshadowed
Kedah as the main isthmian transhipment port. Despite this, the
Melaka Straits ports flourished while Srivijaya held undisputed sway
and kept in check the *orang laut,* who preyed on trading ships in troubled times.

Srivijaya was a centre of Buddhist learning, and during its hegemony
the Malay tongue, the language of southeast Sumatra, spread
throughout the coastal regions of the peninsula and archipelago as the
lingua franca of trade.

Srivijaya's commercial dominance aroused considerable resentment,
and in 1025 the Chola navy of southern India ransacked Srivijaya itself,
together with Malayu, Kedah, Takkola, Langkasuka and many other
vassal states. This was a raid, not a war of conquest, and the Cholas did
not occupy any parts of the empire, but Chola merchants appear to
have remained a powerful influence at the Srivijaya court from that
time. While Srivijaya never recovered its pre-eminence, the eleventh
and twelfth centuries were prosperous trading years for maritime
Southeast Asia, marked by improvements in navigation and the entry of
regular Chinese shipping into the region. The overland isthmian route
lost out to the Melaka Straits as the main trade route, which benefited
Kedah at the expense of Takkola, while the northeastern peninsular
states fell under the sway of the highly cultured Khmer empire.

The northern Borneo coast, which conducted an extensive trade with
Sung China from the tenth to the thirteenth centuries, also came within
Srivijaya's domain, and numbers of Sumatran Malays migrated to nor-
thern Borneo. But the closest contacts were between east Sumatra and

the western part of the Malay peninsula. Contact between the two areas was easier than between the east and west sides of the peninsula, or between the east coast of the peninsula and northern Borneo. The Melaka Straits were as sheltered as an inland sea and allowed the easy passage of people all the year round. Contact with Srivijaya started the process of migration from Sumatra to the Malay peninsula which continued for many centuries.

This influence survived the decline of Srivijaya itself. Apart from its name and language, the Malay peninsula derived from Sumatra its religion in the form of Buddhism, Hinduism and ultimately Islam, its political organization, and its two forms of customary law (*adat*): the indigenous *adat perpateh*, and the *adat temenggong* which was modified for state purposes by Indian practice.

Compared with Indian influence, Chinese impact was slight, although evidence of trade with China goes back to the beginning of the Christian era. Chinese coins and fragments of Han pottery have been discovered near the estuary of the Sarawak river, and China imported birds' nests from Brunei in the seventh century. But this trade was probably carried by Southeast Asian, Indian or Arab traders, and the Chinese themselves do not appear to have entered the Nanyang, or South Seas, trade in force until the time of the Sung dynasty in the eleventh century. By the mid-thirteenth century the Chinese dominated the carrying trade of the South China Sea. The Mongol Yuan dynasty, which supplanted the Sungs, continued their trade policy, and large numbers of Chinese ships came to the Nanyang in the first half of the fourteenth century.

Direct Chinese entry into the trade of Southeast Asia, combined with the long-term jealousy of rival Southeast Asian states, brought about the decline of Srivijaya, so that by the end of the thirteenth century the empire had crumbled away, and Palembang became a pirates' haunt. At first the states on the Malay peninsula and isthmus were independent but quickly became caught between two rising powers: the Thai kingdom centred at Sukhothai, which was founded in the late thirteenth century, and the Hindu empire of Majapahit in east Java, which rose in the fourteenth century. By the second half of the fourteenth century the Thais claimed suzerainty over the whole of the Malay isthmus and peninsula, while Majapahit also claimed as vassal states the Malay peninsula and isthmus as far north as Langkasuka, west Borneo and Brunei, in addition to Java, Bali and south Sumatra.

Temasik/Singapura and the Founding of Melaka

After the fall of the Yuan dynasty in 1368, the first Ming emperor of China reversed the policy of direct trading and forbade private merchants trading in the Nanyang. Srivijaya's decline and the Chinese withdrawal took away controlling moderating influence, and the second half of the fourteenth century was a time of confusion and violence. The southern extremity of the Malay peninsula was in a particularly unenviable position, in that both the Thais and Majapahit claimed to control the area but neither exerted strong authority and protection, and the settlement of Temasik on Singapore island was subject to attacks by both Thais and Javanese.

Temasik's origins are lost in obscurity. Apart from relics of terraces and graves and some Majapahit-type jewellery found on the hill behind the Singapore river, the only physical remains were in the form of a large stone inscribed in supposedly Javanese writing at the mouth of the Singapore river, but this was destroyed in construction work in the nineteenth century. A third century Chinese account mentions P'u-luo-chung, probably Pulau Ujong, 'the island at the end of the peninsula'. Temasik does not appear to have been a station of any importance in the heyday of Srivijaya, when it lay off the main trade route between Palembang and China, but it may have profited initially from the breakup of Srivijaya. Marco Polo in the late-thirteenth century gives a hearsay description of 'Chiamassie' a 'large and noble' town on the island of 'Malayur', which appears to be Temasik. But a Chinese traveller, Wang Ta-yuan, portrayed the island and the Keppel Strait in the early-fourteenth century as a dreaded pirate haunt.

During the turmoil in the last decade of the fourteenth century an adventurer, Parameswara, appeared in Temasik. According to the sixteenth century *Malay Annals* Parameswara was a Palembang prince descended from the Srivijaya royal house, but he may, in fact, have been a refugee from Malayu or Java. Parameswara ousted the ruler of Temasik but was himself driven out shortly afterwards by the Thais or a Malayan–Thai vassal state, which devastated Temasik. Parameswara fled with his small band of followers along the west coast of the Malay peninsula, and about the beginning of the fifteenth century these refugees established themselves in an *orang laut* village at Melaka.

CHAPTER 3

The Founding of Melaka and the Coming of Islam

959
.5

Early Melaka

According to the *Malay Annals* Parameswara named the settlement after a *malaka* tree, under which he was resting when he saw a mousedeer turn and kick one of his hunting dogs, a miraculous omen of good fortune which induced him to put down his roots in this auspicious place. More probably the name derived from the Arab *malakat* or mart, a name long used by traders for nearby Water Island. But the popular myth was figuratively true, since Melaka offered the ambitious and spirited adventurer a chance to make his fortune. Parameswara and his able successors used the opportunity to build Melaka into a flourishing maritime empire and a cultural and religious centre.

The soil was infertile, the surrounding plain swampy and the Melaka river unimportant, but the harbour was sheltered, protected by Sumatra from the monsoon and conveniently placed for the tradewind systems. Moreover the settlement's position at the narrowest point in the Melaka Straits, where the deep water channel lay close to the Malayan coast, gave her command over the passage of shipping.

At first Parameswara and his followers continued their traditional way of life, combining piracy with fishing and petty trading and extracting tolls from passing ships. The settlement was too insignificant to interest the Siamese, whose power stood at its height at the beginning of the fifteenth century, when they received tribute from Kedah, Patani, Kelantan, Trengganu and Pahang and also claimed suzerainty over the southern part of the peninsula.

Within a few years Melaka assumed a new role as a result of a reversal of imperial Chinese policy under the third Ming emperor, Chu Ti. The Chinese decided to trade directly themselves, instead of through tributaries, and in 1403 sent out the first of a series of official trade missions to the Nanyang and the Indian Ocean. The Chinese fleet called at Melaka, and the famous Chinese admiral, Cheng Ho, who made seven voyages to the Indian Ocean between 1405 and 1431, subsequently used Melaka as his supply base. The expeditions, which often comprised more than fifty ships, carrying up to 37 000 men, in themselves

19

stimulated trade, but Parameswara also appreciated the political advantages which Chinese protection could bring Melaka in guarding it against possible Siamese encroachment. China was a more distant, undemanding and benign overlord, bestowing titles and honours, traditionally giving as much in trade as it received in tribute, whereas the Siamese expected tribute without return. Accordingly, Parameswara sent envoys to the Chinese emperor, who in 1409 acknowledged him as a vassal king, and two years later, when Cheng Ho returned to China from his third voyage in the Indian Ocean, Parameswara accompanied him to pay obeisance to the emperor, together with his family, ministers and an entourage of more than 500 followers.

Melaka profited from Chinese trade and protection but expanded slowly. A Chinese Muslim, Ma Huan, who visited Melaka in 1413, a year before Parameswara died, described the settlement as a village of about 2000 inhabitants, most of them fisherfolk.

Parameswara's successors continued to court Chinese protection and took advantage of the chance to travel to China with the fleets which regularly visited the Nanyang. The second ruler went to China soon after his accession in 1414 to have his title confirmed, and again in 1419 to obtain protection in face of Siamese threats. The third ruler, Sri Maharaja, went to China in 1424 to gain recognition and paid a second visit in 1433. But this was the last occasion on which a Melaka ruler visited China in person, since the Chinese authorities decided at this stage to abandon official trading and revert to the tribute system. Quick to appreciate the threat posed by the loss of Chinese patronage, Sri Maharaja hurried home to seek new allies and fresh trade outlets.

The Chinese withdrawal from direct involvement in the Nanyang threatened the very existence of Melaka, yet offered the incentive which spurred its rise from mild prosperity to great wealth and power.

Melaka continued to pay homage to China and private Chinese merchants came in large numbers to trade and sometimes to settle, but they ceased to have any political influence at court. Even during the period of the Ming voyages Chinese cultural impact in Melaka was minimal, not impinging on its traditional links with India, Indonesia, and in particular the east Sumatran port states.

With the decline of Srivijaya, the former empire's commercial prosperity fell to Muslim traders from the middle East and India: Arabs who monopolised the spice trade, and Bengalis, Tamils and Gujaratis, who were attracted to the growing pepper trade of north Sumatra. After the brief period of direct Chinese commercial competition, Muslim dominance remained undisputed.

Seeking an alternative to Chinese protection, Sri Maharaja allied Melaka with Muslim Samudra–Pasai, the most flourishing maritime state in the Straits of Melaka in the mid-1430s. He married the sultan's daughter, embraced Islam and hitched Melaka's fortunes to the rising star of the Muslim trading fraternity.

The Coming of Islam

Much mystery still surrounds early Islamization in Southeast Asia, in which Melaka was destined later to play a vital role. The Muslim religion had originated in Arabia in the seventh century but made little headway in Southeast Asia for hundreds of years, although Arabs had been trading in the Far East since the fourth century and by the ninth century dominated the carrying trade of Southeast Asia. Islam gained a foothold in China, Java and Champa in the eleventh century, probably brought directly from the Middle East. The earliest trace of Islam which has so far been discovered in the Malay peninsula is an inscription found at Kuala Brang in Trengganu, dating from 1303, which ordered the imposition of the Muslim religion and prescribed penalties for infringing its moral rules. Probably Islam was introduced from Champa, but no supporting evidence for a fourteenth-century Muslim state in northeast Malaya has yet been discovered, and this attempt to enforce a puritanical religion may well have succumbed to the rising power of Majapahit.

Islam spread widely in China under the Mongol dynasty, which gave Muslims trading privileges denied to other Chinese. Many Chinese traders who came to the Nanyang were Muslims and enjoyed considerable prestige, particularly in Javanese ports. But neither these merchants nor the Chinese Muslims who came with Admiral Cheng Ho to Melaka in the early-fourteenth century appear to have made many converts.

Hinduism and Buddhism had been widely accepted in Southeast Asia partly because they filled a political need to sanctify the power of rulers, and partly because, originating among Indian people of similar agricultural background, they did not conflict with the animism of the mass of the population. Early Islam was different: a simple, stern, disciplined religion, which suited desert Arabs but had little appeal to the radically different society of Southeast Asia. Many Muslim tenets and practices went against local custom. Its demands of allegiance to one God and his Prophet Muhammad were difficult to adapt to the multitude of spirits and gods. Islam was an individualistic and rational religion, which stressed self reliance rather than propitiating spirits by rituals and ceremonies which were designed to preserve human beings through the crises of birth, puberty, marriage and death. Unlike the earlier Indian religions, it had no ceremonial nor religious hierarchy to bolster the prestige and power of monarchies. A masculine religion in which women played a minor role, Islam did not fit traditional Southeast

Asian agricultural society, in which women held considerable influence and which was often organized along matriarchal lines. Muslim law, with its emphasis on punishment and harsh penalties involving imprisonment, mutilation and death, conflicted with the *adat*, the custom and usage of agricultural societies which was based on arbitration, the payment of compensation for injuries and the conservation of labour.

Islam made little progress in Southeast Asia until the late-thirteenth century, but it then spread fairly quickly and by the sixteenth century was firmly established throughout the coastal regions of the archipelago and the Malay peninsula. This rapid expansion resulted partly from developments in the Islamic world and partly because of changes in Southeast Asia itself.

After the fall of the Baghdad Caliphate to the Mongols in 1258, orders of sufis, or mystic religious teachers, took a leading role in the regeneration of Islam, many travelling to India and some journeying further into Southeast Asia. The travelling teacher had a special place in Islam, which has no established priesthood, and the independent Muslim missionary was welcomed in India and Southeast Asia, as individual Brahmans and Buddhists had been in the past.

Turning away from the simplicity of desert Islam, sufis combined their teaching with local custom, seeking to embrace converts into the new faith by synthesizing the Islamic creed with existing beliefs. Often dynamic and persuasive preachers, claiming powers of magic and healing, they brought a personal charisma, fervour and glamour from the outside world.

Sufis made many Indian converts, particularly in the coastal regions: in Bengal, in the Coromandel coast of south India and later in Gujarat in west India, which became an independent Muslim state in 1298. Long established in the eastern trade, the Indian merchants were often wealthy and respected men, so that their new religion commanded considerable prestige in the ports which they frequented in the archipelago.

The new dynamic Islam came at a time of great change in maritime Southeast Asia, when coastal Malays were carving out new states, which depended so much on individual personality, ability and strong leadership. They sought a different ideology from that which supported the old-established agriculture-based communities and found it in Islam's male dominance, preaching of brotherhood, insistence on self reliance, stress on involvement in the world and approval of trade. Islam was also the religion of foreign merchants whom the new city-states wished to cultivate. Sufis and Muslim merchants were well received in such states, where they often became advisers, sometimes marrying into leading families or becoming rulers in their own right.

A number of north Sumatran states embraced Islam in the late-thirteenth century. The Venetian traveller, Marco Polo, who visited Sumatra in 1292, commented that Perlak was a Muslim town.

Samudra, the modern Pasai, had also been converted by that time, with a ruling house apparently descended from a Bengali Muslim merchant. The mid-fourteenth century Muslim traveller, Ibn Battuta, described Pasai as a big Islamic centre, whose devout sultan attracted foreign Muslim scholars and traders. In turn, these Sumatran ports spread religion further afield in Southeast Asia through the medium of preachers or merchants, and often by royal marriages which led to the conversion of foreign princes.

According to the *Malay Annals* the Prophet Muhammad appeared in a dream to the ruler of Melaka, predicting the imminent arrival of a missionary from Jeddah. The king awoke to find he had been circumcised in his sleep; the following day a ship arrived with a Muslim teacher and the people of Melaka immediately embraced Islam.

Similar tales abound in many parts of island Southeast Asia of rulers' dreams, followed by the arrival of a Muslim preacher, the immediate conversion of the ruler and subsequent speedy conversion of his people. While not strictly true, these legends indicate the form in which Islam arrived in Southeast Asia, coming not as it did to North Africa or Europe through a violent military crusade but as a peaceful adjunct of individual preaching, ordinary trading and dynastic alliances, in much the same way as Hinduism and Buddhism in earlier times. In fact, Sri Maharaja of Melaka appears to have become a Muslim at the time of his marriage to the Pasai princess rather than adopting the religion direct from the Middle East as legend claims.

Assuming the name of Mohamed Shah, Sri Maharaja retained the elaborate Hindu court ceremonial which he had formerly cultivated in order to enhance the ruler's status and made no attempt to enforce Islam as the state religion. He was a much respected, intelligent and just ruler, but the *bendahara,* or chief minister, and the Malay nobility who had retained their Hindu beliefs resented the rising power at court of the Muslim-Tamil group.

Mohamed Shah had no children by his Pasai marriage, and on his death in 1444, Raja Ibrahim, his youngest son by a Hindu-Buddhist Sumatran princess, was chosen as successor. Older sons by non-royal marriages were passed over, including Raja Kassim, who was descended on his mother's side from a cadet branch of the *bendahara's* family, into which the leading Tamil-Muslim merchant, Baginda Mani Purindan, had married. A year after his succession the young ruler was murdered in a palace plot engineered by Raja Kassim's part-Tamil cousin, Tun Ali.[1] Raja Kassim, taking the name Muzaffar Shah, then became sultan, apparently the first Melaka ruler to adopt this Muslim title. He followed tradition by marrying the *bendahara's* daughter, but Tun Ali the kingmaker wielded so much influence at court that the *bendahara,* fearing he had fallen from favour, took poison, and Sultan Muzaffar appointed Tun Ali to the office of *bendahara* in his stead.

Table 3.1   The early rulers of Melaka

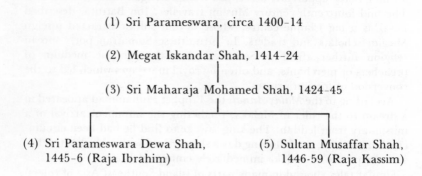

(1) Sri Parameswara, circa 1400–14

(2) Megat Iskandar Shah, 1414–24

(3) Sri Maharaja Mohamed Shah, 1424–45

(4) Sri Parameswara Dewa Shah, 1445–6 (Raja Ibrahim)

(5) Sultan Musaffar Shah, 1446–59 (Raja Kassim)

Table 3.2   Tun Ali and the Melaka royal family

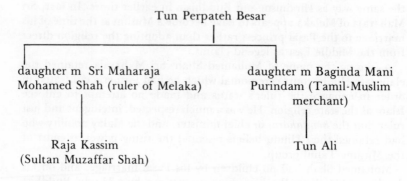

Tun Perpateh Besar

daughter m Sri Maharaja Mohamed Shah (ruler of Melaka)

daughter m Baginda Mani Purindam (Tamil-Muslim merchant)

Raja Kassim (Sultan Muzaffar Shah)

Tun Ali

1. See Wake, C. H., 'Malacca's early kings and the reception of Islam', *Journal of Southeast Asian History* Vol. V (2), 1964 for discussion of these complicated relationships.

CHAPTER 4

The Melaka Sultanate

Sultan Muzaffar Shah

Despite the inauspicious start to Muzaffar's reign, Melaka prospered under his strong rule. He settled the differences between the Malay and Tamil factions, established Islam as the state religion, shook off external threats, extended Melaka's sway over neighbouring states and laid the foundations for its commercial pre-eminence.

Initially Melaka faced great danger. The official adoption of Islam deepened the rift between Melaka and the Buddhist Siamese. Possibly because the new sultan refused to pay tribute, the Siamese sent an army overland from Pahang to attack Melaka in 1445. Still shaken by the troubles which had rent the court, Melaka was weak and vulnerable, but the outlying district chiefs rallied to the sultan's support and defeated the Siamese forces in battle near Muar.

The abortive Siamese invasion proved an indirect blessing since it brought back to Melaka Tun Perak, the former *bendahara's* son, who had retired to the country after his father's suicide to become district chief of Klang. Sultan Muzaffar Shah was so impressed by the young man's intelligence and confident bearing in the campaign against the Siamese that he insisted on retaining him at court, bestowing on him the title of *paduka raja*. Tun Perak was popular with the traditional Malay chiefs, who saw him as the representative of the old regime, untainted by the troubles which had brought Muzaffar to the throne and a counterweight to the part-Tamil Tun Ali. The rivalry between these two able and ambitious men threatened to revive the bitterness of the previous reign. Muzaffar Shah eventually appointed Tun Perak as *bendahara*, relegating Tun Ali to the lesser office of treasurer, but he produced at least a superficial reconciliation between the two, which he consolidated by divorcing one of his own wives, who was Tun Perak's sister, and marrying her to Ali.

Tun Ali remained in the sultan's service, dying during the next reign an old and honoured man, but the real power passed to Bendahara Perak, who for nearly forty years was the power behind the throne, guiding Melaka's fortunes through successive reigns. One of the most outstanding statesmen of his generation, Tun Perak subordinated personal glory to strengthening the sultanate and the state. More than any other single individual he was responsible for making Melaka the most prosperous and influential state in maritime Southeast Asia.

Bendahara Perak put the spectre of Siamese domination to rest. When Siam launched a second attack on Melaka in 1456, this time by sea, Tun Perak led the resistance force in person, supported by all the war chiefs. The rival fleets met in battle off Batu Pahat, where Tun Perak tricked the Siamese by tying firebrands to trees along the shore by night to make it appear that Melaka had a massive fleet. The Siamese fled, pursued as far south as Singapore island by the Melakan ships, and then dispersed.

But Melaka was not seeking military glory. As a trading city it wanted peace and security. Soon after the Siamese had been driven off, Muzaffar Shah sent a conciliatory mission to Siam and a second mission two years later to confirm the peace. In 1456 he also dispatched an embassy to China to obtain recognition of his title.

During Muzaffar's reign Melaka consolidated its hold over Singapore and Bintan, which gave it control over the *orang laut* tribes at this strategic meeting place of the China and Java Seas and the Melaka Straits. Their loyalty was crucial for Melaka's safety and commercial dominance. Parameswara had founded Melaka with the support of *orang laut* and employed them in the early years to force ships to call at Melaka to pay tolls. The *orang laut* provided ships and fighting men to help the sultan in time of trouble and patrolled merchant shipping, preying only on craft which did not have passes from Melaka.

In the words of the *Malay Annals* Muzaffar Shah was respected as 'a raja of high character, just and humane, diligent in inquiry into the pleas of his people'. Under Tun Perak's guidance a well-organized administration developed, patterned on the Srivijayan model from which Melaka claimed descent. The sultan stood at the pinnacle, supported by the *bendahara*, an Indian–Sanskrit title for the prime minister, chief justice and commander-in-chief. Next in the rank came the *penghulu bendahari*, or treasurer, followed by the *temenggong*, who organized court ceremonies and kept law and order, judging all but the most serious criminal cases. Below these dignitaries were the four *orang kaya* or senior chiefs, the *laksamana* or admiral, the army commander, leading courtiers and lesser chiefs and warriors.

About the middle of the century the laws were codified to adapt Islamic practice to the customary *adat temenggong*, which had been derived from Srivijaya. This Melaka digest was subsequently adopted as the model in most other Malayan peninsular states.

Malay officials left the day-to-day supervision of the foreign merchant community and of trade to harbour masters, or *shahbandars*, who were responsible to the treasurer. Fittingly, the title of *shahbandar* was Persian in origin, and these officers were themselves foreign merchants assigned to supervise their own communities.

Sultan Mansur

By the time Muzaffar died in 1458-9 Melaka was stable and prosperous. Building on these firm foundations, it expanded rapidly in wealth, population, territory and prestige under his successor, Mansur, who ruled from 1459 to 1477. He was ably supported by Tun Perak as *bendahara* and in the early years by Tun Ali as treasurer, both of whom were his cousins and brothers-in-law, and also by the *laksamana* Hang Tuah, a flamboyant, virile *orang laut* of legendary prowess, who rose from obscurity to become admiral of Melaka.

Immediately after his accession Sultan Mansur dispatched Tun Perak's younger brother, Perpateh Puteh, on a mission to China, whence he returned, according to the *Malay Annals,* bringing a Chinese princess as wife for Mansur and many Chinese followers, who settled at Bukit China.

Meanwhile, to consolidate protection against Siam, Sultan Mansur launched a naval attack on the Siamese dependency of Pahang, led by Tun Perak, the *laksamana* Hang Tuah, and a fleet of 200 ships. The governor was brought back captive to Melaka, while Pahang was subdued and subsequently placed under the rule of Mansur's eldest son, Muhammad, who was exiled to Pahang after killing Tun Perak's eldest son in a fight.

Pahang was an older state than Melaka, one of the most populous and flourishing regions in the Malay peninsula and famed for its tin and for gold in the upriver Tembeling-Jelai district. As a vassal of Srivijaya, Pahang had covered the whole of the south of the peninsula, but after the collapse of the Srivijaya empire it found itself caught between the expanding kingdoms of Siam and Majapahit, both of which claimed suzerainty over Pahang in the fourteenth century. While Pahang may have had earlier contacts with Muslim traders, it would appear that Islam was introduced as the state religion along with the Melaka pattern of government, with its *bendahara,* treasurer, *temenggong* and hierarchy of lesser officials, as a consequence of the Melakan conquest.

Melaka then went on to extend its sway over Johor, the Riau-Lingga archipelago and the coasts of east Sumatra and the western Malay peninsula by diplomacy, by political and religious influence and where necessary by force. According to the *Malay Annals,* Mansur visited the court of Majapahit, obtaining the hand of the ruler's daughter in marriage, together with suzerainty over the east Sumatran state of Indragiri. Jambi also acknowledged Melaka's overlordship, but when Siak refused to submit, Mansur sent an expedition which killed the ruler and brought his son to Melaka, where he was married to Mansur's daughter and sent back to rule Siak as a vassal. The whole west coast of the Malay peninsula as far north as Perak was brought into submission, giving Melaka the rights to export its tin, which had formerly been shipped through Kedah. Kedah itself came under Melaka's sway about the year 1474.

Melaka also extended its influence through its missionary efforts in propagating the Muslim religion, which blossomed hand in hand with Melaka's trade once it had been adopted as the state religion. It spread to the peninsular states, to Banda, Brunei, and the Javanese ports of Demak, Japara, Tuban and Surabaja, which were breaking away from the crumbling Hindu kingdom of Majapahit.

As in Melaka itself, Islam came peacefully with trade, probably brought by individual preachers and merchants who converted the indigenous population, rather than by large groups of Muslim settlers. Islam forged a common religious bond throughout the archipelago, and its emphasis on the equality of men and the virtues of honest work suited the mobile trade of the merchant communities.

With the advantage of a better harbour and more convenient location, Melaka captured much of Pasai's former trade. Chinese junks preferred to make Melaka their western terminus and a number of Indians, Arabs and Javanese diverted their trade from Pasai to Melaka. Pasai still enjoyed a reputation as a religious centre, but missionaries and scholars from India and the Middle East also began to come to Melaka.

During Mansur's reign the power of the sultanate was consolidated, but this was largely Bendahara Perak's work. Mansur himself was unwarlike and pleasure loving, interested in literature and religion. Living in luxury and surrounded by ceremonial, he developed a glittering court life.

Sultan Alauddin Riayat Shah

Since Mansur's eldest son had been banished to Pahang and his second son killed in an affray, when the sultan died in 1477 he was succeeded by a young boy of fifteen, Alauddin Riayat Shah, Mansur's son by the Majapahit princess. The succession was not universally accepted, and the late sultan's mother plotted unsuccessfully to bring the Pahang ruler back as sultan, but despite his youth, Alauddin revealed many of the leadership qualities displayed by the early Melaka rulers. Vigorous and firm, astute and sensible, the young sultan was independent in spirit. He retained the support of Bendahara Perak and Laksamana Hang Tuah, and on the *bendahara's* death appointed Tun Perak's younger brother, the experienced diplomat Tun Perpateh Puteh, in his place. But Sultan Alauddin intended to be no minister's puppet.

He showed more interest in administration than his father, insisted on enforcing law and order in the port, kept a tight rein on his subject states and extended Melaka's sway still further afield. Alauddin sent expeditions to confirm the allegiance of Pahang and Siak, and he subdued Kampar, installing a new ruler and *bendahara* from Melaka.

In 1481 he dispatched a mission to China to gain confirmation of his title and settle a diplomatic problem which he had inherited. When the Annamese invaded Champa, murdered the king and destroyed the capital in 1471, a Cham prince with a large band of followers fled to Melaka, where he was welcomed by Mansur and made a minister. The Annamese threatened to take reprisals against Melaka, but as a result of Alauddin's mission China forbade such a move.

Sultan Mahmud and Bendahara Mutahir

This promising reign was cut short abruptly in 1488 with the sudden and mysterious death of Sultan Alauddin, allegedly by poisoning, at the age of twenty-six. His elder son was away in Kampar and a younger son, a mere child, was chosen to succeed him as Sultan Mahmud. While the appointment was grudgingly accepted by some of the Malay chiefs, Mahmud did not inherit his father's ability or dedication. He showed some interest in absorbing learning from Muslim scholars, but in general, Mahmud was a headstrong, impetuous and pleasure-loving womanizer, who found his amusements in the company of wild and dashing young men.

Despite the extravagance at court, as long as Mahmud was willing to leave government in his ministers' hands the state did not suffer, and indeed the early years of the sixteenth century saw Melaka reach the height of its wealth, glory and power under the most spectacular of all its *bendaharas*, Tun Mutahir.

The youngest son of Tun Ali by Sultan Muzzafar's divorced wife, Tun Mutahir was a handsome, imposing and ambitious man. Committed by the dying Tun Ali to the care of his uncle, Bendahara Perak, Mutahir was appointed *temenggong* by Sultan Alauddin and was raised to the office of *bendahara* in 1500 when Bendahara Puteh died.

Mutahir was the grandest of all the *bendaharas* and the most powerful. He entrenched his family in all the leading offices of state, so that his elder brother became treasurer, his son *temenggong*, and his niece married Sultan Mahmud.

A commander of ability, Mutahir led a big naval expedition which helped Pahang repel an attack launched, on Siamese instructions, by its vassal state of Ligor. He also led a force which overran and subdued Kelantan.

Melaka now commanded the allegiance of the whole peninsula including Kedah, Kelantan and Trengganu. But it did not succeed in shaking the Siamese hold over Patani. Siam no longer constituted a threat to Melaka or its dependencies, but because of the bad blood between the two states over the eastern coast of the peninsula, Mahmud dispatched a mission to China in 1508, applying belatedly for confirmation of his title and for Chinese protection.

Neither Acheh nor Aru was brought within Melaka's sphere of influence and, as Pasai crumbled, the northern Sumatran states became more troublesome. Aru pirates molested Melaka-bound shipping and in Mansur's reign ravaged the Melaka coast itself. But *orang laut* support kept the southern waters of the Straits a private sea for Melaka.

The Last Years of the Melaka Sultanate

By the end of the fifteenth century Melaka was the premier port in Southeast Asia, the great collecting centre for the Malay peninsula and the archipelago, meeting place of traders from the Middle East, India and the Far East. After the Chinese withdrawal from direct trading, the trade from outside the region and from local feeder ports again converged on one centre. Melaka was ideally situated for this and revived Srivijaya's former role as commercial centre, political overlord, religious and cultural leader of maritime Southeast Asia.

We have a clear picture of Melaka in the last years of Malay rule from two valuable sources, which go into this period in detail from differing points of view: the *Malay Annals,* and the *Suma Oriental,* written by Tome Pires, a Portuguese who spent more than two years in Melaka in the early-sixteenth century.[1]

The population was large, certainly more than 50 000 but unlikely to approach the estimate of 190 000 given in the *Malay Annals.* The splendour of the sultan's court was rivalled by the establishments of the *bendahara* and leading foreign merchants. In addition to a cosmopolitan resident society, hundreds of foreign merchants came every year from India, Persia, Arabia, China, Champa, Cambodia, Siam, Pegu, Sumatra, Java and the eastern islands. By the first decade of the sixteenth century more than 100 large ships called there each year, and at any one time up to 2000 small boats could be seen in the harbour.

Melaka's economy rested entirely on entrepot trade. It produced nothing, except a little tin, and its agriculture was insufficient to feed the population, so that it had to import rice and other foodstuffs from the west Malay coast, the east Sumatran states and sometimes as far afield as Siam and Brunei.

The major trade was in textiles from Gujarat and Coromandel, which were exchanged for eastern luxuries: spices from the Moluccas; silk and porcelain from China; gold and pepper from Sumatra; camphor from Borneo; sandalwood from Timor; and tin from western Malaya.

Trading patterns fitted in with the seasonal monsoons, the Gujaratis coming between March and May; southern Indians from October to January; the Chinese arriving between November and March and leaving in late June; traders from Pegu from March to July; Javanese arriving between May and September and waiting to return in January.

This meant a widely fluctuating merchant body, some transients visiting for a short season, but the Javanese and Chinese in particular having to wait for months to make the return journey. Goods had to be stored and resold, which created an attractive market for trade in the town and encouraged many foreign merchants to put down roots in Melaka.

The Gujaratis were the most important visiting traders and perhaps 1000 of them were resident in Melaka town at the end of the century. But the Tamils and Javanese were the most wealthy, permanent, foreign residents, many owning fine town houses and large landed estates. Utimutiraja, the most prominent Javanese merchant, who controlled the rice trade, almost rivalled Sultan Mahmud in his wealth, living in his own fortified settlement tended by a host of slaves. The Tamils were noted for their gracious living, their cultivation of the arts and notably of music.

The Chinese community flourished. The imperial ban on trade and emigration was not strictly enforced at that time and the late-fifteenth century was a period of active Chinese trading in the Nanyang, of which the main focus switched from Java and Pasai to Melaka. But the Chinese no longer enjoyed political influence, which passed in the second half of the fifteenth century to the Gujaratis, Tamils, Bengalis and Javanese.

There were also smaller communities of Chams, Parsis and Arabs, and a host of Indonesian traders. The east Sumatran trade was one of the mainstays of Melaka's commerce, and it imported gold, pepper, forest produce and food from Indragiri, Palembang, Jambi, Kampar and Siak. Melaka also had close links with the north Java ports and with Brunei, and some contact with the Moluccas and Sulawesi.

Foreign traders were attracted to Melaka by its favourable geographical position and its settled administration and security. Trade taxes were high but fixed, and despite a certain amount of bribery and corruption, trading was more straightforward and less hazardous than in other ports in the region. The sultan and Malay nobility lived luxuriously on the proceeds of trade but ploughed some of the profit into improved facilities, providing warehouses, fair weights and measures, a code of port regulations, and a reliable currency.

The Malay authorities supplied an infrastructure of administration but the skeleton bureaucracy remained a collection of individual officials and did not blossom into more sophisticated machinery of government. Nor did the Malay rulers develop commercial institutions.

While the aristocracy joined in ventures with foreign merchants, they despised trade and left the organization of commerce almost entirely in the hands of foreigners. Although many trading ships were crewed by Malay sailors, all the vessels appear to have been foreign owned. Melaka developed no ship-building industry and, apart from very small craft, imported Pegu-built ships. The considerable capital required to finance the commerce in textiles and luxuries was supplied by foreign merchants.

Speed and good timing were essential for the smooth and fair transaction of trade. Dependence on the changing wind systems required a complicated organization to supervise contracts and enforce price controls in order to avoid extortion. The administration of the foreign community and of trade in general was delegated to four *shahbandars*, chosen from the main foreign communities concerned: the leading *shahbandar* was appointed to deal with the Gujarati merchants; the second with other Indians and traders from Pegu and north Sumatra; the third with the Javanese and traders from Borneo, the Philippines, Moluccas and southern Sumatra; and the fourth with traders from China, Champa and the Far East.

Shahbandars were responsible not only for commercial matters and collecting official trade dues but also for settling minor disputes among their community, each of which lived in its allotted district. As an administrative device the arrangement worked well in facilitating trade and and managing a cosmopolitan society comprising many transients, with a minimum of bureaucracy and interference. This *kapitan* system was later taken over and developed by the Portuguese, the Dutch and in the early days by the British. But it did not encourage the emergence of a local middle class of entrepreneurs. Commercial life at the upper and middle level was dominated by foreign merchants, with some participation by the sultan and leading officials. The majority of the population was not directly concerned with international commerce and those who were confined themselves to a local peddling trade.

Government continued to be a very personal type of rule by the sultan and a chosen handful of ministers, without a formal council or bureaucratic hierarchy. While the later sultans of Melaka lacked the individual drive and ability of their predecessors, the office of sultan was held in great respect.

Islam had no hierarchy to support the monarchy and in this way inhibited the growth of institutions, but it strengthened the monarchy by concentrating political and religious authority in one head of state. In some ways Islam fitted the earlier ideas of the ruler's role as a charismatic father figure, ideally loving his people and commanding their complete devotion. Some of the semi-mystical qualities of the traditional Hindu or Buddhist god-king remained, and Muslim Malay rulers were often believed to have supernatural powers of magic and healing. Surrounded by ceremony, honoured and entitled to the absolute loyalty of his subjects, the sultan was accountable for his actions only to Allah but was not himself regarded as divine. While the office of sultan was held to be sacred, the holder of that office was human. The Malay sultan did not live in the isolation of the Hindu-Buddhist kings but took an active role in direct contact with his people. Succession to the throne was not by divine right of inheritance. The senior chiefs had the right to choose the sultan, the *bendahara* took charge of the royal regalia on the sultan's death and made the formal invitation to his successor. The claims of elder sons could be set aside if their mother's social background or their own personality was considered unsuitable, as in the case of Sultan Mansur's heir, Muhammad.

Under Tun Perak the office of *bendahara* became very powerful, ranking second to the sultan in the state and taking precedence over most foreign vassal rulers. While the office was not hereditary, it was confined to a family group, which traditionally intermarried with the royal house and from which the other two senior ministers, the treasurer and the *temenggong,* were also drawn.

As a commercial state Melaka did not wish to waste its resources by keeping a standing army, so that there were no military forces, powerful chiefs or warriors to threaten internal security. The power of the state lay in the navy, which could be quickly summoned from the *orang laut* tribes, whose loyalty was unwavering. The only threats to the sultanate came in the form of palace revolutions or intrigues.

Melaka took over Srivijaya's role in spreading the form of political government it had inherited from Palembang, together with the Malay language, which became the lingua franca of ports throughout the archipelago. It acted as a focal point for the dissemination of Islam and attracted a number of Muslim scholars and preachers from India and the Middle East, notably the Maulana Abu Bakar, who came in Mansur's reign, and the Maulana Sadar Jahan, who acted as tutor and counsellor to Sultan Mahmud, Bendahara Mutahir and other dignitaries. But Melaka could not be described as a centre of learning, and the court's culture was superficial and brittle, glittering but lacking in depth. It did not develop the sophisticated music, dance forms or shadow play theatre of the traditional Southeast Asian kingdoms but favoured light literature and music, with *pantun* (verse making) competitions as amusements. The qualities in vogue were lively intelligence, sparkling humour and sharp wittedness.

Islam weakened the force of *adat* both in political organization and in law, yet was itself modified by traditional custom. Many Hindu practices were retained as in coronation and marriage ceremonies. The Palembang *adat temenggong,* which had itself been affected by Hindu practice evolved in powerful states, was already an authoritarian patriarchal system of law, and Islam accentuated these features. The Melaka law system underlined the superiority of men who, as household heads, owned and inherited property, and it emphasized their rights in marriage and divorce. It aimed to punish crimes against society and deter criminals, inflicting penalties of imprisonment, mutilation or death. Social offences forbidden by Islam were added to the list of crimes, such as gambling, cock fighting or not observing religious fasts. Fines were paid to the ruler, not to the injured party, so that the legal system supported the position of the ruling class. But in some ways customary *adat* tempered the ferocity of Islamic law which was not administered with the severity common in the Middle East.

Islam weakened the position of women, who in any event did not have the importance in Melaka which they could command in agricultural communities. Among the ruling class their main function was to act as political pawns to cement political relationships through their marriage. This was supported by the practice of polygyny combined with automatic divorce at a husband's will. Beautiful wives were either a status symbol, a monarch's right or a favour to win a vassal's loyalty to the Melakan empire, its political system and religion. But behind the scenes individual mothers, wives and daughters had considerable influence on political affairs.

While Islam preached the equality of men and permitted no caste system, there was a growing distinction between aristocrats, commoners and slaves together with a deepening gulf between rich and poor. At the upper level there was social mixing and intermarriage, particularly between the Malay aristocracy and Indian or Javanese Muslims. Sultans often took foreign-merchants' daughters as wives, later marrying them off to the nobility. The luxurious court life of the sultan and Malay nobility was paralleled by the affluence of leading foreign merchants. But this lifestyle and that of the largely alien trading middle class contrasted with the poverty of the Malay fishermen, who constituted the bulk of the local population.

At the beginning of the sixteenth century Melaka reached the height of its territorial power, commercial prosperity and religious prestige and the sultanate stood at its zenith. In the words of Tome Pires, Melaka was 'a city that was made for merchandise', and it was this reputation which brought the first Portuguese expedition to the port in 1509.

1. Cortesao, A. *The 'Suma Oriental' of Tomé Pires*, 2 vols., Hakluyt Society, second series, Vols. XXXIX and XL, London, 1944.

CHAPTER 5

The Portuguese Conquest of Melaka

Portugal and Asian Trade

In the fifteenth century the Arabs dominated the Middle East trade routes and controlled commerce between Europe and Asia. They held a monopoly over the luxury trade in spices, which were brought from Melaka and Ceylon to Gujarat and Malabar and transhipped by Arab vessels to the Persian Gulf or the Red Sea, whence Venetian merchants carried them to the European market.

In the latter years of the century Portugal set out to break this Venetian–Arab stranglehold by entering into direct trade with the East. The Portuguese, combining lust for profit with Christian fervour, succeeded within the short span of a quarter of a century in upsetting Muslim commercial dominance in Asia and wresting for themselves a large share of the trade.

The states of the Iberian peninsula, which had themselves come under Muslim–Moorish rule, struggled throughout the fifteenth century to throw off the alien yoke, and the impetus of this resistance movement carried them on to an anti-Muslim offensive overseas. Seizing Ceuta on the north African coast from the Moors in 1415, the Portuguese began European expansionism and in the process led the way in naval construction, seamanship, exploration and colonialism. Pushing down the west coast of Africa, they established trading posts and sought a way round the African continent which would bring them to the Indian Ocean. They hoped also to discover the fabled Christian kingdom of Prester John, which they believed existed either in Asia or East Africa, and whose support they wished to enlist in undermining the Muslim religious and commercial hold in Asia.

Throughout the fifteenth century the initiative for expansion rested with the monarchy, which appointed commanders and officers and gave detailed instructions on the purpose and conduct of expeditions. King Manuel I, who reigned from 1495 till 1521, brought Portuguese activities in the East to the peak of their success.

After many exploratory voyages the Portuguese rounded the Cape of Good Hope in 1487, and an expedition under Vasco da Gama reached

Calicut in western India in 1498. The Arabs, Gujaratis and other
Muslims, who monopolized the carrying trade on the west Indian coast,
resented the Portuguese intrusion and put many difficulties in the way
of Vasco da Gama's mission. A second Portuguese expedition, which
came to India in 1500–01 with orders to establish a trading post and
persuade Hindu rulers to expel Muslim traders, came to blows with the
Muslims. The Portuguese post was destroyed, many of the occupants
killed, and the fleet returned to Lisbon badly mauled. This experience
proved that any peaceful infiltration of Asian trade was doomed and the
Muslim commercial monopoly would have to be toppled by force. But
the venture was so financially rewarding that King Manuel decided the
risks were justified.

In 1503 the Portuguese established the first European trading station
in Asia at Cochin in southwest India. Two years later Dom Francisco de
Almeida was appointed first Portuguese viceroy in India and began
harrying Muslim shipping and establishing forts along the coasts of east
Africa and west India, in an attempt to dominate the sea routes. The
Egyptian and Gujarati navies, which combined forces to combat the
Portuguese challenge, initially met with considerable success, but early
in 1509 Almeida defeated the joint fleets to make Portugal the strongest
naval power in the Indian Ocean.

A few months later Almeida was succeeded as viceroy by Afonso de
Albuquerque, an outstanding commander, who in the six years of his
governorship established the foundations for Portuguese power in Asia.
Unlike his predecessor Albuquerque put trading considerations above
political or religious aims. Realizing it was impossible to obliterate
Muslims without also destroying their trade, he called off indiscriminate
attacks upon Muslim shipping and tried to avoid further confrontation
with Egypt and Gujarat. His policy was to forestall any coalition of
Muslim power, to divide the Muslims and to regulate rather than crush
their trade.

Albuquerque also broke with his predecessor's policy in standing clear
of political entanglements, refusing to be drawn into local disputes
unless there was direct profit in this for Portugal. He disapproved of
dispersing limited Portuguese sea power and aimed instead to establish
a few strategically-placed strong bases under direct Portuguese control.
In 1510 he seized Goa in western India, which became the headquarters
of Portuguese power in Asia. The following year he captured Melaka
and in 1515 he established the Portuguese at Ormuz which commanded
the Persian Gulf.

The Portuguese Attack on Melaka

The first Portuguese expedition, commanded by Diogo Lopes de Sequeira, arrived in Melaka in 1509 and was impressed by the city's

opulence and commercial bustle. Bendahara Mutahir received the 'white Bengalis' graciously, presenting to the Portuguese commander the rich robes which were the customary gift to honoured guests and listening sympathetically to their requests for permission to trade. But the Gujaratis, already bitter at the violence and bloodshed which Portuguese competition had brought to India, turned the *bendahara* against the Europeans and persuaded him to kill them.

The plot was revealed, allegedly by a Portuguese officer's Malay mistress, and Sequeira escaped with most of his crew, leaving about twenty of their shipmates as prisoners. Two years later Albuquerque himself came to Melaka to avenge the treachery, rescue his countrymen and seize control of this key to the spice trade.

Many troubles had overtaken Melaka during the course of those two years. The *bendahara,* treasurer and *temenggong* had been killed, the *laksamana* disgraced, and Sultan Mahmud had become a recluse.

For a long time Sultan Mahmud had been increasingly tormented by jealousy and resentment of the *bendahara.* Mutahir, not content, as the wise Tun Perak had been, to keep the substance of power without pretensions to grandeur, flaunted his wealth and position. He counted himself equal to the sultan of Pahang and superior to the sultan of Kedah and all other vassal rulers. Through his contact with foreign merchants his renown spread to other countries, where Melaka came to be identified with his name rather than the sultan's. Mahmud was particularly incensed when Mutahir married his most beautiful daughter, Tun Fatimah, to his nephew instead of offering her as a bride to the sultan in accordance with traditional custom.

As Mutahir used his office to further his own business interests, the foreign merchants became critical of his arrogance, greed and corruption. The *bendahara's* undoing came as a result of a civil dispute between two leading Tamil merchants: Naina Sura Dewana, a wealthy Hindu, and Raja Mendaliar, the *shahbandar.* Naina Sura Dewana allegedly bribed the *bendahara* to give judgment in his favour, whereupon the Raja Mendaliar went to the *laksamana* with allegations that Mutahir was plotting to seize the throne for himself. Laksamana Khoja Husain, son-in-law of Hang Tuah, who had died a few years earlier, reported this to Sultan Mahmud. Already suspicious because Mutahir was acting as ruler of Melaka in all but name, Mahmud gave way to fury and in a mad rage, without further investigation, ordered his men to kill the *bendahara* and confiscate his property. Mutahir perished alongside nearly all his family, including his brother, the treasurer, and his son, the *temenggong.* In his place Mahmud appointed as *bendahara* a son of the late Tun Perak, a frail old man who was half paralysed.

Mahmud married the beautiful Tun Fatimah, but she brought him little happiness. According to the *Malay Annals,* 'never once did she laugh or even smile' but grieved continually for her murdered father. The sultan soon came to realize that the reports about Mutahir's treachery were wrong. He executed the Raja Mendaliar, castrated the *laksamana,* and in remorse went into seclusion. The government was handed over to his son, Ahmad, a rather frivolous young man, who had no bent for matters of state but frittered away his time with worthless companions. When Albuquerque arrived in July 1511, he found a much troubled and weakened Melaka without effective leadership.

The viceroy demanded the release of the prisoners, compensation for Portuguese losses and permission to build a fortified trading post. The Malay authorities were divided about what to do. The ageing *bendahara* advised compromise but most of the chiefs and merchants called for resistance, and the counsels of war prevailed. The Melaka forces were numerically stronger, comprising Malay warriors, supported by able-bodied men from the different foreign communities, in all perhaps 20 000 men. Against these, Albuquerque had a fleet of 18 ships, carrying some 800 Portuguese soldiers with 300 Malabar Indian auxiliaries.

In their initial assault the Portuguese succeeded in capturing the bridge which linked the royal city with the commercial sector on the opposite bank of the river. But the Melaka forces fought back with fierce determination. All the communities rallied to support the Malays. Young Sultan Ahmad bravely entered the thick of the fray on his elephant, and even the ailing *bendahara* took up arms. The vigour of the resistance forced the Portuguese to give up their gains and retreat to their ships to nurse their wounds and reconsider their strategy.

In a second attack a month later, the Portuguese brought the full weight of their artillery to bear on the town, setting it ablaze, and under cover of the bombardment they floated a ship up river on the high tide to recapture the vital bridge. This time they managed to retain their strategic foothold and split the commercial sector from the Malays. Most of the foreign merchants including the elderly, respected Javanese leader, Utimutiraja, came to terms with the invaders, and the motley array of Javanese, Cambodian, Brunei, Mindanao, Pegu and Siamese auxiliaries began to desert the sultan. In a final assault two weeks later the Malay city fell with little resistance. Convinced that the fight was hopeless, Sultan Ahmad fled with his *bendahara,* chieftains, followers and the few foreign merchants who remained loyal to his cause. By nightfall the Portuguese were in complete control of Melaka.

The city of traders had faced no enemy in living memory and was not geared for war. The seemingly superior strength of the defending force was illusory, since it was disunited and leaderless. The *bendahara* was too old to be effective and Sultan Ahmad, despite his courage and will to fight, was no strategist. Furthermore, he was at loggerheads with his father, Mahmud, who hesitated to throw his men into battle. Owing perhaps to the *laksamana's* recent disgrace, the *orang laut* fleet was not marshalled from the Riau–Lingga archipelago, nor could this have faced the larger Portuguese ships in open fight. The Melakan army was a mixed collection from different communities, none of whom, apart from the Malays, had any loyalty to Melaka or any common interest except in making money. This army was no match for the attacking Portuguese force of trained soldiers, equipped with modern weapons, and fighting as one cohesive unit under a single, able commander. The sudden collapse of Melaka at the height of its prosperity also revealed the innate weakness of its personal form of government which was so dependent on strong individual leadership.

Early Portuguese Rule

Albuquerque stayed three months in Melaka to organize administration and try to restore trade to a normal footing. He immediately began to construct a great fortress, *A Famosa*, and, on the site of the sultan's palace on the hill above the river, the Portuguese built St Paul's church. The former Malay town was subsequently enclosed in a walled city to house the Portuguese community, government buildings and Christian churches, while the Malays and other Asian communities lived outside the city walls.

The few alien merchants who fled with the Malays soon returned, and the Portuguese tried to conciliate the business community by working through their accepted leaders. The Chinese and Hindus adapted to the new regime, but there was considerable restiveness among the Muslim merchants. The Javanese leader, Utimutiraja, was executed in December 1511 for allegedly plotting against the Portuguese administration, and his successor, Patih Kadir, met the same fate a year later on similar grounds.

For the first sixty years of Portuguese rule the Captain of the Fortress was the head of the government, but in 1571 Melaka was given its own Governor, who had responsibility for other eastern Portuguese settlements and was subordinate to the Viceroy in Goa. To assist him the Governor had a council, comprising a chief justice, mayor and bishop.

The Portuguese authorities had little direct contact with the Asian inhabitants and kept much of the former Malay administration intact. Headmen, or *kapitans,* were appointed to keep law and order among their own people under the supervision of a Malay *bendahara,* who held civil and criminal jurisdiction over all the non-Portuguese communities living in the suburbs outside the city walls. A Malay *temenggong* was responsible for the Malays of the country districts and a *shahbandar* was put in charge of all non-Portuguese traders.

By the time Albuquerque died in 1515 he had established Portuguese control from the Persian Gulf to Melaka, to the great enrichment of the monarchy. By that time the Portuguese dominated the carrying trade between Asia and Europe, and Lisbon supplanted Venice as the main market in Europe for the Asian trade.

The Portuguese attempted to take over Melaka's commerce intact but under their own control. The spice trade remained the foundation of this commerce. Indian cottons and other piece goods imported from Goa were exchanged in Melaka for spices, which were then sent to Goa for shipment with Indian and Ceylonese spices to the Lisbon market. Spices were also exchanged for Chinese silk and porcelain, which were shipped from Melaka to Europe.

To safeguard this trade the Portuguese government needed to control all competitors, to establish a firm hold over the Moluccas, where spices were produced, and to develop an honest and efficient administration, loyal to the crown's interests. In this they failed.

The Portuguese tried to force all ships to call at Melaka to obtain passes and pay dues, but these vigorous attempts to enforce monopoly and the aggressiveness of Portuguese methods, though initially effective, alienated other traders. In the early years dues were arbitrary, and deterred Asian traders, particularly Muslims, who sought alternative ports such as Acheh, Bantam or Brunei.

At first official Portuguese trade benefited from the backing of a well-organized administration in Goa, but rapid expansion brought great problems for a small country such as Portugal, and particularly for the monarchy. After the death of Manuel I in 1521 royal power began to decline. In theory the crown controlled all administration and trade overseas. Throughout the sixteenth century no Portuguese could go to the East without a royal licence and nearly all of those that did go, were in the service of the king or the church. Neither Portuguese nor foreigners were supposed to trade in pepper, cloves, nutmeg, mace or silk, which were royal monopolies. Nor were officials permitted to engage in private trading.

Albuquerque tried to enforce these rules, but in practice they were constantly infringed, and the crown became increasingly powerless to control its servants overseas. Soldiers and civil servants were not paid regularly and had every inducement to supplement their meagre salaries by trading on their own account. Administration was ineffective and corrupt. The king appointed officials on an individual basis, often as reward for services performed in Portugal. There was no settled civil service, no promotion system and much personal quarrelling.

From the late-1520s the Portuguese government faced mounting troubles and wars in India, which required the kings to finance expensive expeditions and brought them heavily into debt. Increasingly the crown was shouldering responsibility and expense while the profits went to individual Portuguese officials. In 1570 the king was forced to abandon the monopoly of the pepper and spice trades, which were thrown open to foreign consortia, though the Portuguese crown reaped the benefit of taxes on this commerce.

The acquisition of Melaka was a disappointment for the crown. Attempts to capture the spice trade of the Moluccas met with vigorous resistance from local Muslim governments and brought the Portuguese into conflict with Spanish ambitions, so that they established only a precarious hold over the spice islands.

Portugal never gained undisputed mastery over the Melaka Straits. In 1513 Melaka was attacked by a Javanese fleet from Japara, and in the first fifteen years of Portuguese rule suffered repeated assaults by the Malays in attempts to retake their city. Like the Melaka Malays, the Portuguese never succeeded in suppressing the Aru pirates. In 1521 the Portuguese set up a fort at Pasai, but failing to subdue the Sumatran state of Acheh were forced to abandon the Pasai fort three years later. Portuguese attempts to control the Sunda Strait in the late-1520s were thwarted by the Achehnese, who continued to harass the Portuguese for the rest of the century, sometimes threatening to overwhelm Melaka itself.

For 130 years the Portuguese kept a precarious hold on Melaka because, despite their impregnable fortress, dependence on trade and imported food made them vulnerable to siege and blockade. But as long as they controlled the sea route they could be rescued by reinforcements from Goa, and their ultimate safeguard was the division of their enemies: notably the almost constant hostility between Acheh and the ex-Melaka Malays.

At the best of times Melaka was unhealthy, with a high death rate, particularly through malaria. Frequently the Portuguese had to withstand assaults and sieges, which sometimes brought them to the brink of starvation. Yet they clung on, largely because private trading was so profitable.

To compensate for the hazards and dangers, in times of peace the Portuguese lived in elegant luxury and Melaka was then known as 'the Babylon of the Orient'. Private Portuguese trading increased and flourished at the expense of official commerce, particularly in the second half of the century. Embezzlement and dishonesty among officials were so blatant that from 1562 the Portuguese government forbade the transhipment of spices at Melaka. But the port profited from the opening up of Portuguese trade in China and Japan and from the flourishing inter-regional trade in Southeast Asia in which the crown had never been involved. While many ports grew up as rivals to Melaka, they helped to stimulate trade in the archipelago, which in turn benefited Melaka indirectly. A flat rate of trade dues imposed from 1544 made the port more attractive.

Sixteenth-century Melaka was a cosmopolitan city. The bulk of the population was Malay, with a Portuguese ruling class, and commercial activities concentrated in the hands of Portuguese and Chinese. There were also large numbers of African slaves, imported by the Portuguese from Mombasa and Mozambique for sale to settlers for use as troops. The Portuguese population was never large, probably numbering no more than 600 at any one time; other Europeans were rigidly excluded, but officials and soldiers were encouraged to put down roots and marry local women, so that a sizeable Eurasian community grew up.

The Chinese became the most important foreign community in Melaka after many Muslim traders withdrew to alternative ports. They had little political or social influence on the ruling Portuguese community but often entered into joint business ventures with individual Portuguese. From the 1520s for some forty years, the Ming emperors rigorously enforced the regulations banning Chinese from trading in the Nanyang, but the restrictions were relaxed in 1566, after which traders from Fukien and Kwangtung built up a network of commerce throughout the ports of the archipelago.

Apart from some influence on Malay music, the Portuguese had little cultural impact outside their own community. From the earliest days they brought in Roman Catholic priests and built a number of churches, but these catered almost exclusively for Portuguese and their descendants.

They made little attempt to convert the population, regarding the port as a source of personal profit and the guardian of the sea power on which their trade depended, rather than as a missionary field. This indifference persisted even after the Society of Jesus came to propagate Christianity in the East in the 1540s. The celebrated French Jesuit, St Francis Xavier spent two years in Melaka in 1547-8 and founded a school but his major missionary interest was in India and China.

Nor did the Asian population find much to attract them to Christianity. Unlike the earlier religions, Christianity would not adapt to local custom, particularly in the sixteenth century when traditional Roman Catholicism, under challenge from Protestant beliefs in Europe, was unwilling to bend to any unorthodoxy. Portuguese Christians held their beliefs to be unshakable and superior to all other religions. Yet their behaviour did not command respect for Christian virtues. In the words of St. Francis Xavier, 'There is a very rich merchandise which the traders regard of little account. It is called a man's conscience, and so little esteemed is it in these parts, that all the merchants believe they would go bankrupt if they invested in it'.

Christianity was also distasteful to Melakans because it came through war, not as the companion of peaceful trading like the earlier religions. While the Portuguese did not persecute Muslims in Melaka, reports of their anti-Muslim harshness in India, the Moluccas and elsewhere alienated Muslims throughout the region and consolidated Islam in opposition to this violent, foreign intrusion.

Conversion to Christianity offered no enhanced social status. The Portuguese showed no respect for converts, and King Manuel's orders that Portuguese and Asian Christians should be treated as equals were ignored, so that Christianity was confined to an arrogant Portuguese ruling class on one hand and a socially despised Eurasian community on the other.

The Portuguese never tried to extend their influence beyond Melaka town. Their interest was in trade, not territory, and they believed that in capturing Melaka they would automatically inherit her commerce and control of the vital sea lanes. While the Portuguese recognized Melaka as the key to trade in the East, they were not able to exploit their acquisition fully, partly because Portugal was a small country, lacking the naval power to patrol Asian shipping, curb smuggling or crush piracy. But their failure also stemmed from the fact that they did not recognize the foundations on which Melaka's past prosperity was based. The sultanate's pre-eminence had rested not on military might but on commerce backed by a political system of vassal states, which ensured peace and stability. While Portuguese fleets were impressive in battle, they were not as effective in patrolling trade as the *orang laut* tribes over whom the Malays held suzerainty. *Orang laut* were invaluable allies, helping to enforce a suzerain's monopoly, but dangerous enemies, preying on rival merchantmen. While the Portuguese never had the opportunity of harnessing the *orang laut* to their system, initially some of the Melakan vassal states in Sumatra were willing to accept Portugal as their new overlord, but the Portuguese avoided such commitments.

Melaka's commercial effectiveness under Malay rule had stemmed largely from its political, cultural and religious leadership, and in rejecting this role the Portuguese forfeited popular allegiance.

CHAPTER 6

Johor, Acheh and Brunei in the Sixteenth Century

The Founding of Johor

The Portuguese capture of Melaka did not mean the destruction of Malay power. Displaced from Melaka, it re-emerged in new principalities in other parts of the archipelago, notably Johor, Acheh and Brunei, all of which became important states during the sixteenth century. They carried on the Malayo–Muslim pattern of maritime power, and between them they were able, in some measure, to balance the power of the Portuguese.

Mahmud, Ahmad and their followers retreated first to Muar, thence overland to Pahang. After sending fruitless appeals to China, they moved to the Johor river and finally in 1513 to Bintan. Mahmud, despairing of Ahmad's political ineptitude, had his son murdered and resumed power himself, re-establishing his court on the island, the source of *orang laut* support.

Mahmud's primary objective was to recapture Melaka, against which the Malays launched repeated attacks in the years that followed: in 1512, 1515, 1516, 1519, 1523 and again in 1524. In retaliation for these raids and blockades, which brought Melaka to the brink of starvation and disrupted her trade, the Portuguese staged a number of counter-attacks, culminating in the destruction of Mahmud's capital at Bintan in 1526.

The sultan fled to Kampar, where he died two years later. His widow, Tun Fatimah, persuaded the chiefs to choose her son as successor in preference to Mahmud's eldest son, Muzaffar. Thus the late Bendahara Mutahir's grandson became Sultan Alauddin Riayat Shah, while Muzaffar accepted an invitation to become first sultan of Perak. Muzaffar set up his capital on the middle stretches of the Perak river about the year 1529, introducing the Melaka system of government and appointing the raja of Selangor as his *bendahara*.

Meanwhile in the early-1530s Sultan Alauddin established a new capital on the Johor river, near to the modern Kota Tinggi. It was not a convenient centre for trading but offered an escape route in time of crisis, and the successors to the Melaka empire retained their seat of power on the Johor river during most of the two centuries that followed.

From their new headquarters the Malays continued to harass Portuguese shipping and instigate plots in Melaka. To put an end to these threats the Portuguese tried to destroy Johor. In 1535 they razed the capital to the ground, but the inhabitants fled upriver and rebuilt their town. The following year another Portuguese expedition wiped out this new settlement but once more the Malays sprang back to life, and in the 1540s they established their capital at Johor Lama, fifteen kilometres from the mouth of the Johor river.

While the loss of Melaka dealt a heavy blow to Malay economic power, it did not destroy the sultan's political standing in the region. When the Portuguese rebuffed requests for help from a deposed ruler of Pasai in 1512, Sultan Mahmud helped expel the usurper and gave his daughter in marriage to the restored ruler. Shortly afterwards when the Sultan of Kampar tried to throw off Johor's suzerainty and put himself under Portuguese protection, Mahmud allegedly spread false reports which led the Portuguese to execute the ruler of Kampar on suspicion of treason.

These events proved to neighbouring states that Johor was still the most effective overlord in the region. Kampar was brought back into Johor's fold. Lingga, Indragiri, Siak and Pahang paid homage, and Mahmud continued to build up alliances with vassal states through royal marriages. His son, Sultan Alauddin Riayat Shah, in a long reign lasting from 1529 until 1564, set an example which his successors followed by insisting on etiquette, formal homage and the manifestations of vassalage.

The Portuguese opposed Johor only in so far as the Malays were a continuing threat to trade, and, with one exception, all the Portuguese attacks on them were made in the first quarter century of their occupation of Melaka. The Portuguese were not interested in challenging Malay political hegemony, unlike the emerging Sumatran state of Acheh, which aspired to take over both Johor's economic and political role.

Acheh

Acheh's rise was meteoric. At the beginning of the sixteenth century this small state at the northern tip of Sumatra produced a little pepper but lived mainly on piracy. The fall of Melaka stimulated the Muslim rulers of Acheh to take the lead in resisting the Christian Portuguese intruders and then going on to battle with Johor for political and economic leadership in Sumatra and the Melaka Straits. A combination of religious fervour and political ambition made Acheh the most powerful force in the western Nanyang in the sixteenth and early-seventeenth centuries.

Sultan Ali Mughayat Shah of Acheh led neighbouring states in expelling the Portuguese from Pedir and Pasai in 1524, after which the small northern kingdoms united to form a larger Acheh Besar. Many Muslim traders were attracted away from Portuguese Melaka to Achehnese ports and the country expanded in wealth and population. The capital at Bandar Acheh was well placed for ships sailing along the western coast of Sumatra to the Sunda Straits, and Acheh developed this route to by-pass Portuguese Melaka. In the late-1520s it successfully thwarted Portuguese attempts to establish control over the Sunda Straits and created friendly links with Bantam in west Java to dominate this increasingly important gateway. Acheh also co-operated with Japara and the north Java sultanates to tap the Moluccas trade.

During a long reign, which lasted from 1537 to 1571, the aggressive and powerful Sultan Alauddin Riayat Shah al-Kahar, the Strong, extended Acheh's control south in Sumatra. He carried anti-Portuguese hostility to Melaka itself and soon after coming to the throne launched a direct but unsuccessful attack on the fortress. The only hope of overthrowing the Portuguese lay in a united effort by Acheh and Johor, but Acheh's ambitions threw these two Muslim powers into conflict and their occasional attempts to put up a common front against the Portuguese were half hearted and short lived.

Acheh, Melaka and Johor

After calling off the attack on Melaka, in 1539 the Achehnese fleet turned against Aru, overthrowing the government and killing the ruler, whose widow appealed to Johor. Sultan Alauddin Riayat Shah of Johor married the widowed queen and sent a fleet, which, with the backing of his Siak vassals, defeated the Achehnese at the mouth of the Panai river and restored the former regime.

This began a hostility between Acheh and Johor which lasted for a century, but it was the only occasion on which Johor sought out and defeated her rival. After that the southern kingdom of Johor was constantly on the defensive, while Acheh increased in power and ambition.

Carrying the holy Islamic war and forcing conversion on the hitherto animist Minangkabau people of central Sumatra, Sultan Alauddin Riayat Shah al-Kahar claimed suzerainty over the pepper ports of north Sumatra and the gold-producing region of Minangkabau. By the middle of the century Acheh was the main headquarters for Muslim Indian and Arab traders. It was also the most vigorous Islamic centre in the archipelago, and to stress this the Sultan put Acheh under the suzerainty of the Ottoman empire and hired mercenary soldiers from Turkey.

When Acheh prepared a second attack on Melaka in 1547, the Johor fleet stood by, ready apparently to defy the invaders. When Johor itself attacked Melaka four years later, the Achehnese did not help, although their intervention might have forced a Portuguese capitulation since the Johor force almost starved Melaka out. Their fleet of some 200 vessels blockaded the port, while an army reputedly 5000 strong occupied the suburbs and cut off all supplies. The Portuguese were besieged in their fortress for three months and relieved only by reinforcements from Goa.

Johor hated and resented the Portuguese but feared Achehnese aspirations even more, and the fundamental clash of material interests outweighed racial and religious sympathies. In 1564 Acheh wrested Aru from Johor and attacked the heart of the empire in the first of a series of raids which were to terrorize Johor for the next sixty years. In the initial attack the Achehnese destroyed Johor Lama and took the entire royal family back to Acheh, where Sultan Alauddin died. The Achehnese sent his son back to Johor as Sultan Muzaffar Shah, but the new ruler immediately threw off Achehnese suzerainty and in 1568 sent men to help Melaka resist a further Achehnese attack. The large Sumatran force of some 20 000 fighting men was again unable to storm the fortress. Instead they threw themselves against Johor in retaliation for Muzaffar's defection. In 1570 they burned all Malay settlements along the Johor river, forcing Muzaffar to flee far upstream to Seluyut.

Johor obtained some respite while Acheh turned to battle once more with the Portuguese. In 1571 the Portuguese commander's status in Melaka was raised to governor, and Goa sent reinforcements with orders to eliminate the Achehnese menace. But the war continued for another seventy years, with the Achehnese almost constantly on the offensive though unable to storm the fortress of *A Famosa*.

In 1574 and again the following year the Achehnese launched further attacks on Melaka, but failing to dislodge the Portuguese at the centre, they turned to gain mastery of the peninsular side of the Melaka Straits. Acheh built a fort in Perlis and in 1575 turned against Perak, which had hitherto supported Johor's cause. The Achehnese subdued the country and carried off the royal family to Acheh, sending the sultan's son back to rule Perak as a vassal state. Perak remained under Achehnese domination for almost a century, although except for short periods the Achehnese preferred not to rule the country directly but through the local royal house.

The Achehnese threat in Sumatra and the Malay peninsula drove the Portuguese and Malays together for a time. In 1582 the Portuguese helped Johor ward off a further Achehnese attack, and Sultan Abdul Jalil Riayat Shah of Johor visited Melaka in person to thank the Portuguese, the first of the former Malay royal house to set foot in Melaka. But this friendship soon wilted, and in 1587 Johor launched a further large-scale land and sea attack on the Portuguese. Again Melaka was saved only by reinforcements from Goa, and in retribution the Portuguese employed this relieving force to destroy Johor Lama. In this first

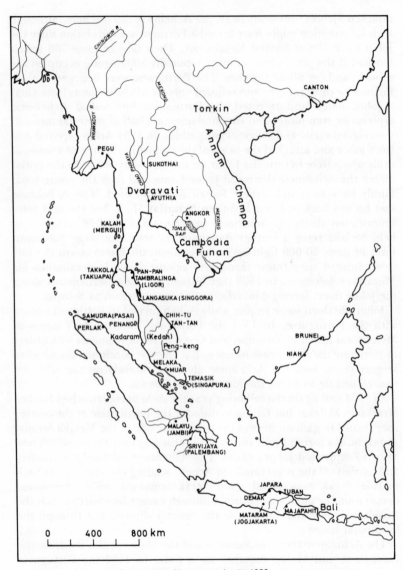

The western Nanyang prior to 1600

Portuguese punitive raid in more than half a century the town was looted and razed to the ground. The inhabitants fled up river to Batu Sawar, and it was many years before Johor recovered from the disaster.

Eye-witness descriptions of Acheh at the end of the sixteenth century portray a court of rather uncouth magnificence. Its gross but intelligent

Sultan Alauddin Riayat Shah, was a hard-drinking glutton who ate off gold plates and fine porcelain, but had acquired his throne by murder and punished his subjects with barbaric cruelty. His successor, Iskandar Muda or Mahkota Alam, Crown of the World, who also murdered his way to the throne in 1607, was the most powerful and ruthless of Achehnese rulers. A masterful warrior, he brought the sultanate to the peak of its tyranny within the country and extended Acheh's sway furthest afield. He claimed suzerainty over the whole west coast of Sumatra and the east coast as far south as Asahan and aimed to control the entire Malay peninsula including Johor and Melaka. By means of its powerful fleet Acheh achieved such a position of dominance in the peninsula that Johor could no longer guarantee protection to its vassals, nor even offer refuge from Achehnese attacks.

In a raid on Johor in 1613, the Achehnese destroyed Batu Sawar and again brought the royal family and ministers as prisoners to Acheh. Iskandar Muda sent the ex-sultan's half brother back as Sultan Hammat Shah, with an Achehnese bride and a force of Sumatran soldiers, to rule Johor as a vassal state. In 1617 Acheh devastated Pahang, carrying off the royal family and thousands of prisoners. Two years later it obtained the submission of Kedah, formerly Siam's vassal, and took its ruler a prisoner to Acheh. In 1620 it again invaded Perak, taking 5000 prisoners away and placing a more pliant ruler on the throne.

Meanwhile Hammat Shah had the temerity to repudiate Achehnese control and moved his capital from the comparative safety of the Johor river to the island of Lingga. At first the new settlement prospered, largely as a feeder port for Melaka. Traders came from Siam, Patani, Makassar and Java, bringing mainly rice and other foodstuffs and necessities, which were then transhipped into small local craft bound for the Portuguese settlement. But these good times soon came to an end. In 1623 Acheh destroyed the capital at Lingga, driving out Sultan Hammat, who died shortly afterwards and was succeeded by Abdul Jalil Riayat Shah. For many years after this the Johor Malays had no fixed capital.

In 1629 the Achehnese attacked Melaka once more in great force, capturing Bukit China, St John's Hill and the suburbs outside the walls. But again reinforcements from Goa saved the Portuguese defenders, who were then able to turn on their assailants and inflict a crushing defeat on the Achehnese navy, killing about 19 000 men.

This disaster heralded the decline of Acheh. In 1635 it launched a further punitive raid on Pahang, but the following year Iskandar Muda died. Having no male heir, he adopted his son-in-law Iskandar Thani, a Pahang prince taken captive in childhood. This ambitious successor survived only until 1641, after which Acheh came under the rule of a succession of queens and collapsed under the strains of the past century of brutal expansion, the depopulation of war and the murder and violence of palace intrigues. At home the *orang kaya* took advantage of ineffective female rule to shake free from the domination of centralized royal power, while abroad a weakened Acheh quickly lost its grip over its vassal states.

The devastation Johor suffered in 1623 was the last blow which the Achehnese were to inflict upon it. After Acheh's defeat at the hands of the Portuguese in 1629 Johor began to recover and its fortunes took a dramatic turn with the advent of new allies from the Netherlands.

The Netherlands and Asian Trade

Originally part of the Habsburg empire, the Netherlands revolted against Spain in the late 1560s. In the ensuing struggle, which culminated in the northern provinces forming an independent Dutch republic, they built up a profitable trade, distributing Asian goods from Lisbon throughout northern Europe. This livelihood was threatened when the Portuguese crown passed to Spain in 1580 and King Philip II of Spain closed Lisbon to the Dutch in 1594.

Seeking to enter directly into the Eastern spice trade, the first Dutch expedition set out in 1595 sailing round the Cape of Good Hope, direct to the Sunda Strait and the west Javanese port of Bantam. Despite difficulties and misfortunes the venture encouraged a spate of further expeditions in the next few years. Some were profitable, but competition threatened the success of the separate Dutch undertakings. To eliminate a price war among themselves and to strengthen their hand against the Portuguese and other European rivals, in 1602 the Netherlands formed the Vereenigde Oostindische Compagnie, or United East India Company, under the overall direction of the Heeren XVII, the Seventeen Gentlemen, who represented the leading cities of the Netherlands.

Originally the Dutch hoped to avoid open conflict with the Portuguese by keeping clear of the Melaka Straits route, but Goa put pressure on Indonesian ports to turn away Dutch traders. This led to violence and a running war between Dutch and Portuguese ships, embittered by religious and nationalist animosity between Dutch Protestant rebels and Roman Catholic Portugal, which was now part of Spain.

Early Dutch expeditions ranged widely round Sumatra, Java, Borneo and Celebes. Since they were not strong enough themselves to dislodge the Portuguese from Melaka, the Dutch attempted to make offensive alliances with Portugal's enemies, notably Johor and Acheh. The first Dutch expedition which visited Batu Sawar in 1602 was warmly welcomed and the Dutch established a trading post there the following year. In 1606 the Dutch Admiral Matelieff de Jonge made a treaty with Johor for a joint attack on Melaka but had to lift the siege after three months when Portuguese reinforcements arrived from Goa. The next year the Dutch made an agreement with Acheh, which gave them favourable trading terms.

A truce in Europe, which lasted from 1609 until 1621, brought open warfare between Holland and the Iberian powers to a temporary halt, during which the Dutch consolidated their position in the East. The main Dutch objectives were Banda and the Moluccas, where they made treaties with local rulers and built forts in an attempt to monopolize the spice trade. They eliminated competition from Indian, Chinese and Indonesian traders in Bantam and Jambi, sacked Japara, and in 1618 a new governor general, Jan Pieterszoon Coen, set up his base in Jakarta, which was renamed Batavia and became the headquarters for Dutch activities in the East.

At the same time the Dutch set out to crush English rivalry. The English East India Company, founded in 1600, lacked the financial backing and centralized organization of its Dutch counterpart. Its early voyages came mainly in search of pepper, to Acheh, Jambi and Bantam. Finding the Dutch already well entrenched, the English traders tried to infringe Dutch monopolies and open rival stations. Despite attempts by the British and Netherlands governments in Europe to promote co-operation, by 1615 English and Dutch traders were engaged in open war in the East, which culminated in 1623 in the Dutch executing ten British traders resident at Amboina on charges of treason.

By the time Holland again found itself at war with Spain and Portugal in Europe its position in the East was much stronger, while Portugal's energies were dispersed in north Africa, west Africa, Brazil, Ceylon and India, in addition to defending Melaka and the tenuous link with the Moluccas. Portugal faced growing hostility in India and competition from English and French as well as Dutch privateers. On the other hand the bitter hostility between Portugal's enemies, Acheh and Johor, made it impossible for the Dutch to unite them in confronting Melaka.

While Acheh had granted Holland very favourable trade terms in the past, the Dutch were alarmed at Iskandar Muda's current campaigns to conquer Kedah, Perak, Johor and east Sumatra, which they saw as a risk to the valuable pepper trade. The Dutch preferred, therefore, to seek an alliance with Johor. In the 1630s they kept up a persistent campaign to prevent shipping calling at Melaka, as a result of which the port's prosperity declined rapidly. In 1639 the Dutch made a further agreement with Johor for a joint attack on Melaka. The Dutch fleet began its blockade in June 1640. In August Dutch forces landed and forced the defenders to retreat into the fortress. Meanwhile the Johor Malays encircled the town, preventing refugees escaping or supplies coming in. Hunger and disease brought great privation to the defenders, while malaria and dysentery decimated the Dutch attacking force and made Johor's support the more vital. When the final assault came in January 1641, the Dutch had fewer than 700 fit soldiers. The Portuguese put up a tough defence but the end was inevitable. This time they could expect no reinforcements from Goa nor count on divisions in their enemies' ranks, and finally the fortress was compelled to surrender.

The Dutch Conquest of Melaka

The fall of Portuguese Melaka in January 1641 and the death of the last male ruler of Acheh a month later meant that within a few weeks Johor was saved from both the enemies which had threatened it for more than a century, and a long, gloomy chapter of its history came to an end.

The events of 1641 also brought to a close the long ordeal of Pahang, which had led a chequered existence in the sixteenth century. Originally it remained loyal to the former Malay regime and helped Bintan in besieging Portuguese Melaka in 1523 and in defending Bintan against Portuguese retaliation two years later. After that it reverted to sending tribute to Siam. Several rulers were murdered in palace intrigues but its economy flourished in the reflected prosperity of Patani and Brunei, with which states its ruling house had marriage connections.

In 1607 the Dutch set up a trading post in Pahang and Admiral Matelieff visited Pahang in that year looking for help against the Portuguese. But from that time Pahang was drawn into the bitter four-cornered rivalry of Johor, Acheh, the Dutch and Portuguese. It was sacked in 1612 by Johor, who put a Johor prince on its throne, and devastated five years later by Acheh who expelled this ruler. It was again laid waste by Acheh in 1635 and three years later suffered the same fate at Johor's hands after Pahang had made its peace with Acheh. In less than thirty years Pahang had been ravaged repeatedly, a large part of its population killed or carried into slavery, its economy ruined.

The Malay Peninsula in the Mid-Seventeeth Century

The Portuguese left little permanent impression upon the Malay peninsula. *A Famosa* continued to dominate the town and harbour until the British demolished the fortifications during the Napoleonic Wars, leaving only the Santiago gate and the ruins of St Paul's church on the hill. A small Roman Catholic enclave survived and a Eurasian community, most of whom degenerated into poverty, living as fishermen and continuing, until recent years, to speak an outdated Portuguese patois.

The Achehnese also appear to have made little lasting impact on the peninsula. A harsher, more ruthless power than the Melaka sultanate, their brand of Islam was an intense, militant, anti-Christian creed, which Achehnese scholars and sufis carried to Makassar, to Mataram in

Java and further afield in the archipelago. But in the Malay peninsula the immediate object was to capture and deport large numbers of prisoners to restock their own depopulated country, and apart from traces of Achehnese titles and styles of dress which survived in Perak for centuries, their legacy in the peninsula was largely negative and destructive. Acheh's effect on state administration was minimal. The traditional Srivijaya–Melaka political pattern was retained and Melaka's legal system extended. The Pahang Digest of 1596 was drawn up when Johor's fortunes were at a low ebb, and the Melaka-based ninety-nine laws of Perak were extended in the eighteenth century to the state which had come most firmly under Achehnese influence. At the height of its imperial power, policy was dictated from Acheh itself and it was customary for it to retain relatives of vassal rulers as hostages for amenable behaviour. Sometimes Acheh sent its own men to support or supervise subject rulers and it deposed those who did not follow its wishes. But usually the Achehnese ruled through puppet chiefs from the traditional local ruling families.

The Johor sultanate survived the Achehnese menace partly because Acheh's energies were largely absorbed in trying to overturn the Portuguese, but also because of innate strengths in the Johor system. The same resilience which allowed Melaka to rise so quickly in the fifteenth century enabled it to surmount the vicissitudes which followed. Mobile and adaptable to their environment, living by a combination of piracy and trade, without a fixed agricultural base or large, permanent city, the Johor Malays could quickly recover from the destruction of their settlements. Their wood-built villages could easily be reconstructed and the *orang laut* fleet re-assembled to exploit shipping.

In the long term Johor was a more acceptable overlord than the exacting, cruel, aggressive Acheh. Throughout the humiliations of the sixteenth and early-seventeenth centuries the Johor sultanate clung to its traditions and ceremonies and increased its demands for obedience from its subjects. Disloyalty and even regicide were not unknown in the days of the Melaka sultanate, but by the time the *Sejarah Melayu* came to recount the history of Melaka's golden age, more than a century after its downfall, loyalty to the ruler was the paramount quality, and the writer stressed the self sacrifice of Tun Perak, the calm resignation of Tun Mutahir in accepting his fate. The legitimacy of officials' power and the stability of the state stemmed from the institution of monarchy, so that unquestioning submission became even more essential in the subsequent diaspora of the Melaka Malays.

The experiences of the dark years of the sixteenth and early-seventeenth centuries helped to mould Malay political attitudes, and the personal religious and political autocracy of the sultanate became the pattern of Malay political organization.

Brunei

While the sixteenth century was a time of confusion and bitter conflict in the Malay peninsula, the fall of Melaka to the Portuguese brought new opportunities to other parts of maritime Southeast Asia. The Portuguese did not fulfil their ambition to monopolize certain branches of Asian trade but their presence led to a general expansion of commercial activity. The decentralization of Melaka's former trade profited not only Acheh but also Brunei, Patani, and the northern Muslim Javanese sultanates of Bantam, Demak and Japara. These latter had thrown off Majapahit's yoke in the late-fifteenth century and came to control the Javanese coastal trade. Bantam in northwest Java dominated the Sunda Straits passage, while Japara in the northeast had the strongest navy in the archipelago in the sixteenth century, challenging the Portuguese in their attempts to monopolize the Moluccas trade and on two occasions attacking Melaka itself.

Lying on the main trade route between China and the western part of the archipelago, Brunei had built up a flourishing trade with China for several centuries and had come under the influence of Srivijaya and later of Majapahit. A large resident Chinese community was settled in Brunei by the time Cheng Ho's navy visited the city, and Ong Sum Ping, a trader who arrived with one of these expeditions, married a daughter of the ruler of Brunei.

About the middle of the fifteenth century Awang Alak ber Tabar, raja of Brunei, married a Muslim princess from Melaka and adopted Islam. Brunei built up a considerable trade with Melaka, sending camphor, rice, gold and sago in exchange for Indian textiles.

For some years Islam was probably confined to the royal family, until Sharif Ali, an Arab from Taif, who married a niece of Awang Alak ber Tabar, became ruler of Brunei as Sultan Berkat. He converted the population of Brunei town, built several mosques, and developed an efficient administration patterned on the Melaka model.

The first European visitors, who arrived with Magellan's expedition in 1521 during the reign of Sultan Bulkeiah, found an impressive and cultivated court. Pigafetta, a member of that expedition, described Brunei, although perhaps with exaggeration, as a large and wealthy city of some 25 000 households. Apart from the sultan's palace, which was lavishly furnished and well defended, most of the houses were built on stilts over the water.

Already a flourishing trade centre, Brunei blossomed after Melaka's fall to the Portuguese. Many Muslim traders diverted their custom to Brunei, but the sultanate followed Melakan tradition in tolerating other religions, and, unlike Acheh, Brunei kept on friendly terms with the Portuguese. It shared the Portuguese interest in boosting the China trade, without being involved in the struggle for mastery of the Malay peninsula and the Melaka Straits. In 1526 Brunei and the Portuguese came to a commercial understanding and the Portuguese set up a trading post there. As Portuguese trade with China and Japan expanded Brunei became a regular port of call on the route between Melaka and Macao. Increasing numbers of Chinese settled in Brunei to conduct trade with south China and Patani.

Brunei also assumed importance in the Moluccas trade, since the hostility of Japara and Demak compelled the Portuguese to avoid the normal route through the Java Sea and instead to take the long northern route via Sulu and the Celebes Sea.

The first half of the sixteenth century was Brunei's golden age, when it claimed suzerainty over the riverine communities along the whole west and north Borneo coasts, the Sulu archipelago and Mindanao, and forced Manila to pay tribute. In this way it dominated commercial traffic along the coast and in the islands to the north.

During this period many of the Borneo coastal communities followed Brunei in adopting Islam. There is no evidence of any widespread migration of Malays from Sumatra or the peninsula, and most of the Borneo 'Malays' were indigenous inhabitants, who became Muslims. Islam made no headway outside of the coastal settlements, and the semi-nomadic tribes of the interior clung to their animist beliefs.

While Brunei continued to maintain friendly terms with the Portuguese, whose interests were complementary to its own, it clashed with the Spaniards, who were attempting to establish their rule in the Philippines in the latter part of the sixteenth century. In 1577 the Spaniards took temporary possession of Brunei and raided it again in 1588 and in 1645. When Portugal was brought under the Spanish crown in 1580 Brunei lost its European ally. By the end of the sixteenth century Brunei's hold on its northern dependencies was slipping, as the Spaniards gained a firmer foothold and the Sultan of Sulu asserted his independence.

CHAPTER 7

The Revival of Johor, 1641–99

Johor and the Dutch

Sultan Abdul Jalil Riayat Shah, who had ruled from a number of settlements in the Riau archipelago since the Achehnese devastation of Lingga in 1623, rebuilt his capital at Batu Sawar on the Johor river in 1641. At that time Johor could claim suzerainty only over the southern part of the Malay peninsula, Singapore, the Riau-Lingga archipelago, Siak and Kampar. Perak, Pahang, Trengganu, Kelantan and Kedah, together with the Sumatran states of Indragiri and Rokan were lost to it. This shrunken kingdom had few natural resources but was well placed for trading and, taking advantage of their friendship with the Dutch, the Johor Malays attempted to revive the political and economic power of the former Melaka sultanate.

Like the Iberian powers, the Dutch based their commercial policy upon monopoly, aiming to exclude Asian and European rivals, to buy as cheaply as possible from Asian producers and to sell at the highest price in Europe. As the greatest naval power in the seventeenth century, they were far more effective than their Portuguese predecessors in dominating the trade of the eastern archipelago, and they also had no territorial ambitions in Sumatra or the Malay peninsula to bring them into collision with Johor.

Whereas Portugal had tried, though unsuccessfully, to maintain Melaka's traditional role as central pivot of the archipelago trade, the Dutch based their central market, collecting centre and administrative capital at Batavia, which guarded the Sunda Straits, their main gateway to Europe.

Their prime interest was to corner the spice trade, and to this end they seized the spice-producing islands, removed their populations and substituted slave plantation labour. Elsewhere the Dutch made treaties with local rulers, which sought to guarantee them a monopoly of vital commercial products, such as pepper or tin.

Dutch attempts to squeeze all rivals out of the spice trade brought them into conflict with the Javanese sultanates and with Makassar in southwest Celebes. Makassar had developed in the early-seventeenth century as a flourishing centre of independent commerce, frequented by Indonesian, Chinese, Indian and European traders. From the second decade of the century the Dutch were at open war with Makassar, and violence grew more bitter until finally in 1667 the Dutch conquered Makassar, extended their control over the neighbouring states and slammed shut this back door to the spice trade.

In Java the Dutch confronted the rising Muslim kingdom of Mataram, based near Jogjakarta, whose vigorous Sultan Agung extended his sway in the second decade of the seventeenth century over the northern Javanese sultanates, Palembang and west Borneo. The Netherlands refused to acknowledge Mataram's claim to suzerainty over the whole of Java, but after 1674, when the northern Javanese states rose in revolt, Mataram enlisted Dutch support to re-assert its rule in return for commercial privileges, so that the Dutch East India Company became increasingly immersed in Javanese politics and in territorial acquisitions on the island.

In Sumatra and the Malay peninsula the Dutch attempted to draw Acheh into their treaty system, making a number of commercial agreements to give the Dutch East India Company a monopoly of Sumatran pepper exports and the lion's share of the Perak tin trade. But by the middle of the century the Achehnese were no longer strong enough to see that these treaties were honoured, even if they so wished. Frequent infringements led the Dutch to instal Residents in the west coast Sumatran states in the 1660s, and to build up the power of the Minangkabau ruler in the Padang highlands over the west coast of Sumatra, to replace Achehnese authority.

The Dutch harried Asian rivals and effectively drove out all serious European competition from the Malay peninsula and the archipelago. The most formidable potential rival, the English East India Company, could not withstand the pressure of the government-backed Dutch counterpart. After the Dutch executions of 1623 the English withdrew from Amboina and abandoned Patani that same year. They kept a tenuous hold in Banjermasin until 1651, in Makassar till 1667, and in Jambi until 1679, but were driven from their final effective post at Bantam in 1682. The English company kept a foothold at remote Benkulen in west Sumatra but transferred its major attentions from Southeast Asia to India.

For more than a century the Dutch faced no serious threat to their position in the archipelago, either from European or Asian rivals, and while their naval supremacy lasted they kept a firm hold over spices and a fairly effective grip on pepper exports, although they never gained complete control over the tin trade of the Malay peninsula. In most parts of the archipelago their monopoly and treaty system disrupted former trade, precluded the emergence of prosperous ports, apart from

feeder outlets for Dutch commerce, and roused considerable objection
from local and international producers and merchants.

Johor was unique in being a beneficiary of the Dutch system. Friendship with Johor was a cornerstone of Batavia's policy throughout the
seventeenth century, and Johor recovered and blossomed in the warmth
of Dutch protection. Despite occasional friction, both parties
appreciated the value of their co-operation. Batavia wanted to see a
strong, stable, prosperous Johor, in firm control of its dependencies in
Sumatra and the Malay peninsula, ensuring peace in Melaka's hinterland and committing the *orang laut* to keeping the Melaka Straits safe
for peaceful trading, while Johor consolidated and enlarged the commercial benefits which it reaped from Dutch gratitude for its part in the
conquest of Portuguese Melaka.

The initial Johor–Dutch pact of 1639 was followed, in 1642, by a
treaty permitting the sultan and *orang kaya* of Johor to trade freely with
neighbouring states and exempting them from paying tariffs in Melaka
itself. As the years passed Johor insisted on increasing these privileges
until it managed to escape virtually all the restrictions of the Dutch
monopoly. The more enterprising *orang kaya* became very rich,
attracting followers and acquiring slaves to enhance their power and
status. They extended their passes to proteges of other nationalities.
Indonesian, Chinese, Arab, Indian, and occasionally individual Dutch
traders put themselves under the patronage of the Johor chiefs,
including Muslim Indian and Arab traders who married into noble
Johor families.

Much of the Melaka sultanate's commercial organization was revived
in seventeenth century Johor: officials to handle trade and supervise
transactions, facilities for storage, fixed and fair tariffs, accurate
weights and measures. As in previous centuries the *orang laut* patrolled
the seas, directing shipping into Johor ports.

With Dutch permission, Johor reforged direct commercial links with
China and India and developed a prosperous trade with Makassar,
although the Dutch excluded it from the Moluccas spice trade. Indian,
Arab, Indonesian and Chinese traders found Johor a more convenient
port and the choice, quality and price of its merchandise more attrac-
tive than that in Dutch Melaka. Europeans, such as Spaniards from
Manila, Danes and even individual English traders, found a welcome in
Johor and its tolerance attracted a cosmopolitan trading community.

By the middle of the century the port of Johor bustled with trade, and
the extension of its political control over east Sumatra strengthened its
commercial position. The sultan sent a *shahbandar* to rule Siak in 1662,
appointed a Johor governor to Indragiri in 1669, and ten years later
made Jambi a vassal state. In this way Johor acquired control of the
newly discovered Siak tin mines and dominated the trade outlets for

Minangkabau gold, so that many Asian ships frequented Johor's vassal ports of Bengkalis and Indragiri in preference to Melaka.

As Dutch Melaka's trade languished in the face of Johor's privileged competition, the authorities came increasingly to feel that too high a price had been paid for Johor's co-operation. Such complaints were dismissed by Batavia. Melaka was merely an outpost, though an important one, and its interests were always subordinated to wider Dutch concerns in the Indies.

Dutch Trade in the Malay Peninsula

Apart from its role of enforcing Dutch supremacy in the Straits of Melaka and keeping interlopers out, Melaka's main function was to act as a collecting centre for commercial products from Sumatra and the Malay peninsula. The Netherlands' chief interest in the peninsula lay in the tin trade of the west-coast states, where throughout the seventeenth century they attempted to enforce a monopoly but with little success. They made a treaty with Kedah in 1642 and with Ujong Salang, the modern Phuket, the following year, but the rulers constantly evaded these agreements, despite repeated Dutch blockades of the Kedah coast.

In 1639 the Dutch made an agreement with Acheh for the purchase of Perak's tin but the trade was precarious. A Dutch trading post set up at the mouth of the Perak river in 1650 was wiped out by local Malays the following year. Blockading Acheh to obtain redress, the Dutch forced it to make a fresh treaty in 1659, providing compensation for the destruction of the factory and giving the Dutch the sole right along with Acheh to trade in Perak. But Acheh's weakness made this agreement a dead letter. The Dutch re-opened their Perak post in 1659 but were forced to close it down four years later. In 1670 they built a fort on Pangkor island to intercept exports of tin, transported overland from the Kinta valley to Lumut to evade the Dutch, but this station was overrun by Perak Malays in 1690 and abandoned.

Local rulers in Ujong Salang, Kedah, and Perak carried on a regular smuggling trade with Indian, Arab and occasional British interlopers, but the major part of tin exports from Perak, Selangor, Klang and Sungei Ujong went to Johor traders.

The Dutch kept up attempts to dominate the tin trade but it continued to be uncertain throughout the seventeenth and eighteenth centuries. The Dutch East India Company's main trading interests remained in spices and pepper, so that it was concerned primarily with Java and the Moluccas, and to a lesser extent with Sumatra. By the early-eighteenth century the Company was turning from trade to commercial agriculture and narrowing its interests to the island of Java.

In the Malay peninsula the Dutch never attempted to extend their territorial authority beyond Melaka town and the adjoining Naning. Concerned solely with trade, they made even less cultural impact than their Portuguese predecessors. No effort was made to spread the Protestant Christian religion and the Dutch left little tangible evidence of their regime in Melaka, apart from some picturesque public buildings and houses.

Indirect Dutch influence was more profound. They helped to weaken the Achehnese yoke and curb the ambitions of Mataram, which had sought to create a new empire in Java, south Sumatra and the Malay peninsula. They provided the opportunity for the resurgence of Johor as a leading Malay power. Their activities in Sumatra and Celebes encouraged the displacement and migration of Minangkabaus, Bugis and Makassarese, who were to play significant roles in the Malay peninsula. The Dutch helped to create a power vacuum in the northern part of the peninsula which opened the way for a renewed, if initially weak, southern push by Siam.

Brunei

Dutch preoccupation with the Melaka Straits and the Java Sea meant a decline in commercial activity in the south China Sea and northern Borneo. The Dutch were on friendly terms with Brunei but it became a backwater and by the end of the seventeenth century had few resident foreign merchants. Chinese junks no longer patronized the port, which became little more than a pirate base. Further, as a result of Spanish incursions, the Brunei sultanate lost control over their vassal chiefs in the Sulu archipelago and Mindanao.

Decline of Acheh

While Johor recovered much of its commercial prosperity and control over many of its former dependencies, it never became the focal point of the archipelago as the Melaka sultanate had been, and no state ever again came to dominate both sides of the Melaka Straits. For a brief moment it appeared that Johor might achieve this goal when, immediately after the death of Iskandar Thani of Acheh in 1641, it proposed to bury the discord between the two countries by a marriage between the sultan of Johor and the queen of Acheh. The Achehnese *orang kaya* refused this offer which threatened to absorb Acheh into Johor, to the relief of the Dutch, who had no wish to see the Melaka Straits converted into an Acheh–Johor lake.

Acheh's rapid decline saved Johor from further threat. After 1641 Acheh gave up claims over Pahang, which soon came under the direct rule of the sultan of Johor and was governed as an integral part of Johor

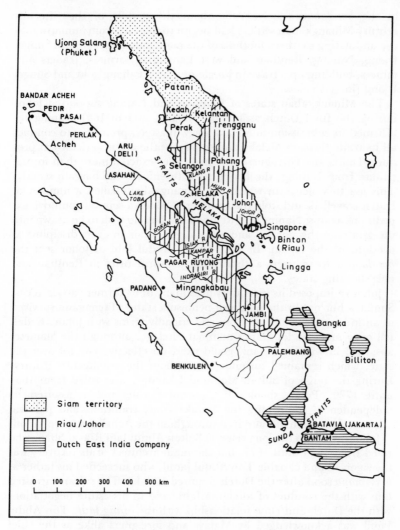

The Malay Peninsula and Sumatra circa A.D. 1700

for the next 200 years. By the late-1650s Acheh had lost its last foothold in the Malay peninsula and was in full retreat in Sumatra.

The Minangkabau States

With Dutch encouragement, Johor also revived its suzerainty over its dependencies in the region inland from Melaka, which were traditionally in the *bendahara's* fief. From about the middle of the fifteenth century Minangkabau settlers had begun to migrate from Sumatra into the undulating southern foothills of the main mountain range in Sungei Ujong, Naning, Rembau and west Pahang as farmers, traders and miners, building up a trade in jungle produce, Pahang gold and Sungei Ujong tin.

The Minangkabau states of Rembau and Naning supported Johor during the final Dutch assault on Melaka, and in 1641 Naning re-affirmed its submission to Melaka's new masters, promising to conduct all its trade through Melaka and to pay a tithe on its agricultural produce. Unlike the Portuguese who had never exacted more than formal tribute from Naning, the Dutch tried to enforce the bargain strictly. This led to violence in which the Minangkabaus killed a number of Dutch travellers and stole their property. Melaka sent out punitive expeditions against Naning and Rembau but had no wish to be drawn into the affairs of the interior and encouraged Johor to exert discipline as overlord of the region. In 1644 Sultan Abdul Jalil of Johor sent the *bendahara* to re-assert authority and confirm titles in Rembau and neighbouring states.

Johor re-imposed its suzerainty over many of its former vassals in east Sumatra but not in the northern peninsula states. Trengganu survived as an independent unit on close and friendly terms with Johor. Kedah fell once more under Siam's nominal tutelage, although the Siamese, absorbed in wars in Patani, could exert no effective control over the state, which remained turbulent throughout the seventeenth century. During the reign of Sultan Mahmud Iskandar, who ruled from 1654 until 1720, Perak shook off Achehnese rule and re-asserted its independence, confirming the Melaka court traditions and political organization which had survived throughout the Achehnese occupation.

Johor revived in the long reign of Sultan Abdul Jalil Riayat Shah, who ruled from 1623 until 1677, but the main architect of its recovery was the vigorous and capable Tun Abdul Jamil, who succeeded his father as *laksamana* soon after the Dutch acquired Melaka. The sultan entrusted him with the conduct of foreign affairs, and in his astute negotiations with the Dutch and close relationship with the *orang laut,* Tun Abdul Jamil was acknowledged by Malays and foreigners alike as the chief minister, and indeed the real power, in the state, fulfilling the role normally reserved for the *bendahara*.

Johor-Jambi Wars

By 1660 Johor was the strongest Asian economic power in the region, but this peace and prosperity were rudely shattered by the outbreak of war between Johor and Jambi, arising from the marriage in 1659 of the *raja muda* of Johor and a Jambi princess. Designed to cement friendship between the two states, this union roused suspicions in the ageing Sultan Abdul Jalil Riayat Shah of Johor that the *raja muda* and his Jambi relatives intended to seize his throne. Laksamana Tun Abdul Jamil, fearing a threat to his own authority, encouraged the sultan's fears.

Slights and insults led to violence in which Johor and Jambi used their *orang laut* tribes to molest not only each other's shipping but also neutral traders frequenting their rival's ports. Dutch attempts at mediation to bring to an end this long drawn out conflict, which was damaging to trade, broke down, and in 1673 Jambi looted and destroyed Johor Lama, taking into captivity the *bendahara*, many *orang kaya* and about 1200 inhabitants, together with a fleet of boats laden with booty. The sultan fled to Pahang and the *laksamana* to Bintan, where at the sultan's command he rebuilt the capital at Riau.

Despite the terrible disaster at Johor and the loss of so many of its leaders, people and treasure, the ruler had escaped, and most of Johor's peninsular and Sumatran vassal states remained loyal. The *orang laut* forces were quickly reassembled, and within a few months the *laksamana* inflicted defeat on Jambi's navy.

While Johor speedily recovered its political and commercial position and ultimately triumphed over Jambi, the wars set in motion events which were eventually to lead to the downfall of the Johor empire by bringing two new components into its politics: the Minangkabaus and Buginese.

The Minangkabaus

The slow process of Minangkabau migration into the Malay peninsula speeded up from the mid-seventeenth century. It was customary among the Minangkabau for young men to leave their villages in the hands of elders and women while they went on *merantau*, or wandering, and from the mid-seventeenth century they migrated in large numbers from the Padang highlands down the Siak and Kampar rivers to the east coast of Sumatra and across the Melaka Straits. Avoiding the water-logged plains and acid soils of the west coast lowlands, they moved to the hilly region inland, which closely resembled the terrain of their Sumatran homeland. Here skilled Minangkabau farmers recreated their traditional mixed farming, based upon rice, fruit and animal husbandry, and introduced irrigation techniques.

While the Minangkabau belonged to the same ethnic and linguistic stock as the Johor Malays and were devotedly Muslim, they differed in their matrilinear social organization and re-established themselves on a lineage basis in their new homeland. Property, vested in the clan or *suku*, was handed down from mother to daughter, and Minangkabau men entered their wife's *suku* on marriage. The legal system followed the *adat perpateh*, a milder form of the Melaka *adat temenggong* and more appropriate to their agricultural society. It emphasized compensation for the victim rather than punishment of the guilty or retribution for society and the state. Under its provisions for collective responsibility and shared burdens, a wrongdoer's family was responsible for any member's faults. The Minangkabau settlers, themselves fairly recent converts but devout if somewhat unorthodox in their way of life, brought Islam to the interior of the peninsula. They appear to have intermarried with the Jakun of the lower rivers and were probably a more pervasive, peaceful missionary influence than Acheh.

The Minangkabau settled in virgin land on the fringes of Malay kingdoms in the peninsula and Sumatra. The peninsular Minangkabau established their own clan leadership, in which the heads of the various *suku* formed a council. At the same time they accepted the political authority of local Malay headmen, or *waris*, who were responsible to the *bendahara* of Melaka-Johor and acknowledged the vague suzerainty of the sultan. There was occasional trouble, such as the embarrassment between Johor and the Dutch over Minangkabau activities immediately after the Dutch conquest of Melaka, but in general the Minangkabau were left undisturbed to live their own way of life, having little contact either with the Malay authorities or with their own homeland.

Achehnese control of the east Sumatran coast in the sixteenth century and early-seventeenth century cut emigrant Minangkabau links with Sumatra but as the Achehnese withdrew and the Sumatran Minangkabau court at Pagar Ruyong began to revive in the sunshine of Dutch approval, old ties were revived and a continual stream of immigrants forged new bonds between the peninsular Minangkabaus and their spiritual overlord at Pagar Ruyong.

After Johor was sacked in 1673 the Minangkabaus of Sungei Ujong and Rembau took the opportunity to assert their independence. In 1677 they joined with the neighbouring state of Naning, which was nominally subject to Dutch Melaka, and appealed to Pagar Ruyong to send them a ruler of their own, one Raja Ibrahim.

This move was unwelcome both to Johor and the Dutch, who feared a combination of Minangkabau power across the Melaka Straits. Raja Ibrahim appealed to his Sumatran countrymen for help in attacking Melaka in 1678, when the Minangkabaus raided the outskirts of the city and the inhabitants fled into the fort. But the threat ended temporarily when Raja Ibrahim was murdered in Rembau in 1679. Rembau and Naning sued for peace, their treaties with the Dutch were renewed and Melaka appointed puppet chiefs in Naning to keep the territory under its control.

The Buginese

Shortly before his death Raja Ibrahim had appealed to Buginese and Makassarese settlers in Klang to join in a holy war against the Christian

Dutch, and these Celebes people also came to play a vital part in Malaysian history.

Traditionally the southwest peninsula of Celebes comprised a number of loosely confederated small kingdoms, of which the most important were the kingdom of Goa, centred on Makassar, and the nearby Buginese kingdom of Bone. The region lacked natural resources, so that young Bugis and Makassarese went out as rovers to make a living by trade and piracy. They were often found in the ports of Melaka, Borneo, Java and the east coast of the Malay peninsula in the fifteenth and sixteenth centuries, and in turn the kingdom of Goa became a haven for refugees: Malays, who fled from Melaka after the Portuguese conquest, fugitives from Champa, Patani and elsewhere. Makassar flourished in the first half of the seventeenth century and became converted at this late time to Islam, which provided the impetus for carrying a trading crusade into the interior and to other parts of the archipelago.

Dutch efforts to wrest trade from Makassar and to enforce commercial monopolies provoked a long drawn out holy war, culminating in the Dutch conquest of the kingdom of Goa in 1667. Roving bands under independent chieftains fled from Celebes to seek their fortunes elsewhere in the archipelago, carrying hatred of the Dutch wherever they went. They tended to keep in separate groups but shared a pride in their homeland, and colonies of Bugis and Makassarese provided havens for ever increasing bands of new refugees fleeing from unsettled conditions in the Celebes.

The political system of southwest Celebes bred a fiercely independent people and a competitive, masculine society. While they resembled the coastal Malays in the mobile, restless zest for adventure and in their ability to adapt to their geographical environment, the Bugis and Makassarese found difficulty in assimilating peacefully in their new countries of settlement. Local rulers sometimes called on the support of these energetic, intrepid fighters, but invariably the Bugis proved a disruptive force in their host societies.

This happened in Jambi, where, after fruitless appeals for help against Johor to the Dutch and to Mataram, which was still his nominal overlord, the ruler called on the support of Daeng Mangika, a refugee Makassarese prince. Daeng Mangika's following settled in Jambi and attracted such an influx of other Makassarese and Buginese refugees that Jambi became alarmed. Relations were so strained that when Johor attacked Jambi in 1679, Daeng Mangika deserted his hosts and went over to Johor's side. Johor then defeated and established suzerainty over Jambi, while Daeng Mangika moved to Palembang.

Johor in the Late Seventeenth Century

The conquest of Jambi was a great triumph for Johor and for the

Laksamana Tun Abdul Jamil, who now assumed the rank of *Paduka Raja*. Only six years after its humiliating destruction by Jambi, Johor had not only destroyed its rival but also thrown off the dangers of Minangkabau revolt. The *Paduka Raja* went on to further victory two years later, when Jambi called on its new suzerain to repel another incursion from Daeng Mangika. Johor's intervention was successful, Daeng Mangika was killed and the Makassarese–Palembang force expelled.

While the sultan remained on the mainland, the *Paduka Raja* was left in full mastery of the state in Riau. Sultan Abdul Jalil Riayat Shah, who died in Pahang in 1677 at the age of ninety, was succeeded by a nephew, Sultan Ibrahim, who sought to assert his rightful authority as head of state. But the setback to the *Paduka Raja's* authority was only temporary, since Sultan Ibrahim died two years later, and his widow, the *Paduka Raja's* daughter, though childless herself, acted as regent for Ibrahim's seven-year-old son, Mahmud. The *Paduka Raja* gave leading offices of state to his sons, making one *laksamana* and a second *temenggong*, so that by virtue of his own authority and through his immediate family the *Paduka Raja* came to dominate every aspect of the state, political, commercial and diplomatic. Ruling as an autocrat, he ignored the *bendahara* and the *orang kaya*.

Johor prospered greatly in these years, and in 1685 the *Paduka Raja* negotiated a favourable commercial treaty with the Dutch, which formalized all the privileges Johor had acquired over the years. But the *bendahara* and *orang kaya*, growing restive at their exclusion from affairs of state, banded together against Tun Abdul Jamil. When the *bendahara* seized custody of the young Sultan Mahmud, most of the *orang laut* rallied behind him, while the *Paduka Raja* and his sons fled with their treasure and part of the royal regalia to seek sanctuary in Patani. The Johor fleet overtook them off the Trengganu coast where the *Paduka Raja* Tun Abdul Jamil put up a stout resistance, using his Spanish silver rials as cannon fodder when all his ammunition was spent. Eventually he was overpowered and executed with a slave's *kris* together with those sons who had accompanied him, while his daughter, the regent, was drowned.

Such was the humiliating fate of the ageing Paduka Raja Tun Abdul Jamil, who had guided the destinies of Johor for nearly half a century but was defeated in the end by his own success and overweening arrogance.

After the *Paduka Raja's* overthrow Bendahara Tun Habib Abdul Majid became chief minister, and the whole population was removed to Kota Tinggi on the Johor river. Internally the change of leadership caused little upset. The *bendahara* restored the *orang kaya* to their accustomed offices and ruled closely in consultation with them.

Bendahara Tun Habib Abdul Majid was a capable man, who kept a firm grip on the state and died in 1697 leaving a united and prosperous Johor. His son, Tun Abdul Jalil, who succeeded as *bendahara,* was mild and respected, but he lacked his father's forcefulness and could not control Sultan Mahmud, now nineteen years old, a vindictive sadist and homosexual pervert. The *orang laut* degenerated into an undisciplined pirate mob, Sultan Mahmud's reputation for unpredictable savagery frightened off foreign traders, and Johor's trade plummeted. Mahmud's wanton cruelty, which included shooting men at random to test a new gun, reached its height in 1699 when he ordered the pregnant wife of an *orang kaya,* Megat Sri Rama, to be ripped apart because she had eaten a jackfruit from his garden. In revulsion, the *bendahara, temenggong* and *orang kaya* decided the sultan was mad, and, with the exception of one influential *orang laut* leader, they agreed to support the injured husband in killing Mahmud. The dissenting leader was executed, since by *adat* the deposition of a mad ruler could only be made by unanimous agreement of the *orang kaya*. Megat Sri Rama then attacked Mahmud as he rode openly through the city, and the other *orang kaya* joined him in stabbing the sultan to death.

Since Mahmud had no heir, the *bendahara* was proclaimed Sultan Abdul Jalil Riayat Shah, and the old house of Melaka, which had claimed descent from the rulers of Srivijaya, came to an ignominious end.

CHAPTER 8

The Eighteenth Century: Malays, Bugis and Minangkabaus

Bendahara/Sultan Abdul Jalil Riayat Shah

The murder of Sultan Mahmud meant not only the death of the king and end of the Melaka dynasty but also dealt a blow to the Malay system of government from which it never recovered. While many of Mahmud's ancestors had exerted little real power, their symbolic supremacy guaranteed stability and legitimacy. In principle the Malay sultan was inviolable, and while a number of earlier sultans had suffered unnatural deaths, there had never been a case of open regicide at the hands of the *orang kaya*. The terrible offence of *derhaka*, or treason to the ruler and the state, left great rifts and divisions among the leadership. According to legend, the dying sultan had stabbed Megat Sri Rama in the foot, and grass grew in the wound until the murderer died four years later. Similarly the festering wounds inflicted on the state never healed.

The *orang laut*, who had been unwaveringly loyal to the sultanate since the founding of Melaka, were shocked by the murder of Sultan Mahmud. While some *orang laut* tribes submitted to the new regime, many sought an alternative overlord. The Perak ruling family, the only survivors of the former Melaka royal house, were in no position to exert any authority outside of their own state, so that some *orang laut* transferred their service to Palembang, whence the Srivijaya–Melaka royal house had originally derived its title, while many refused to acknowledge any master and drifted into indiscriminate piracy.

The refusal of outlying provinces to accept the new sultan, particularly in those regions of the Johor empire in the peninsula and east Sumatra settled by Minangkabau immigrants, led to revolts in Selangor, Klang, Rembau, Siak and Indragiri.

Sultan Abdul Jalil Riayat Shah was not the man to pull the shaken country together. Worthy but weak and impractical, the former *bendahara* became increasingly immersed in religious superstition and left the running of the country to his brothers: Tun Mas Anum, who suc-

68

ceeded him as *bendahara,* and Tun Mahmud, the *shahbandar.* Domineering, unpopular and somewhat disreputable, Bendahara Tun Mas Anum made little headway in suppressing the rebellions and it was Tun Mahmud who pulled Johor out of chaos, Slight in stature and unimpressive physically, but clever and intensely ambitious, Tun Mahmud was recognized as the sultan's heir after the death of *bendahara* Tun Mas Anum in 1708. For the next ten years Raja Muda Tun Mahmud remained the real power in the state supported by his elder brother, Tun Abdullah, as *bendahara* and a younger brother as *temenggong.*

In 1705 Sultan Abdul Jalil built a new capital at Pancor on the Johor river but deserted this inauspicious site four years later, when an accidental fire destroyed the town. The bulk of the population followed the sultan and *raja muda* to Riau, where they attempted to revive the empire's former prosperity.

Soon Indonesian, Chinese, Siamese and Cambodian shipping began to return to Riau, which once more drained away trade from Dutch Melaka. The *raja muda* maintained his predecessors' 'iron fist in a velvet glove' policy towards the Dutch, receiving them with courtesy but refusing to surrender any of Johor's privileges. He claimed that the commercial treaty made during the former sultan's minority was now void and prevaricated when the Dutch tried to negotiate a fresh agreement.

With its trade continuing to decline, Melaka again called on Batavia to redress Johor's alleged abuse of commercial privilege, but the Dutch East India Company continued to subordinate Melaka's interests to wider Dutch policy in the archipelago. Preoccupied with territorial and political affairs in Java and with the development of commercial agriculture on that island, Batavia was less inclined to pay heed to problems in Johor, the Melaka Straits and the Malay peninsula.

With provincial revolts suppressed and Riau returning to prosperity, by the second decade of the century the empire seemed to be recovering under the firm guidance of Raja Muda Tun Mahmud. But stability was superficial, and the fragile peace was broken in 1715 by conflict with the Bugis which set the Riau-Johor empire on the path to ruin.

During the latter years of the seventeenth century Bugis refugees had come to settle in increasing numbers in the frontier territories of the Johor empire. A Bugis community formed a settlement at the mouth of the Selangor river about the year 1681, another group established itself at the estuary of the Linggi early in the eighteenth century, and in 1702 Johor granted formal permission for the Bugis to take up residence in its dominions. In these hitherto uninhabited districts on the west coast of the peninsula the Bugis tried to reconstruct the independent mode of life which they had enjoyed in their homeland without coming into conflict with the central Johor authorities, to whom they paid nominal allegiance. Initially Raja Muda Tun Mahmud welcomed the Bugis as a

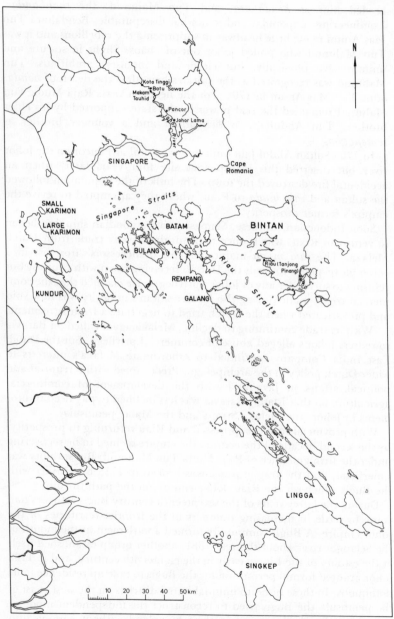

The Johor River and the Riau-Lingga Archipelago

counterweight to the troublesome Minangkabaus, and the Bugis found favour at court.

But the adventurous spirit of the Bugis and their activities as soldiers of fortune spelt danger, and their involvement in civil war in Kedah in 1715 triggered off a chain of disaster for Johor. Called into the Kedah succession dispute, two Buginese chieftains from Linggi, Daeng Marewa and Daeng Manompok, were dissatisfied with their reward and proceeded to ravage and loot Kedah. Their refusal to comply with Raja Muda Tun Mahmud's demands that they surrender half of their booty to the sultan according to Johor custom, provoked a two-year struggle which exposed the fundamental weakness and divisions of the seemingly prosperous Johor empire. Tun Mahmud found difficulty in rallying support from Johor's Sumatran vassal states which were still smarting from the suppression of their recent rebellions. But the Bugis of Selangor and Linggi joined ranks to form a well-disciplined, cohesive force. Keen fighters, the Bugis from the start held the upper hand. In 1716 Daeng Manompok seized the island of Bengkalis, while Daeng Marewa defeated the Johor army, led by Raja Muda Tun Mahmud and his brother, the *temenggong*. Daeng Marewa then seized Selangor and promptly made a bargain with the Dutch to export all Selangor tin to Melaka.

The Raja Muda Tun Mahmud tried to win Dutch backing, agreeing finally to sign the trade treaty over which Johor had been haggling for years. But the Dutch did not want to become involved in the political affairs of the Malay peninsula and were happy to profit from the Selangor tin trade which Bugis–Johor rivalry diverted to Melaka.

Riau's trade fell dramatically, and in 1716 Sultan Abdul Jalil moved the capital back to the safety of the Johor river.

The Bugis war weakened the Johor empire, posing the threat of secession by its vassal provinces and laying bare deep divisions in the heart of the empire itself. The *orang kaya* grew increasingly critical of military defeats of the *raja muda* and the *temenggong* and the failure of the colourless and timid sultan to offer any leadership.

The Malay political system, lacking formal institutions and offering opportunities for able individuals to acquire wealth through trade, provided a framework in which ambitious leaders could acquire great power. In the past, men such as Bendahara Mutahir or the Paduka Raja Abdul Jamil, had installed close relatives in all the major offices spreading their tentacles like an octopus throughout the state. Such men were tolerated until they assumed such an arrogance of power that they ignored the unwritten custom of consulting the *orang kaya* and allotting the aristocracy its rightful place in the body politic, at which point, since there was no constitutional means to check them, they were forcibly destroyed. Normally the sultan's presence meant that overweening ministers could be swept aside without inflicting lasting injury on the state. But at this stage the sultanate itself was in question. The accession of a non-royal sultan had never been happily accepted, and it appeared as if the Bugis plague was a judgement of Allah on the legitimate monarch's killers.

Raja Kechil

At this crucial moment, late in 1717, a young pretender to the Johor throne appeared, in the person of Raja Kechil of Siak, who claimed to be the murdered Sultan Mahmud's posthumous son. His maternal grandfather was alleged to have smuggled the baby out to Muar and later to have brought him back to Johor. But the child was said to bear such a striking resemblance to the dead sultan that he was again sent away, this time in the safe keeping of a Minangkabau trader, who took him to Pagar Ruyong. The youth joined a band of fighters, saw service in Sumatran civil wars and subsequently found favour at the Pagar Ruyong court. Gathering about him a following of Minangkabaus, Raja Kechil then went to Siak and at Bengkalis met the Bugis invaders: Daeng Manompok and two of Daeng Marewa's brothers, Daeng Parani and Daeng Cellak. Raja Kechil promised to reward the Bugis chiefs if they helped him gain the Johor throne and to make Daeng Parani his *raja muda*.

Raja Kechil's claims about his parentage were dubious, but he had the support of Pagar Ruyong and his appearance at this period of stress released latent tensions and discontent with the existing regime. The royal family commanded no respect. The *orang kaya* despised the sultan's cowardice and blamed the *raja muda* and his brothers for the empire's troubles. The *orang laut* were delighted to acknowledge an alternative heir who claimed legitimate descent from the Melaka house, and the Raja Negara Selat, head of the Singapore *orang laut*, came immediately to Bengkalis to pay homage. Command of the *orang laut* fleet was crucial for the Minangkabau leader, who had no naval force of his own, and with the support of the Bugis and Minangkabaus of Pagar Ruyong, east Sumatra and the Malay peninsula, Raja Kechil overthrew the already discredited and unpopular Johor regime in 1719 and seized the throne for himself. Both the *temenggong* and *laksamana* were executed, and the Raja Muda Tun Mahmud was slain after running amok and killing his wife and children. The *bendahara* escaped but Raja Kechil permitted the toppled Sultan Abdul Jalil to revert to his office of *bendahara* after he agreed to pay homage.

By reinstating Abdul Jalil and marrying his daughter according to Malay custom, Raja Kechil went a long way to asserting the legitimacy of his position, but strains soon appeared in the new state. Raja Kechil felt insecure in his capital at Riau, since his main power base remained in Siak. The ex-*bendahara*, Tun Abdullah, and other *émigrés* who had taken refuge in Melaka plotted to restore the ex-sultan. Abdul Jalil himself soon fled to Trengganu, a pathetic exile, described by an English visitor, Alexander Hamilton, as 'a poor distrest king, who by his senseless devotion to superstition ruined his country and his family'. The former sultan found scant welcome and in 1721 he withdrew to Kuala Pahang, where his former *bendahara*, Tun Abdullah, and other refugee chiefs joined him.

Meanwhile Tun Abdullah exploited friction between the Minangkabaus and their Buginese allies, making a bargain with Daeng Marewa in 1721 to drive Raja Kechil out. To forestall attack, Raja Kechil dispatched a force against the Bugis and sent his *laksamana* to kill the ex-sultan. Abdul Jalil was murdered while he was at prayer and his young son, Sulaiman, brought back to Riau as a prisoner. But Raja Kechil's pre-emptive strike against the Bugis failed. Daeng Marewa and Daeng Manompok attacked Riau, where they put Raja Kechil to flight, slaughtered all the Minangkabaus they could find, looted the town and captured the royal regalia. The Bugis leaders then released Sulaiman and installed him as sultan in accordance with Malay ceremony. At the same time Sultan Sulaiman formally admitted Daeng Marewa as *yamtuan muda,* or underking, and Daeng Manompok as *raja tua.*

Sultan Sulaiman and the Bugis

Thus the succession to the Riau-Johor empire was finally settled in 1722, bringing to an end more than twenty years of restless uncertainty. In the absence of any male heir to the Melaka–Johor royal line, the throne legally devolved by Malay custom on the *bendahara's* house. Abdul Jalil's violent death atoned for his involvement in Sultan Mahmud's murder and his progeny, who were innocent of that crime, were recognized as the legitimate rulers. Sulaiman, born after Abdul Jalil mounted the throne, became sultan and his descendants continued to rule Riau-Johor until the empire disappeared in the early-twentieth century. Abdul Jalil's older sons, born before their father was elevated to the sultanate, became *bendahara* and *temenggong* and from them the non-royal senior officers of state traced their descent. As in the past there was much intermarriage between the royal and aristocratic houses and also after this time with the Bugis nobility.

The installation of Sultan Sulaiman, backed by the Bugis, set the pattern for a more peaceful and settled Johor. But the nature of the empire had changed. While Sulaiman and his successors could claim legal legitimacy, they lacked the mystical aura of the old Melaka–Srivijaya house. The power of the sultanate now depended upon the ability of the individual ruler or the physical might of the Bugis. The sultan and the Bugis depended on each other, since Sulaiman owed his throne to the Bugis and relied on their continued military support, while in his turn,

Table 8.1   Sultans of Johor, Riau-Lingga, Trengganu, Singapore, Pahang in the eighteenth-nineteenth centuries

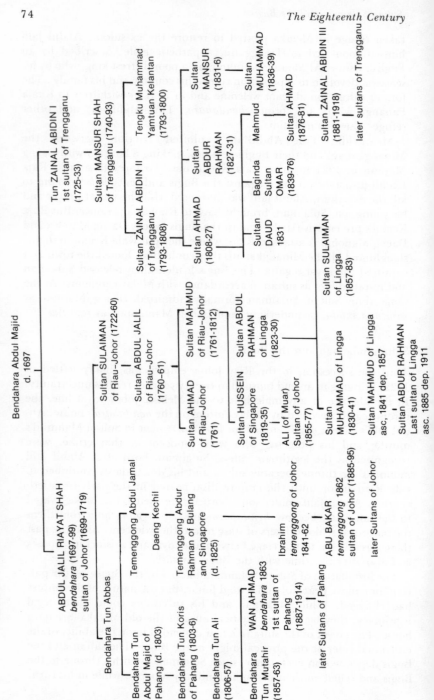

Table 8.2   Bendaharas and temenggongs in the eighteenth-nineteenth centuries

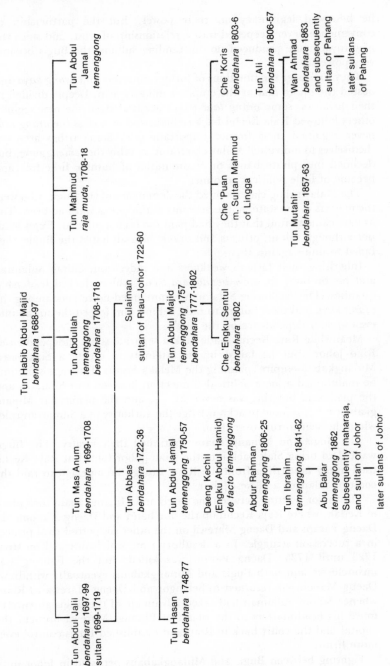

he bestowed legitimacy on their power. But the partnership of convenience never deepened into a relationship of trust, and since the new royal house produced no outstanding sultans, the Bugis became very powerful.

They took over the functions of former ministers and *orang kaya* and ousted the *orang laut* as the empire's military arm. Deeply divided in their loyalties, some *orang laut* tribes acknowledged the new regime, others followed Raja Kechil back to Siak, and as a class the *orang laut* never regained their former important role. Some tribes attached themselves to individual Malay chieftains, notably the *temenggong,* but declined into pirate bands or communities of humble fisherfolk and became of little political account.

The Malay ruling class resented the dominance of the Bugis, who were the masters of the state, not its servants as the *orang laut* had been. The Malays came to find that they had paid too high a price for Bugis help, but although sultan, officers and *orang kaya* all hated the Bugis, they failed to unite against them.

Inheriting their father's weakness and indecision, Sultan Sulaiman and his brother, the new *bendahara,* Tun Abbas, lacked leadership qualities. The vacillating Sulaiman commanded no respect among the *orang kaya* and their failure to rally behind him forced the sultan into even greater dependence on the Bugis.

Meanwhile Raja Kechil made Siak a separate state, independent of Riau–Johor. But he failed in his attempts to create a Siak-based Minangkabau empire spanning the Melaka Straits. During his lifetime he maintained a loose political connection between east Sumatra and the peninsula but this was never strong, and the peninsular Minangkabau states refused to acknowledge the authority of a Sumatran ruler whom he sent to rule over them.

The Bugis and Minangkabaus continued their rivalry. The Bugis wanted to bring Siak back into the Riau–Johor fold, but Raja Kechil used *orang laut* tribes from the Riau-Lingga archipelago to raid the coast of Selangor and west Johor.

The major fighting between the Bugis and Minangkabaus took place in Kedah, where Raja Kechil on the one hand and Daeng Manompok, Daeng Parani and Daeng Marewa on the other supported rival princes in a succession struggle. In a desultory war, which dragged on from 1723 until 1725, Daeng Parani was killed, but the fighting was inconclusive and both Bugis and Minangkabaus eventually withdrew. Daeng Manompok returned to Selangor and Daeng Marewa to Riau, whence Sultan Sulaiman had taken advantage of the Bugis absence to move his headquarters to the island of Bulang. Marewa brought the capital and the court back to Riau and established Bugis control even more firmly.

Fighting between Bugis and Minangkabaus persisted in Johor until

Daeng Marewa's death in 1728. But by that time Raja Kechil's hopes were dashed and soon afterwards he degenerated into mad melancholia.

The alliance between the Bugis and the Johor Malays survived for most of the eighteenth century but throughout that time the pact depended very much on the Buginese strength to enforce it. There were two points of allegiance: the Malay sultan and the Bugis *yamtuan muda*, but the latter held the real power. The office of *yamtuan muda* remained in the family of Daeng Marewa, his brothers and descendants. Originally Raja Tua Daeng Manompok enjoyed almost equal status, but his family's influence was eclipsed when the third *yamtuan muda* drove the *raja tua's* community out of Riau in 1767.

Daeng Marewa was succeeded as *yamtuan muda* in 1728 by his brother, Daeng Cellak, who extended Buginese power further along the west coast of the peninsula. In 1742 he invaded Perak, captured the royal regalia and installed the *raja muda* of Perak as sultan in opposition to the incumbent ruler. In the same year Daeng Cellak's son, Raja Lumu became first sultan of Selangor as Sultan Sallehuddin and established Selangor as an independent state, free of Johor's overlordship.

When Daeng Cellak died in 1745 the Bugis were strongly entrenched in Riau and the west coast peninsular states, but a new champion of Malay rights appeared at this stage in the person of Sultan Mansur of Trengganu.

Trengganu and the Riau/Johor Empire

While the western and southern states of the Malay peninsula were ravaged by wars in the early decades of the eighteenth century, the east coast enjoyed a period of prosperous tranquillity. To the north, Siamese ambitions at the time were confined to subduing Patani, while Johor was preoccupied with its own affairs in the south. Meanwhile Trengganu developed a thriving textile industry and conducted a profitable trade with Siam, Cambodia, west Borneo and China based on exports of pepper and gold.

Trengganu had close traditional ties with the Johor empire dating from the days of the Melaka Sultanate, but about the year 1724 Tun Zainal Abidin, a younger brother of the former Sultan Abdul Jalil of Johor, established Trengganu as an independent state and became its first sultan, founding the present ruling house. Trengganu maintained and strengthened its friendship with Johor. Hitherto the state had been a sympathetic bystander, often offering refuge to Malay leaders in time of trouble, but in the mid-eighteenth century it began for the first time to play an active role in the politics of the Riau-Johor empire.

Zainal Abidin's son, Mansur, succeeded his father as sultan of

Trengganu in 1740 at the age of fourteen and ruled the state for more than fifty years. The royal houses of Trengganu and Riau-Johor were closely linked. Mansur's uncle, Sultan Sulaiman of Riau-Johor, visited Trengganu frequently, while the young Mansur spent much time at the Riau court, where he married daughters of both the sultan and Yamtuan Muda Daeng Cellak.

A much more determined character than his uncle, Sultan Sulaiman, Mansur believed that Riau-Johor could only free itself from Bugis subjection by renewing its traditional co-operation with the Dutch. By the mid-1740s such a policy was opportune, since the Dutch, although initially happy to profit from dissensions in the Johor empire, did not want to see a strong Johor supplanted by a stronger and more aggressive Bugis kingdom. The Buginese ravaging of Kedah and Perak and their harassment of shipping disrupted trade and the Dutch feared Buginese power would envelope Melaka and threaten the town itself.

Revisiting Riau in 1745, Mansur tried to use the opportunity presented by Daeng Cellak's death to rally anti-Bugis sentiment. He spent the next fifteen years at the Johor capital, bringing in a large force of Trengganu followers and leaving his own state to his ministers' care.

The new *yamtuan muda*, Daeng Kemboja of Linggi, did not immediately come to Riau, and in his absence Mansur built up anti-Bugis sympathies among the *bendahara, temenggong* and the *orang kaya*. The Malay party's chance to assert an independent line came as a result of civil war which broke out in Siak after Raja Kechil's death in 1745, when his two sons quarrelled over the succession. One claimant appealed for help from Riau-Johor, and despite Daeng Kemboja's refusal to become involved, Mansur persuaded Sulaiman to lend support and to court Dutch backing. But this scheme foundered. In 1748 Daeng Kemboja came to Riau and was formally installed as *yamtuan muda*, the oath of loyalty between Malays and Bugis was re-affirmed, and Bugis power was more firmly entrenched in Riau than ever.

In 1753 Daeng Kemboja returned to Linggi and set out to strengthen the Buginese position in the peninsular Minangkabau states. Numbers of Bugis had migrated to the interior, attracted mainly by the profits of the tin trade, and in the late-1750s Daeng Kemboja invaded the tin mining state of Sungei Ujong, where he established a Bugis as territorial chief, changing the traditional title of that office to the Bugis term, *klana putra*.

Meanwhile Mansur of Trengganu took advantage of Daeng Kemboja's absence from Riau to rebuild the influence of the Malay party at court. He also exploited Dutch fears about the Buginese triumph in Sungei Ujong, which was the major source of Melaka's tin trade. In 1756 Mansur of Trengganu accompanied Sultan Sulaiman and the *bendahara* of Riau-Johor on a state visit to Melaka, where they signed a treaty, by which the Dutch promised to help the Malays against the Bugis in exchange for a joint monopoly of Siak's trade and sole rights to the tin trade of Selangor, Klang and Linggi once Sulaiman regained control of his vassal states.

In the war which ensued, the Bugis and their Rembau allies ravaged Melaka's suburbs, while a combined Dutch–Trengganu force seized Linggi. In 1757 Sultan Sulaiman offered to cede Linggi and Rembau to the Dutch if they helped him recover Siak and Selangor, and he asked for a Dutch garrison to be posted at Riau to protect him against the Bugis.

Despite fierce Bugis resistance, the Dutch gained the upper hand. But Batavia did not want to become involved at that stage in the politics of Riau or the Malay peninsular states. The Company was not prepared to set up a garrison in Riau, nor for his part did Sulaiman intend to carry out his pledges. The Dutch were content instead to make a treaty in 1759 with Rembau, Klang and Daeng Kemboja of Linggi, which assured the Dutch East India Company of a monopoly of their tin trade. Despite the Dutch withdrawal, Mansur advocated a further attack on Linggi, but Sulaiman, now over sixty years old and near to death, wanted an end to fighting. In 1760 he invited Yamtuan Muda Daeng Cellak to return to court and renewed the bargain of co-operation between Malays and Bugis.

Mansur retired to Trengganu in disgust, leaving the Bugis to consolidate their power. Sulaiman died in 1760, followed quickly by two successors, and in 1761 the Bugis proclaimed an infant, Mahmud, as sultan, under the guardianship of Daeng Kemboja.

The Zenith of Buginese Power

For more than twenty years the Bugis then ruled without challenge in Riau and their west coast states. Daeng Kemboja reigned supreme, supported by his cousin, the vigorous warrior Raja Haji, Daeng Cellak's son, who succeeded him as *yamtuan muda* in 1777.

The Bugis forced Jambi and Indragiri to renew their pledges of loyalty to Riau–Johor in the 1760s. In 1770 Raja Haji and his brother, Sultan Sallehuddin of Selangor, went in force to Perak, where they exacted allegiance and compelled the sultan to give his daughter in marriage to Sallehuddin.

The two brothers then went on to Kedah, where once more the Bugis were invited in as mercenary soldiers in a succession dispute. In 1770 the ageing sultan of Kedah, Muhammad Jiwa, handed over administration of the country to Tunku Abdullah, his only son by a commoner wife. This appointment angered a faction at the Kedah court, who preferred a nominee of pure royal blood and who invited Raja Haji and his Buginese force to help them overthrow Sultan Muhammad Jiwa and his son. As a reward the Bugis were promised free rein to pillage the property of Indian and Chinese residents in Kedah. When the Bugis arrived at Kuala Kedah in 1771, the sultan's relatives staged a palace revolt, and the old sultan, taken unawares and appalled at this family treachery, retreated to Perlis. The Bugis plundered not only alien merchants' property but took away everything they could carry, including Malay women and children to sell into slavery. They destroyed and burned Alor Star, Kuala Kedah and all the settlements along the Kedah river and then withdrew. Meanwhile the royal rebels found no support either among the Kedah *orang kaya* or the general population and had to flee with their Buginese partners to find refuge in Selangor.

The Bugis reached the height of their power in the 1770s, at which time they were in direct control of Selangor, Sungei Ujong and the west coast south to Melaka. They commanded the allegiance of part of east Sumatra, while the rulers of Riau-Johor and Perak were their puppets.

The senior Malay officers and *orang kaya* were disgruntled but powerless to resist. Sultan Mansur of Trengganu turned a deaf ear to appeals for help from the *bendahara* and *temenggong*, and from this time the major Johor chiefs withdrew to their fiefs: the *temenggong* to Bulang and the nearby islands, and the *bendahara* to Pahang. The first *bendahara* of Pahang, Tun Abdul Majid, assumed this title about 1770. His successors continued to be acknowledged as senior chief of the Riau-Johor empire and retained the honour of formally installing the sultan. Pahang remained part of the Johor empire with each *bendahara's* title being confirmed by the sultan, but it was the one province of the empire where the Bugis had no influence. The link with Riau weakened as the eighteenth century went on, and in practice the *bendaharas* came to rule Pahang as a semi-autonomous vassal state.

The capital of the empire remained at Riau and never returned to the Johor river after Raja Kechil abandoned his position there in 1719. From the middle of the century Riau was a flourishing commercial centre, frequented by Asian and European traders, who were attracted by its moderate tariffs and relative freedom from restrictions. As in previous times, Riau-Johor flouted treaty undertakings with the Dutch, who were not strong enough to enforce their monopolies, and Riau became the centre of the Sumatran pepper trade and the tin trade of the western peninsular states.

Riau-Johor Empire and the Dutch

Yamtuan Muda Raja Haji maintained the traditional Riau-Johor policy towards the Dutch of outward amicability, cloaking a hard and uncompromising attitude. This uneasy relationship was strained to breaking point in 1782, when the Dutch governor of Melaka provoked a quarrel with Raja Haji over the seizure of an English ship in Riau. The Dutch blockaded Riau but had to call their forces off in face of a threat to Melaka itself by the combined forces of Riau, Selangor and Rembau. In 1784 Raja Haji landed to the south of the city, while his nephew, Ibrahim, who had recently succeeded as sultan of Selangor, attacked from the north. The Bugis and Minangkabaus laid siege to Melaka for six months, repeatedly raiding its suburbs. The Dutch plight was grave but the attackers could not storm the fortress, and a Dutch fleet, which arrived in Batavia from Europe and was immediately diverted to relieve Melaka, took the assailants by surprise. Some 500 Bugis soldiers were slaughtered and at the height of the battle Raja Haji was shot through by a musket ball. His followers fled in confusion, dismayed by the death of their dynamic and charismatic leader, whom they had believed to be invulnerable.

The Dutch force then turned against Selangor, forcing Ibrahim to flee overland to Pahang, after which the Dutch set up a fort at Kuala Selangor and blockaded the Selangor river. The Dutch fleet then attacked Riau, where the Bugis had installed Daeng Kemboja's son, Raja Ali, as the new *yamtuan muda*. Overpowering the Bugis garrison, the Dutch made a treaty with Sultan Mahmud in 1784, whereby Riau-Johor acknowledged the Dutch East India Company's suzerainty. The succession to the throne was to be subject to Dutch approval. All previous agreements with the Bugis were to be rescinded, no Bugis could hold official rank and Mahmud was to expel all those who were not born in Riau. The Dutch were accorded freedom to trade throughout Johor's territories, but all other Europeans were to be excluded, and restrictions were also imposed on Asian traders dealing in spices or tin.

The following year a Dutch resident, supported by a garrison of Dutch soldiers, was installed in Riau to see that the treaty was enforced and to supervise trade. In 1787 Sultan Mahmud paid a visit to Melaka, where he signed an agreement promising to follow the Dutch resident's advice.

The Dutch triumph was impressive but fragile. The Bugis showed their customary resilience. After his expulsion from Riau Yamtuan Muda Raja Ali, establishing his base in the Natuna Islands, turned pirate and harassed shipping. In 1787 the Buginese Sultan Ibrahim of Selangor returned with a Pahang force, took the Kuala Selangor fort by surprise and drove the Dutch out.

Meanwhile in Riau, Sultan Mahmud, distressed to find that in freeing himself from the Bugis he had merely acquired a more exacting Dutch master, intrigued with pirate bands to attack the Dutch. When a powerful Illanun pirate fleet from Mindanao attacked Riau in 1787, only the Chinese community came to the support of the Dutch. Sultan Mahmud's men held back, the Dutch trading post was destroyed and the survivors fled to Melaka.

Mahmud retired to Pahang, where it was alleged he was trying to

arrange for an overland attack on Melaka. Meanwhile the Dutch quickly re-established themselves in Riau, but they found the settlement
almost deserted. A six months' free-trade period failed to attract merchants back, and the Dutch were anxious to restore peace and re-instate
the Malay regime. But they made a mistake in contemptuously dismiss-
ing a mediation offer made by the ageing Sultan Mansur of Trengganu. Incensed by this insult, Mansur built up an anti-Dutch coalition
comprising Johor, Lingga, Siak, Indragiri and Rembau, but the
alliance crumbled with his death in 1793. Eventually Mahmud made his
peace with the Dutch and returned to Riau in 1795.

Negri Sembilan

While the Riau–Johor empire and the Bugis were pre-occupied in
troubles, the other states of the peninsula went their separate ways.

Despite the fact that the Minangkabaus of Rembau had supported
Raja Haji in attacking Melaka in 1784, Buginese influence in the
interior had already begun to decline from the time Daeng Kemboja
returned to Riau in 1760 to resume the office of *yamtuan muda* of
Riau–Johor. With Daeng Kemboja absorbed in the affairs of Riau, and
Raja Haji and Sultan Sallehuddin of Selangor engaged in adventures in
Perak and Kedah, the link between the Minangkabau states and Riau–
Johor became even more tenuous, and in 1773 the Minangkabaus of the
peninsular states appealed to Pagar Ruyong to appoint a ruler over
them. A Sumatran, Raja Melewar, supposedly of the royal house of
Pagar Ruyong, was installed as first *yang di-pertuan besar* of the Negri
Sembilan (literally, nine states) confederacy by the four *undang,* or
territorial chiefs, of Sungei Ujong, Jelebu, Johol and Rembau. Negri
Sembilan was a loose coalition, never a formal confederacy, and there is
some confusion as to the composition and origin of the 'nine states.'*

Raja Melewar set up his capital at Sri Menanti in the hitherto
insignificant state of Ulu Muar, where he indulged in ceremonial but
had little power. He was given neither lands nor rights to raise revenue
but received a fixed tribute in the form of rice and coconuts. With no
opportunity to build up wealth, attract followers and create a power
base, the *yang di-pertuan besar* could not vie with major chiefs, such as
the *klana putra* of Sungei Ujong or the *penghulu* of Rembau. In practice Raja Melewar had little political authority outside of the Ulu Muar
district and none at all over the Bugis chiefs of Sungei Ujong, Klang or
Rembau.

* The original nine districts of Minangkabau settlement were Sungei Ujong, Jelebu, Johol, Rembau,
Klang, Naning, Jelai, Ulu Pahang and Segamat. But of these, Klang came under Bugis rule and eventually became part of Selangor. Naning was a vassal state of Melaka and subsequently absorbed into it.
Ulu Pahang and Jelai became part of Pahang, and Segamat of Johor. The 'nine states' of twentieth-
century Negri Sembilan comprised the much smaller area of Sungei Ujong, Jelebu, Johol, Rembau,
with Ulu Muar, Inas, Gunong Pasir, Terachi and Jempul.

The death of Raja Haji, the expulsion of Sultan Ibrahim from Selangor and the Dutch seizure of Riau in 1784 freed Negri Sembilan from the fear of Buginese domination and sapped any sense of unity. Internal quarrels sprang up once more, now further embittered by rivalries over the growing profits of the tin trade. Tin-producing states, such as Sungei Ujong and Jelebu, or districts such as Rembau on the Linggi river, which was the major highway for the tin trade, waxed rich, leaving behind other purely agricultural areas, such as the *yang dipertuan besar*'s own district of Sri Menanti.

Once the danger of outside interference had evaporated, the local *undang* were unwilling to surrender any authority to the *yang dipertuan besar*. When Raja Melewar died in 1795, he was succeeded by other Sumatran chieftains: Raja Hitam, who held the office from 1795 until 1808; Raja Lenggang, who reigned from 1808 to 1824; and Raja Laboh, who arrived in 1824. But Raja Laboh, the last ruler sent from Minangkabau, never succeeded in establishing his position. Wars for control of the tin areas and the Linggi river, which raged from 1824 until 1832, ended political ties with Sumatra and led to the establishment of an indigenous, hereditary royal family in Negri Sembilan.

The Sumatran link had little political significance but important social consequences. The arrival of the Sumatran princes strengthened the influence of Minangkabau law and enhanced the status of the *adat perpateh*, which up to that time had probably been merely used as personal family law within the *suku*. While the majority of the population were Minangkabaus, the territorial chiefs were descended from Melaka–Johor Malays, who later intermarried with Buginese chieftains, and both the coastal Malays and the Bugis had patrilinear societies. The Johor territorial chiefs traditionally used the *adat temenggong*, and purely Buginese communities, such as Linggi, or Bugis-dominated states such as Sungei Ujong or Rembau, were organized on patriarchal lines.

Hitherto matriarchal *suku* organization had co-existed with a patriarchal political system, but from the latter quarter of the eighteenth century Minangkabau matriarchal custom spread and was finally adopted in Sungei Ujong in the second or third decade of the nineteenth century.

Trengganu in the Late-Eighteenth Century

After washing his hands of Riau–Johor's troubles in 1760, Sultan Mansur returned to rule Trengganu and to expand the influence of his prosperous state. He saw a potential threat in the neighbouring state of Kelantan, where central authority was reviving after more than a century, during which time the state had splintered into a number of petty chiefdoms. In 1775 Mansur mounted a campaign in person and after bitter fighting succeeded in putting his own nominee on the throne of

Kelantan. Subsequently Mansur's son married the Kelantan ruler's daughter and eventually became ruler of Kelantan himself.

While Mansur was a vigorous and independent-minded ruler, he unintentionally brought Trengganu into the Siamese net. In 1781 he agreed to a Siamese request to attack Ligor and at that time sent the *bunga mas,* a traditional tribute of gold and silver flowers, to the Siamese capital at Ayuthia. This was the first occasion on which Trengganu sent tribute, and although it apparently began as a voluntary gesture of friendship, Siam came to interpret it as a token of vassalage.

Mansur died in 1793, leaving Trengganu flourishing, but already there were indications of troubles to come. His son, Zainal Abidin II, who was known as the Red-Eyed Ruler, faced a series of revolts in Kelantan, culminating in the expulsion of the ruler, Zainal Abidin's brother. Kelantan asserted its independence, and in 1800 a local chief, Long Mohamed, was proclaimed Muhammad I, first sultan of Kelantan.

Kedah

The northwestern state of Kedah was less successful in avoiding the troubles of other peninsular states but enjoyed periods of great prosperity in the eighteenth century. The rich, fertile and well drained basin of the Kedah river in the northern part of the state was the only region in the peninsula at that time which could produce a surplus of rice for export. Kedah was probably the major pepper-producing state in the peninsula in the eighteenth century, and exported tin which was produced in its southern districts or transported overland from Patani and the mines of Klian Intan and Kroh in the interior. Although its early glory of Srivijayan days had faded, Alor Star, Kuala Kedah and Kuala Muda conducted a thriving international trade. Its population numbered perhaps as many as 100 000 in the last decade of the eighteenth century, including prosperous communities of Indian and Chinese traders.

While its geographical position and natural resources brought Kedah wealth, they also excited the jealousy of its neighbours, particularly Siam, but in general Kedah succeeded in balancing its foreign policy to achieve peace and independence. Its relationship with the Siamese was particularly delicate. Divided from the Siamese on ethnic, religious and linguistic grounds, the Kedah Malays resisted Siam's domination but where necessary invoked its protection. During the seventeenth century it had turned to Siam for support after the Achehnese devastation in 1619, but re-asserted its independence in the 1630s when the Achehnese threat disappeared. For the rest of the century it had played off the Dutch and Siamese somewhat precariously, aiming to avoid dependence on either.

Kedah's main troubles arose from internal succession disputes as in 1721 and 1771, when it foolishly invited in Buginese mercenaries and brought about its own devastation. But international developments in the second half of the eighteenth century brought new and more dangerous threats. When Ayuthia fell to the Burmese in 1767, Kedah repudiated Siamese suzerainty and for a time sent tribute to the Burmese capital of Ava. Within a year Siam's swift recovery compelled Kedah to acknowledge Siamese overlordship afresh, but the ensuing struggle between Burma and Siam left Kedah in an invidious and vulnerable position.

Despite this threat of involvement in the strife of its more powerful neighbours, Kedah recovered comparatively quickly from the abortive coup of 1771. Savage though it was, the Bugis incursion was merely a raid and did not seek to establish any permanent political hold in Kedah. The rebellion had not shaken the system of government. Sultan Muhammad's treacherous relatives had fled and he soon returned as un-disputed master to rebuild the state. Kedah continued to send the tribute of gold and silver flowers every three years to Siam, but regarded this as a voluntary offering.

The Malay World in the Eighteenth Century

The eighteenth century was a time of drift for the Malay world, when the Minangkabaus and Bugis played an active role, overshadowing the Malays, who produced no outstanding leaders in this period. But neither the Minangkabaus nor the Bugis succeeded in strengthening the Riau–Johor empire or in creating a new one of their own.

Raja Kechil had a sense of vision. Had he retained the Johor throne, he might have carved out a powerful Minangkabau empire astride the Melaka Straits, a successor to Srivijaya and Melaka, but his defeat ended this prospect. Various attempts were subsequently made to draw the Minangkabaus of the peninsula and Sumatra closer together, but this essentially inland, agricultural people lacked the naval power and commercial interest to create a maritime empire. Despite this, the steady influx of Minangkabau migrants from Sumatra to Negri Sembilan continued throughout the century, opening up new areas of the interior to farming and tin mining, and strengthening the influence of Minangkabau matriarchal custom in Negri Sembilan.

The Bugis achieved greater and more lasting power but did not employ this to consolidate or extend the Riau–Johor empire. While they were skilled seamen, disciplined warriors and fiercely loyal to their com-patriots, the traditional background of the Bugis did not endow them with the conception of a united political state. They lacked diplomacy to match their fighting prowess and divided their energies between Riau and the western peninsular states, ever thirsting for adventure and relishing a fight.

Bugis chiefs married into Malay noble families but the Buginese community as a whole kept a separate identity throughout the eighteenth century and was not assimilated into Malay society, despite strong similarities in the ecological background and character of the two peoples.

In general Buginese influence was disruptive. The Bugis brought war and destruction to Selangor, Perak and Kedah and, despite their power, they let the Riau-Johor empire crumble. The Sumatran states broke away, Negri Sembilan and Trengganu established their independence, and the Bugis' own state of Selangor established itself as a separate unit.

Struck down in 1784, apparently at the very height of their power, the Bugis were never again destined to play a crucial role in the Malay peninsula. But they established a Buginese sultanate in Selangor, left large communities of restless, enterprising colonists in Johor, Negri Sembilan and Perak, and became a strong element in the ruling houses of most Malay peninsular states.

Table 8.3   Early Buginese rulers of Riau and Selangor

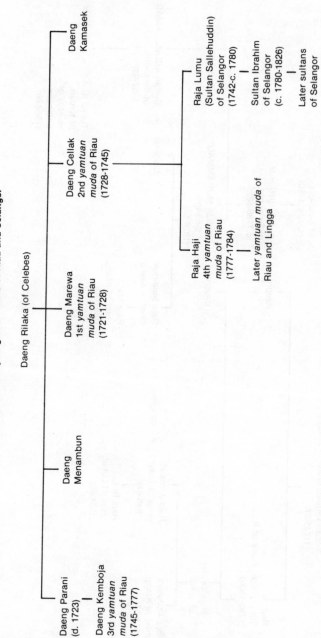

Daeng Rilaka (of Celebes)

Daeng Parani
(d. 1723)

Daeng Kemboja
3rd *yamtuan
muda* of Riau
(1745-1777)

Daeng Menambun

Daeng Marewa
1st *yamtuan
muda* of Riau
(1721-1728)

Daeng Cellak
2nd *yamtuan
muda* of Riau
(1728-1745)

Daeng Kamasek

Raja Haji
4th *yamtuan
muda* of Riau
(1777-1784)

Later *yamtuan muda* of
Riau and Lingga

Raja Lumu
(Sultan Sallehuddin)
of Selangor
(1742-c. 1780)

Sultan Ibrahim
of Selangor
(c. 1780-1826)

Later sultans
of Selangor

Table 8.4 The Buginese rulers of Selangor

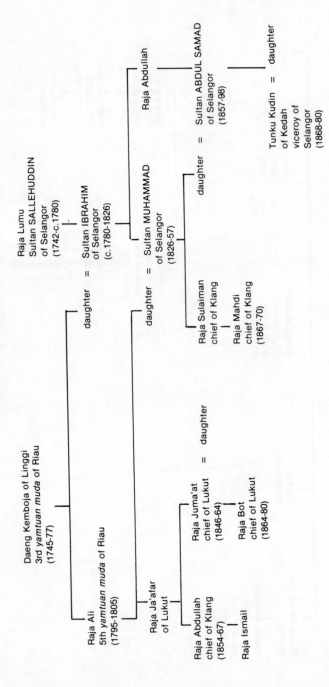

CHAPTER 9

Early British Contacts,
1761–1824

The English East India Company's Quest for a Base

For more than a century the Malay peninsula and northern Borneo had attracted little outside attention, but in the latter years of the eighteenth century the region was once more drawn into international affairs, notably through the activities of the English East India Company.

From the days when the East India Company had first attempted to establish a foothold in the spice trade of the eastern archipelago, the English were aware of the rich tin deposits of the Malay peninsula. But an expedition sent by the Company in 1647 reported adversely on trading prospects in Perak and Johor. They decided conditions in Johor were too competitive and found Acheh, Perak's overlord, bound by treaty obligations to uphold a Dutch trading monopoly in Perak.

After the Dutch drove the English factors out of Bantam in 1682, the English East India Company turned its back on the archipelago and the Malay peninsula. Confining its activities in Southeast Asia to remote Benkulen in west Sumatra, the Company concentrated on building up its economic and political interests in India. Its major concern was trade between Britain, India and China, and it was content to leave trade with Southeast Asia in the hands of English private or 'country' traders, who maintained their headquarters in India but were not Company employees. Chiefly interested in tin, individual English traders were to be found in many peninsular and archipelago ports, frequently infringing Dutch treaty rights.

The English East India Company held a monopoly over the China trade, which became increasingly lucrative during the second half of the eighteenth century, particularly the trade in Chinese tea. To protect and stimulate this commerce the Company began to look for a base in the East, as a refitting station for the Company's ships and a possible collecting centre for produce to feed the China trade. At that time the Company was forced to pay for its tea imports in silver and sought an alternative in the pepper, tin and other 'Straits produce' which Southeast Asia traditionally supplied to China.

The British did not want to jeopardize their European interests by clashing with the Dutch or the Spaniards in their search for an Eastern base, and they were thus attracted to northern Borneo which fell outside the sphere of any other European power. Northern Borneo also lay on a new route to China, which was discovered in 1757 and offered greater freedom from dependence on monsoon winds.

Accordingly in 1759 the governor of Madras dispatched an official, Alexander Dalrymple, to investigate the north coast of Borneo. In 1761 Dalrymple made an agreement with the sultan of Sulu, who offered the Company permission to establish a trading post and freedom of trade in his dominions in return for military defence aid. Two years later Sulu offered the Company the island of Balambangan off the northern tip of Borneo, and eventually in 1773 a Benkulen official, John Herbert, was sent to establish a post on the island.

Balambangan had no resources of its own but provided many attractions. It seemed ideally situated to tap the Bugis trade, and lay close to China on a coast which had attracted Chinese traders for centuries. The Company hoped Chinese traders might be drawn to the new centre to escape the commercial restrictions imposed by the authorities in Canton.

But the venture was short lived. The Sulu court was a centre of intrigue and violence, and in 1775, barely a year after it came into being, the trading post was destroyed by Suluks. Herbert withdrew south to the island of Labuan in the territory of Brunei, where he recommended founding an alternative post, which would be able to tap the Brunei pepper trade. Brunei was anxious to accept British protection, but the East India Company wanted no further involvement in the unsettled conditions in northern Borneo and ordered Herbert to abandon Labuan. The Company re-occupied Balambangan briefly from 1803 until 1805 during the French wars, when it considered building up a naval base there, but the idea was quickly abandoned.

Instead the Company's attention was diverted south to the Straits of Melaka and the Malay peninsula, where a base could also serve a strategic purpose. During the struggle against the French for mastery in India, the British found themselves at a disadvantage since the Company based its fleet in Bombay and possessed no naval station in the Bay of Bengal. The French, with facilities in Mergui and Acheh, had readier access to the Coromandel coast, and during one campaign in 1746 briefly managed to wrest Madras from the British. This induced the Company to begin searching for a suitable Eastern base. A station set up in Negrais, off the Burmese coast, was destroyed by the Burmese in 1759, and missions to seek sites in Acheh or the Sunda Straits in the mid-1760s came to nothing. After looking at possibilities in the Nicobars, Phuket island and the Andamans, in 1771 the Company's attention was drawn to Kedah, where Sultan Muhammad Jiwa was seeking allies to help recover his throne.

Having fled to Perlis at the time of the rebellion and Bugis incursion,

Sultan Muhammad Jiwa appealed for aid to the governor of Madras and to an English trading agency in Acheh. The latter immediately responded to the sultan's pleas by sending Francis Light, an English country trader employed by the Madras firm of Jourdain, Sulivan and de Souza, who brought two ships, arms, ammunition and a band of sepoys.

By that stage the Kedah revolt had collapsed but Sultan Muhammad Jiwa was prepared to give Jourdains a licence to trade and to establish a post at Kuala Kedah, in return for retaining a force of troops to protect Kedah in the event of any further attack. He also offered to cede Kuala Kedah or even the whole coast south to Penang if Jourdains would help him mount a retaliatory campaign against the Bugis in Selangor to recover stolen booty and recapture his rebellious relatives. But the Madras firm was not willing to take on this commitment.

At this point the Madras government, interested in Light's enthusiastic reports about Kedah, sent a mission in 1772 under the command of the Hon. Edward Monckton, with instructions to explore the suitability of Kedah as a potential base. Sultan Muhammad Jiwa welcomed Monckton and offered to cede Kuala Kedah to the Company, together with a monopoly of tin and pepper exports, if the British would help him punish Selangor. But the Company would not consider an offensive alliance, particularly against the Bugis, whom they regarded as valuable trading partners. The sultan was not interested in granting concessions on any other terms and, urged on by the Indian merchants in Kedah who dominated its commerce at that time, he sent the 'stuttering boy' Monckton packing, and the negotiations collapsed.

The Company was impelled to renew its quest in the early-1780s, when British shipping in the East suffered greatly from French naval attacks in the closing stages of the War of American Independence and the Dutch closed their ports to British shipping. In 1784 the Company dispatched one mission to Acheh and a second under Captain Thomas Forrest to Kedah and Riau. Both expeditions received a chilling welcome. Sultan Abdullah Mukarram Shah, who had succeeded his father, Muhammad Jiwa, in 1778, refused to grant a site, so Forrest sailed on to Riau, where the situation in June 1784 looked more promising for the East India Company. The Bugis, in full command, had driven the Dutch out of Riau and Raja Haji was laying siege to Melaka. But within a few months British hopes were crushed. Raja Haji was killed, his attack on Melaka dispersed, the Bugis expelled from Riau, and Mahmud's cession of Riau to the Dutch late in 1784 put an end to Forrest's plans. At the same time the Dutch victory in the Melaka Straits and their new hold in Riau alarmed the English East India Company, who feared a Dutch stranglehold on the China trade route. The British renewed their search for a base with added intensity, and when Francis Light informed Calcutta in February 1786 that the sultan of Kedah was now willing to cede the island of Penang, the Company accepted the offer and appointed Light superintendent.

The reversal in Kedah's policy arose from renewed hostility between Burma and Siam and a change in the nature of its relationship with Siam, which threatened Kedah's security and eventually led to its downfall. According to Kedah tradition, the royal houses of Ayuthia and Kedah originated from common stock, and Kedah had always regarded the *bunga mas* or tribute of gold and silver flowers, which it paid to Ayuthia, as a voluntary gesture of friendship. In return it received goods of equal value and Siam made no heavy demands.

The final destruction of Ayuthia by the Burmese in 1767 and the collapse of the Siamese dynasty broke the blood link with Kedah, who regarded the new Siamese kings as usurpers. For a time it stopped sending the *bunga mas* but was eventually forced by Burma–Siam rivalry and by its own internal power struggles into a position of vassalage towards Siam.

Two strong kings came to the throne in 1782: Bodawpaya in Burma and General Chakri, who became Rama I, in Siam. Three years later Bodawpaya invaded Siam, and Sultan Abdullah Mukarram Shah of Kedah, wanting to keep his country neutral but pressed by both sides for help, played off one against the other, promising homage and sending supplies to both. In this dangerous situation he offered to lease Penang island to the East India Company in return for protection.

The Founding of Penang

After signing a preliminary letter with Sultan Abdullah, Francis Light occupied Penang in August 1786 on Calcutta's orders, pending reference to the Directors in London, but no formal written contract was made. The sultan continued to ask for protection and the Company to haggle over the price and terms of the lease. Relations reached breaking point in 1790 when Sultan Abdullah tried to force the Company's hand by enlisting the aid of Illanun pirates, part of the fleet which had driven the Dutch from Riau and then turned north to ravage the west coast of the Malay peninsula. Sultan Abdullah made a bargain with the Illanuns, blockaded Penang and demanded that the Company should either agree to terms, guarantee him military aid and pay him a rent of Spanish $10 000 a year, or they should evacuate the island. The plan misfired, Light taking the threat as a declaration of war, and in 1791 the British attacked Prai, dispersed the Kedah naval force and compelled Abdullah to make a treaty, in which he accepted $6000 a year for Penang and promised not to obstruct supplies to the settlement.

In 1800 this agreement was superseded by a further Treaty of Peace, Friendship and Alliance, which the Company held to be the basis of its relationship with Kedah. According to this pact, Kedah ceded to the

East India Company the strip of territory which came to be known as Province Wellesley on the coast opposite Penang, stretching from the Muda to the Krian rivers, in return for which the sultan's pension was increased to Spanish $10 000. The Company undertook to guard the Province Wellesley coast, but no mention was made of military assistance to Kedah, either defensive or offensive.

Penang was virtually uninhabited when Francis Light took possession in 1786, renamed the island Prince of Wales Island and founded the settlement of Georgetown, in honour of George, Prince of Wales, who later became George IV. To attract settlers and traders, Light allowed immigrants to claim whatever land they could clear and threw the port open to ships of all nations free of duties. This policy, which was in direct contrast to the monopoly hitherto practised in the region by the Portuguese and Dutch, quickly attracted a cosmopolitan population: Malays, Sumatrans, Indians from Kedah, and Chinese who came from Kedah, Phuket and other ports in the area. Within ten years the population numbered nearly 7000 and this figure rose by 1801 to over 10 000.

Penang attracted much of the trade which had formerly gone to Kedah. It became a centre for north Sumatran pepper, and a large proportion of Malayan tin exports was smuggled through Penang in contravention of the Dutch monopoly.

Light hoped to make the island a production centre for pepper and spices for the China trade. In 1790 he introduced pepper plants from Sumatra and pepper planting became popular, particularly among Chinese farmers. Spice plants were imported from the Moluccas in 1795 but the growing of cloves and nutmegs developed slowly. Only European planters were prepared to accept the considerable capital outlay and the delay on return in these slow maturing crops, and plantation owners were hampered by a shortage of labour.

Light remained as superintendent until his death in 1794, running the settlement on a shoestring budget and administering the population through their own headmen, or *kapitans,* in the way that the Malays, Portuguese and Dutch had governed Melaka. *Kapitans* were responsible for keeping law and order and settling disputes within their communities, while more difficult cases were referred to the superintendent, who passed judgment according to common sense.

From the beginning of the nineteenth century more sophisticated administration was introduced. In 1800 a lieutenant-governor replaced the superintendent and a professional lawyer was sent to administer justice. In 1805, when it was proposed to develop Georgetown as a naval base, Penang was raised to the status of a presidency government, equivalent to Bengal, Bombay and Madras, and was allocated an elaborate establishment of governor and officials. In 1808 a charter of justice introduced British law and created courts separate from the administration and presided over by a professional judge.

The expense involved brought no compensating advantage to the Company. In its bid to encourage settlement, the Penang government had deprived itself of the opportunity to raise any appreciable revenue from land, commerce or poll taxes. From 1801 it introduced a 5 per cent tariff on imports and exports but had to rely mainly on farming out the rights to sell opium and arrack, or Asian spirits, and selling market and pawnbrokers' licences. After the expensive presidency establishment was introduced in 1805 the settlement was constantly in debt.

As a collecting centre for the China trade Penang was a disappointment. While trade continued to expand for the first twenty years, Penang was on the periphery of the archipelago and its commerce continued to be mainly a local regional trade covering north Sumatra, northwest Malaya, southern Burma and southwest Thailand.

Penang also lost its strategic attraction. In 1805 the Company planned to turn the island into a naval base, but the defeat of the French navy at Trafalgar later that year, coupled with the British occupation of Dutch bases in the East during the French wars, made this proposal redundant. In 1810 it was finally abandoned in favour of developing Trincomalee in Ceylon.

Despite these disappointments, Penang became the base for the expansion of British power during the wars against France, which persisted with two brief interludes from 1793 until 1815. When the French overran the Netherlands in 1795 and insisted on the right to use Dutch ports in the East, the British countered by making an agreement with the exiled Dutch government to take over temporary control of strategic Dutch possessions. The English East India Company occupied Melaka in 1795, the Moluccas the following year and Java in 1811.

With the acquisition of Dutch ports and the removal of Dutch restrictions, English country traders flourished. But for the East India Company the administration of Dutch territories was expensive and unrewarding, while Penang lost trade since, with Java in the Company's hands, British shipping found the Sunda Strait safe and more convenient.

Raffles and the Founding of Singapore

While London regarded the temporary occupation of Dutch territory as a friendly caretaker operation, British officials and merchants on the spot saw an opportunity to build up British trade and to make it difficult for the Dutch to restore their monopoly in future. To this end the Penang government began demolishing Melaka's fortifications in 1806 and proposed to transfer its population to Penang. The destruction was nearly completed by 1808, when Thomas Stamford Raffles, assistant

Sir Thomas Stamford Raffles. Portrait by G. F. Joseph,
A.R.A., 1817 *(By permission of the Trustees of the
National Portrait Gallery, London).*

secretary to the Penang government, arrived on holiday. As a result of
his recommendations Melaka was preserved and the plan to evacuate
the population abandoned.

Raffles, a former East India Company clerk, posted from London to
the new Penang presidency in 1805, was the most outstanding advocate
among those Englishmen who wanted to exploit war-time expansion to
extend and consolidate British commercial and naval strength in
Southeast Asia. A man of vision and ambition for himself and his country, Raffles was governor of Java from 1811 until 1816, during which
time he installed a British resident in Banjermasin in south Borneo in
1812, sent expeditions to help local rulers put down piracy in north and
west Borneo and the Sulu archipelago, advocated British occupation of
the Marudu Bay area of northern Borneo, and tried to win Calcutta's
backing for a far-reaching scheme of protection treaties. By making
Britain the paramount power in the archipelago, supporting the power
of indigenous rulers, Raffles hoped to restore order and peace, suppress

piracy and slavery, and bring prosperity and development to the region, which he considered was inhibited by Dutch monopoly and the dominance of Chinese and Arabs in the Asian commercial sector.

Neither the East India Company nor the British government wanted to extend commitments in Southeast Asia. They were no longer interested in collecting Straits produce, since Indian opium now sufficed to finance the China trade. Their only concern was to guard the route to China and they believed the Dutch, as a friendly European neighbour, would co-operate in this. In 1814 an Anglo-Dutch convention agreed to the restoration of Dutch colonies, with the exception of Ceylon and the Cape of Good Hope. By 1818 the Dutch were back in possession of Melaka, Java and their other Southeast Asian territories.

Before the Dutch returned, the Penang authorities attempted to safeguard British commercial interests by making agreements with local rulers. In 1818 Governor James Bannerman sent representatives to make arrangements for the tin trade in Perak and Selangor, and he dispatched Colonel William Farquhar, resident of Melaka from 1803 until 1818, to make a treaty with Riau, in which the sultan guaranteed the British trading rights in Riau-Johor and its dependencies and promised not to grant any monopolies.

Once the Dutch were restored they attempted to re-impose their restrictive pacts. They forced Sultan Ibrahim of Selangor to renew his former commercial treaty and compelled the sultan of Riau-Johor to repudiate his recent agreement with the British, to accept a Dutch resident and garrison at Riau and to exclude other European traders from his empire, outside of Riau and Lingga themselves.

Meanwhile Raffles continued in vain to push his schemes in London, and when he returned to the East as lieutenant-governor of Benkulen in 1818, he carried out an unremitting but unsuccessful one-man campaign to thwart the restoration of Dutch influence in southern Sumatra.

While Raffles's views roused no sympathy in London, Dutch policy began to worry the Company's officials in Calcutta, and when Raffles visited Calcutta in person late in 1818, he persuaded the governor-general to send him on a mission to set up a British post at the southern end of the Melaka Straits, provided this did not bring the Company into any conflict with the Dutch.

Initially Raffles favoured Riau but arrived in Penang to learn that the Dutch had already re-established themselves there. After inspecting the Karimon islands, Raffles's expedition sailed on to Singapore, where in January 1819 he made an agreement with the local chieftain, Temenggong Abdur Rahman of Riau-Johor, which permitted the British to establish a trading post. To give the Company a clear title to such a station, the pact needed the approval of the sultan of Riau-Johor, but here Raffles was faced with a difficulty, and an opportunity, since the succession to the empire was in dispute.

In 1799, four years after the French conquered Holland, the Dutch East India Company ended in bankruptcy and the Dutch removed their post from Riau. Raja Ali then forced his way back to Riau, and in 1804 Sultan Mahmud restored him to his office of *yamtuan muda*. The renewed Bugis paramountcy annoyed the traditional 'Malay' leaders, although they themselves after generations of intermarriage had a strong Buginese streak. Particularly displeased was the Temenggong Engku Muda Muhammad, who from his headquarters at Bulang had acted as *yamtuan muda* in Raja Ali's absence. In 1805 Raja Ali died and was succeeded as *yamtuan muda* by the Bugis Raja Ja'afar. But Engku Muda Muhammad, continuing to consider himself as *yamtuan muda*, refused to use his own title of *temenggong*. This passed to his nephew, Daeng Abdur Rahman, who was formally installed *temenggong* in 1806 by Sultan Mahmud and shortly afterwards moved from Bulang to Singapore.

Resistance to central authority, which had built up in the Riau–Johor empire in the past century, was pulling it apart. The sultan was effective only in Lingga, the *yamtuan muda* in Riau, while the *temenggong* controlled Johor, Singapore, Bulang and the Karimons, and the *bendahara* ruled Pahang. When Sultan Mahmud died in 1812, he left no sons by his royal wives but two sons by Bugis commoners: Hussein, the elder, who was closely connected with the *temenggong*'s family by marriage, and Abdul Rahman. Hussein seemed to be marked out for the succession by his father: traditional royal marriages were arranged for him and he was absent in Pahang for his wedding with the *bendahara*'s daughter when Mahmud died. But the Bugis faction favoured the younger son, Abdul Rahman, who was of a religious turn of mind and prepared to leave the running of government to the *yamtuan muda*. No formal coronation could take place because Sultan Mahmud's widow, Tengku Putri Hamidah, formidable daughter of the warrior Raja Haji, refused to give up the regalia. But the Yamtuan Muda Raja Ja'afar acknowledged Abdul Rahman, who was recognized as sultan by the Dutch on their return and in effect by the British, since Farquhar's treaty of 1818 was made with Abdul Rahman. Hussein appeared to accept the situation and returned to live at Riau in semi-retirement.

Raffles formally approached Sultan Abdul Rahman to approve his arrangement in Singapore but realized the sultan's Dutch masters would refuse any such sanction, and in order to give a cloak of legality to his action decided to recognize Hussein as the rightful sultan. Accordingly he sent secretly for the startled Hussein to come to Singapore and in February 1819 signed a formal agreement with 'His Highness the Sultan Hussein Mohamed Shah, Sultan of Johor' and with the *temenggong*, under which the two chiefs permitted the East India Company to establish a post at Singapore on payment of Spanish $5000 a year to Hussein and Spanish $3000 to the *temenggong*.

The Treaty of London, 1824

The legality of these arrangements was shaky. The Dutch were furious, the Penang authorities jealous and the British government embarrassed. The Dutch, claiming Raffles's intervention infringed their treaty rights in Riau-Johor, contemplated expelling the British from Singapore by force, but they decided to restrain themselves to diplomatic channels, since they were confident Britain itself would repudiate Raffles's action.

Slow communications saved the British settlement at Singapore. Calcutta referred the matter to London, which included it in issues already under discussion between England and Holland, with a view to drawing up a comprehensive agreement.

The long-drawn-out negotiations resulted in the Treaty of London of 1824, which sought to consolidate Anglo-Dutch friendship in Europe by settling all points of dispute in the East. According to the territorial stipulations, which demarcated spheres of influence, Holland withdrew its objection to the British occupation of Singapore, surrendered Melaka to the East India Company and undertook not to make any engagements in the Malay peninsula. In return Britain transferred Benkulen to the Dutch and promised not to interfere in Sumatra nor in the islands south of the Singapore Strait. The exchange of territory was formally completed in 1825, and the following year the English East India Company united Penang, Province Wellesley, Melaka and Singapore under one Straits Settlements presidency government, with its headquarters in Penang.

The intention behind the Anglo-Dutch treaty was merely to remove sources of friction between the two countries, and as such the territorial clauses were effective, although twenty years later the question was raised as to whether Borneo came within the scope of the agreement. But the Treaty of London had far-reaching consequences for the Malay world. Unintentionally it partitioned the Riau-Johor empire. The British were ignorant of the implications but the Dutch, who had been so largely responsible for resurrecting the Johor empire in the seventeenth century were instrumental in destroying it 200 years later. In undertaking to restrain the sultan from 'interfering' in domains north of the line of demarcation, they converted him into a Dutch puppet and confined him to the Riau-Lingga archipelago. The *temenggong*'s patrimony was cut in half; the Karimons and his traditional base at Bulang falling within the Dutch sphere of interest. He chose to identify himself instead with Singapore and Johor. The treaty gave further impetus for the *temenggong* and *bendahara* to move towards independence, and both were destined by the end of the nineteenth century to emerge as sultans of their own states.

The Treaty of London also cut the Malay peninsula off from

Sumatra, whence it had derived its language, religion, political, cultural and social traditions, thus destroying a link which stretched back through the centuries from Raja Kechil of Minangkabau, through the Johor and Melaka sultanates to Malayu-Jambi and Srivijaya.

After 1824 the Malay peninsula was isolated from former influences and was destined ultimately to come under British rule.

CHAPTER 10

The Straits Settlements, 1826–73

The East India Company regarded the Straits Settlements as links in the chain of staging posts on the China route, not launching pads for expansion into the Malay peninsula, and it soon lost interest even in the settlements themselves.

From the beginning the united settlements failed to pay their way, and revenue was insufficient to finance the elaborate administrative and judicial establishment, which was extended from Penang to cover Melaka and Singapore in 1826. The union coincided with a time of financial crisis in India, and the Company decided to economize by pruning top-heavy Straits administration. In 1830 the settlements were reduced to the status of a residency, part of the Bengal presidency. The civil service was slashed and the governor reduced to the rank of resident in all but name. Shortly after this, in 1833, the British parliament abolished the East India Company's China-trade monopoly. The Straits Settlements then became a useless burden to the Company, which it was forced to maintain for the benefit of others' trade.

Geographically dispersed, the settlements were difficult and expensive to administer and, despite the 1830 retrenchment, the authorities faced perennial revenue problems. A combination of confused land policy and practical agricultural difficulties prevented the collection of an adequate land revenue. The government was forbidden to tax trade, and various suggestions to impose poll taxes, income tax or levies on exported capital were abandoned, partly through lack of machinery to enforce them but mainly for fear they would deter immigration. The Straits authorities had to rely on excise revenue, raised almost entirely from the 'vices and pleasures' of the Asian inhabitants by tax farmers, who purchased from the government exclusive rights to sell opium, arrack, toddy (coconut palm wine) and other commodities.

The excise farms, which were first introduced in Penang in 1789, continued to be the mainstay of the Straits revenue throughout the nineteenth century. Initially the Penang and Singapore gambling farms were the most lucrative revenue earners but were abolished on moral grounds in Penang in 1810 and in Singapore in 1829, leaving opium as the major source of revenue. This method of taxation had been adapted by the Dutch and by the East India Company in Benkulen from the traditional practice of local rulers. It provided an assured income at no administrative cost and protected the authorities from coming into conflict with the local population, since the tax farmers were invariably Asian merchants. But the system prevented the government from profiting to the full from the Straits Settlements' increasing prosperity.

Until 1863, when the introduction of stamp duties first enabled the Straits government to balance its budget, the government of India was forced to subsidize the Straits Settlements, and there was never enough revenue to provide better administration, commercial reforms, port improvements or adequate police protection, let alone social welfare measures such as the provision of education, poor relief, medical facilities or labour protection.

But the very laxness of government, the modicum of law and order combined with freedom from commercial taxation and unrestricted immigration, quickly attracted population and trade. By 1860 the inhabitants numbered 274 000. Penang, together with Province Wellesley, had the largest population, numbering nearly 125 000 people. Singapore, which at the time of its first census in 1824 comprised only 10 000 inhabitants, stood in second place with 81 000. Melaka, which in 1826 had been the most populous of the settlements with 31 000 inhabitants, was now the smallest, although its population had more than doubled to 68 000.

Singapore, the most urbanized, commercially developed and prosperous settlement, became the capital in the 1830s. From the time of its foundation it acted as a magnet drawing in trade which was already highly developed in the region. More conveniently situated than Penang and free from Riau's impositions, Singapore attracted Bugis, Sumatran, Malay and Chinese traders, who already frequented the Straits of Melaka, the Riau archipelago and the east coast of the Malay peninsula. Within a few years it became a centre for ships from Europe, India and China. Singapore's trade with China grew rapidly following the abolition of the East India Company's monopoly, as did trade with the Netherlands Indies after Batavia lifted many restrictions in the 1840s. New commercial channels opened up: with Cochin China, with northwest Borneo from the 1840s after the Brooke regime was established in Sarawak, and with Siam after the Bowring treaty with Bangkok was signed in 1855. Singapore's trade multiplied more than fourfold in the period from 1824 to 1868, by which time it stood at an annual value of nearly $59 million.

It was an entrepôt trade based largely on textiles, metal goods and firearms from Britain, opium and textiles from India, silk and tea from China, gold and coffee from Minangkabau, pepper from north Sumatra, salt from Siam, gold and tin from Pahang, tin from Perak, Selangor and Sungei Ujong, gutta-percha (rubber gum) from Johor, birds' nests, agar-agar (derived from sea-weed) and other Straits produce from the eastern archipelago.

Singapore's prosperity developed in fits and starts, with periodic booms and slumps, and its fickle entrepôt trade depended on preserving an exemption from commercial exactions which was unique to the Straits Settlements. The East India Company's board of control in London laid down the principle of permanent free trade in the Straits. In 1826 it extended to Penang and Melaka the freedom from tariffs which Raffles had initially established as a temporary measure to get trade started in Singapore, and ten years later this exemption was widened to cover port charges too. Singapore's mercantile community zealously upheld this principle of free trade, which survived virtually intact until the 1930s.

The development of steamships put Singapore's trade on firmer foundations. The Peninsular and Oriental Steam Navigation Company extended its service to Penang, Singapore and Hong Kong in 1845, and regular steamship communications were established the following year between Calcutta and the Straits ports. Singapore's New Harbour, coming into use from the middle of the century and renamed Keppel Harbour in 1900, was admirably adapted to cope with the advent of steamers and the growing volume of shipping. Deep, well protected and requiring no dredging, it was one of the world's finest natural harbours.

The opening of the Suez Canal in 1869 confirmed Singapore's pre-eminence as a pivot of international trade. The canal speeded up the change from sail to steam, established the India–Melaka Straits route in preference to the Cape–Sunda Straits route as the main highway to the East and made Singapore vital to British imperial power.

Agriculture

In contrast to trade, the development of commercial agriculture was disappointing, except in the southern half of Province Wellesley. Here Chinese planters began growing sugar-cane for export on a small scale in the first decade of the nineteenth century, and from the 1840s Europeans opened up large plantations for sugar, which remained a major estate crop in the area for another sixty years.

Elsewhere the story of plantation agriculture was one of failure. Initially this was attributed to deficient land laws and in the early-1830s the land situation in Penang and Singapore was described as one of 'wild confusion'. A Straits Land Act passed in 1839 stimulated enthusiasm for agricultural development, and many new nutmeg plantations were opened up in Penang and Singapore, mainly by Europeans. But from the middle of the century blight began to attack the Penang spice trees, spreading subsequently to Singapore, and by the mid-1860s most estates had been wiped out.

Coconuts were grown along Singapore's sandy southeast coast, but they were not very profitable. Singapore's two sugar plantations went bankrupt in the middle of the century, and experiments to grow coffee, cotton, cinnamon, indigo and cloves all ended in failure.

The only commercially viable crops in Singapore were pepper and gambier, grown exclusively by the Chinese, some plantations pre-dating the British occupation. Gambier and pepper cultivation expanded in the 1830s and reached a peak in the 1840s, when gambier plantations covered much of the interior of the island. But this form of farming quickly exhausted the soil and by the middle of the century many abandoned estates had reverted to secondary jungle.

Though different in character, Chinese and European methods of agriculture were equally ill suited to the Straits. The Chinese, anxious to make money quickly and return to China, forsook the meticulous care of the soil to which they were traditionally accustomed, in favour of a slash and burn technique which destroyed the earth's fertility. The Europeans, trying to develop long-term landed estates, applied their traditional practice of weeding, clearing and widely-spaced planting with disastrous effect in hot, wet tropical conditions.

Melaka's problems were different from Singapore's and its land tenure question much more complex. The former Dutch administration had granted title to all lands in Melaka, apart from Naning, to a few individual landlords, who had not developed the land but claimed the right to collect one-tenth of the value of the produce from their territory.

Convinced that Melaka could become the granary of the Straits, in 1828 the East India Company decided to clear the way for development by buying out the proprietors' rights and paying them fixed annuities in compensation. But the authorities then found it impossible to collect the tenth, the proceeds of which amounted to only a fraction of the annuities paid out to the proprietors. The Straits Land Act of 1839, which commuted the tenth to a cash land rent, and a special Melaka Land Act passed in 1861 failed to remedy the situation.

Apart from its land-law problems, Melaka presented physical difficulties. The extensive plain behind the slightly raised sandy coastline was an acid freshwater swamp, subject to frequent flooding, and requiring irrigation works to develop its potential as a rich, rice-growing region. All the Straits authorities' attempts to improve Melaka's agriculture ended in disappointment. As in Singapore, the only successful commercial agricultural enterprise was Chinese, and from the mid-1850s thousands of Chinese planters poured into uninhabited upland areas to grow tapioca.

Given peaceful conditions and freed from obligations for forced labour or military service, Malay peasant agriculture flourished. In particular from the 1820s refugees and immigrants from Kedah opened up the hitherto uninhabited northern tracts of Province Wellesley to the cultivation of rice. Employing traditional methods, subsistence peasant farming became partly commercialized, geared to selling a surplus to Melaka or Georgetown.

Population

Apart from Melaka, which was the only territory with a long-settled population, most inhabitants of the Straits Settlements were immigrants of varied ethnic origin. Even in Melaka there was a large influx of population from nearby states and overseas.

Three-quarters of Melaka's population in 1860 were Malays, most of them peasant farmers, but in Melaka town the biggest single community were the Chinese, and the rest of the urban population comprised Malays, Indians, and Eurasians of Portuguese or Dutch extraction.

Province Wellesley was also predominantly Malay in population. In 1820 the territory supported only 6000 people, but an influx of refugees from war-torn Kedah increased the population to 47 000 by 1835. By 1860 the inhabitants exceeded 67 000, of whom the majority was Malay but there were some 8000 Chinese and 5000 Indians, mostly working on sugar plantations in the south. The numbers of Indians increased steadily in the later years of the century as they came to replace Chinese on European plantations.

In 1826 the bulk of Penang's population was Malay, the country areas exclusively so, with Indians predominating in the town. But many Chinese immigrants came into Penang during the 1830s and 1840s and by the late-1850s the Chinese constituted the largest single community on the island. In 1858 they numbered 24 000, compared with 20 000 Malays and 12 000 Indians.

When the East India Company first acquired Singapore the island supported about 1000 people, mainly aborigine tribes living along the Kallang and Seletar rivers and *orang laut,* together with a few Malays attached to the *temenggong*'s settlement and a handful of Chinese gambier planters. Many Malays subsequently came to Singapore from the peninsular states, Sumatra and the Riau archipelago, but Chinese immigration was heavier. By 1827 nearly half the population was Chinese and by 1860 the proportion had risen to 65 per cent. At that date the Indians were the second largest community, outnumbering the Malays, and there were smaller communities of Bugis, Arabs, Javanese, Boyanese from Bawean island, Armenians and other minorities.

The Indian and Chinese communities themselves were of heterogeneous background. Most Indians, whether traders or labourers, came from southern India, but were divided into several dialect and religious groups, Hindu and Muslim. There were also numbers of Parsee, Gujerati and Bengali traders in Penang and Singapore.

Nearly all Chinese immigrants came from southeast China, from the provinces of Kwangtung and Fukien, but belonged to a variety of dialect groups, mainly Hokkien, Teochew, Cantonese and Hakka. Most urban Chinese in Penang, Melaka and Singapore, including the majority of traders, were Hokkien, from the Amoy district of Fukien, while Teochews from the Swatow region were the second most important trading group. The labouring classes were chiefly Cantonese or Hakka. Most artisans were Cantonese, while the Hakkas predominated in agriculture and tin mining. Later in the century large numbers of Hailams emigrated from Hainan island to take up labouring jobs in Singapore.

Initially all communities were organized under their own headmen or *kapitans,* who were responsible for keeping order in their community and settling minor disputes, but the *kapitan* system formally came to an end when the Charters of Justice introduced British law into Penang in 1808 and into Singapore and Melaka in 1826. From that time all residents were technically subject to British courts, except in questions of Muslim custom. In practice, lack of officials and difficulties in adapting to the British legal system meant that the various communities continued to administer themselves and the authorities still relied on prominent Asian merchants as unofficial *kapitans* or go-betweens.

The economic opportunities, comparative safety and lack of restrictions made the Straits Settlements the most attractive goal for Chinese emigrants, while the British authorities, admiring the Chinese ability to organize themselves and face any hardship in their search for success, regarded them as ideal pioneers.

The Manchu government forbade emigration but in practice this prohibition was ignored by young men, who left China in their thousands in the nineteenth century, partly driven by over-population and civil war, partly drawn by the prospects of making their fortunes in the Nanyang. Most were penniless, illiterate youths, who aimed to make good and return within a few years to settle down in China. Apart from prostitutes, no Chinese women came to the Straits in the first half of the nineteenth century.

On arrival in the Straits, the immigrant, or *sinkheh,* was hired by Chinese employers, who paid his passage to the junk captain. The *sinkheh* was then required to work without wages for one year to repay his passage, after which he was free to find his own employment. Some prospered and returned to China, but many fell ill, succumbed to excessive opium smoking or lost their savings in gambling. Many remained trapped in poverty. kept permanently in debt under the system whereby wealthy Hokkien and Teochew entrepreneurs advanced capital to those beginning a business in exchange for rights to purchase produce at low prices and supply workers' needs, often at exorbitant rates.

Since emigration from China broke traditional family and village links, social organization came to be concentrated largely in secret societies. The most powerful of these was the Triad, or Heaven and Earth Society, a political organization founded in Fukien in the first half of the eighteenth century to oppose Manchu rule. The Triad did not transplant its political activities to the Straits Settlements and it avoided conflict with the British authorities. The societies were legal in the Straits until 1890 and only their membership and ritual were secret. Serving a useful purpose at that stage, they provided help for the inexperienced immigrant, organized the coolie trade and hiring of labour, and settled diputes. The societies protected but also exploited the mass of Chinese and impeded the assimilation of immigrants into the new society, particularly their assimilation into the British judicial system. Standing outside the colonial pale, they offered alternative tribunals, more effective protection and more terrible retribution.

As the number of immigrants increased, the struggle of rival societies for a greater share in the lucrative traffic in coolies and prostitutes led to clashes and disturbed the peace. But violence was confined to the Chinese themselves and was not directed against the government or other communities. Lacking machinery to rule the Chinese and reluctant to put any curb on immigration, the Straits authorities were unwilling to enforce measures against the societies or declare them illegal. They aimed to work in co-operation with their leaders rather than drive them underground.

Transfer to Colonial Rule

The European population was small, in 1860 numbering 466 in Singapore, 316 in Penang and only a handful of officials in Melaka. But the European merchants were very vocal and as they prospered became increasingly critical of alleged official parsimony and inaction, although they were equally vociferous in resisting any proposals for new taxes. During the 1850s the European merchants of Singapore mounted an increasingly bitter campaign of protest against Calcutta's alleged indifference and ignorance in governing the Straits Settlements, and agitated for a Straits legislative council. They complained about the authorities' failure to provide port improvements and town amenities, to discipline Chinese secret societies or to provide adequate police protection. They criticized the Company for using the Straits as penal settlements and for failing to extend British influence in the Malay states. Into well-intentioned currency reforms they read sinister plots to oust the Spanish dollar in favour of the little used but official rupee currency. Finally, when the Indian Mutiny erupted in 1857, the Singapore merchants petitioned the British parliament to separate the Straits Settlements from India and convert them into a British crown colony.

Ten years of haggling ensued, since Britain had no wish to extend its colonial commitments at that time nor to assume any new financial burden. Eventually in 1867, after the Stamp Act of 1863 did away with the Straits deficit, the Colonial Office agreed to the transfer. But the decision was taken with some reluctance and on condition that the new colony shouldered the major part of its military expenditure. London had no intention of introducing costly administrative reforms or taking action to curb Chinese secret societies, nor did it intend to extend Britain's activities in the Malay peninsula.

The transfer to colonial rule in 1867 meant the introduction of the usual colonial institutions: an executive council comprising the governor and senior officials, and a legislative council which included three non-officials nominated by the governor. The first nominees were all British, but a Cantonese, Hoo Ah Kay, nicknamed Whampoa after his birthplace, was appointed to the legislative council in 1869.

Initially colonial rule brought disappointment to the politically vocal Europeans who had agitated for the transfer but then found they had little real power on the legislative council. They clashed constantly with the first colonial governor, Sir Harry St George Ord, a forthright, domineering man. In 1868 former Singapore merchants who had retired to London founded a Straits Settlements Association to argue the cause of Straits mercantile interests with the British government, and the Association set up branches in Singapore and Penang. The battle between Ord and the Singapore merchants persisted throughout his tenure of office, culminating shortly before Ord's retirement in 1873 in the resignation of all the non-official legislative councillors, with the exception of Whampoa.

Despite these teething troubles, the Straits Settlements crown colony was by that time firmly established, riding a new wave of commercial success and poised to play a positive role in the Malay states.

CHAPTER 11

The Malay States, 1824-73

When the Straits Settlements were formed in 1826 the Malay peninsula was still thinly peopled and, apart from aborigines, probably supported little more than a quarter of a million inhabitants. Most of the population lived in pockets of settlement in the middle reaches of the rivers, avoiding the inhospitable mangrove swamps and water-logged coastal plains, which remained the domain of roving bands of *orang laut* fishermen–pirates. The rivers provided almost the sole means of communication, and peasant farming communities had little contact with their counterparts on other river systems, from which they were separated by vast tracts of impenetrable rain forest. Nor in most regions did their lives touch those of the up-river swidden farmers, hunters and food gatherers. Many Jakun of the southern regions intermarried and merged with the Malays, settling down as peasant farmers and adopting the Muslim religion, but the Temiar, Semai and Semang of the more remote northern hill forests continued to hold themselves aloof and rejected Islam, which had no appeal to their traditional way of life.

No peninsular state emerged with a strong economic base either in agriculture or commerce to succeed the Melaka sultanate. Apart from the Minangkabaus, who used irrigation for rice cultivation on a small scale, no attempts were made anywhere in the peninsula prior to the late-nineteenth century to introduce drainage and irrigation works or to develop the land sufficiently to support a powerful state. Dutch attempts to open up Melaka to agricultural development by leasing occupation rights to individuals failed, since the Dutch 'proprietors' contented themselves with appointing agents to collect a tithe on the produce of these lands and did nothing to promote improvements. In times of peace and stability Kedah, which was the most fertile state, produced sufficient rice to support a modest export trade, but the other states were at best self sufficient in agriculture.

Traditionally the most prosperous states were in the north and east of the peninsula, but by the 1820s Kedah was reduced by war and rebellion to little more than 10 000 people, about a tenth of the number it had supported at the beginning of the century. Kelantan took its place as the most populous state, with some 50 000 inhabitants; Pahang numbered about 40 000; Perak about 35 000; Negri Sembilan, Johor and Trengganu about 25 000 to 30 000 each; while Selangor boasted probably no more than 5000 people.

A variety of historical experience had produced distinctive characteristics, particularly between the states of the west and east coasts. Cut off from the rest of the peninsula to the west and south by mountain ranges, Kelantan and Trengganu looked naturally to Siam, Indochina and the South China Sea. For centuries these states had been open to cultural influences from Funan and maybe Langkasuka, from the Khmer empire, Majapahit and Ayuthia, whence the silversmiths of Kelantan and the weavers and metal workers of Trengganu derived their craftsmanship. In the early-nineteenth century they were the most prosperous and highly developed states in the peninsula, largely because they had enjoyed longer periods of peace, escaping ravaging by Acheh and most of the troubles engendered by the Minangkabau–Bugis wars. Both states supported a thriving, mixed peasant economy, based on rice, supplemented by cattle, fruit and fishing. Trengganu was less fertile than Kelantan but was the most urbanized of the Malay states, with half its population living in the capital at Kuala Trengganu.

The war-torn states to the south and west were less developed economically, and more influenced culturally by Sumatra, notably through Srivijaya, Acheh and Minangkabau, and later by the Bugis. The only flourishing agricultural settlements were the Minangkabau villages of Negri Sembilan, which produced sufficient rice, fruit and meat to export a small surplus to Melaka. The vast state of Pahang supported only pockets of peasant farmers scattered along the Pahang river, although it also produced some tin near the coast and gold in the interior. Perak exported some tin, but most of its people lived as peasants on the middle stretches of the Perak river. Selangor produced a little tin in the Klang valley, but its tiny population was scattered among five separate valleys: Selangor, Bernam, Klang, Langat and Lukut. Johor had scarcely any agriculture, and its sparse population lived mainly along the Johor river or in the Muar region, deriving a living from fishing and small-scale trading.

Despite differences of experience and the comparative isolation of the various communities, the peninsular states had many features in common: a subsistence rice economy, an affinity in language and culture, submission to Islam, and a joint political tradition, inherited from the Melaka sultanate, which was perpetuated not only in Riau–Johor as its direct successor state, but in former vassal states too.

The sultan was honoured and surrounded by elaborate and ancient ceremonial, which was strictly observed through the centuries despite the ruler's shrinking economic and physical power. He continued to combine religious and political autocracy in a personal form of government, which lacked formal institutions, a recruited civil service or religious bureaucracy.

While the sultan was revered, his actual powers were vague and undefined. Despite the absence of a council he was supposed to rule in conjunction with his *orang kaya*. These powerful vassals had the right to raise revenue and labour in their districts and often commanded more wealth and manpower than the sultan himself. But it was in the aristocracy's interests to respect and uphold the sultanate, since their own power depended on maintaining the royal dignity.

Local authority rested with district chiefs or rajas, who in turn deputed village administration to headmen, with responsibility for judging disputes, raising local taxes and marshalling labour.

Rajas had followings of *rakyat* or freemen, who constituted the bulk of the peasantry, together with bondsmen and slaves who worked either as field labourers or household servants. Slaves were often convicted criminals, prisoners of war or captured aborigines, but were less common than bondsmen, who pledged their own services and sometimes those of their whole families to a chieftain in repayment of debts.

Except among the Minangkabau communities of Negri Sembilan, the Melaka system tended to suppress the equality and freedom of traditional village life but provided overall protection, generally leaving villages to manage their own affairs as long as they paid their dues. While chiefs were free to raise whatever revenue they could extract, in practice there was a limit to the oppression which peasants would tolerate, and if a raja's impositions grew too heavy, whole communities would run away to create new settlements elsewhere.

Except among the Minangkabau clans, ownership of land was assumed to rest with the sultan. Land as such had little meaning or value in pre-colonial times, and this precluded the chiefs emerging as a landed-gentry class. Rajas had rights over labour and the produce of the soil rather than over territory, so that peasants had obligations to their raja but were not tied to the soil, as in Western feudal practice. Peasants might migrate as a band with their chieftain to escape natural or military disaster or to seek a better livelihood. This was easy with such a scattered population amid vast tracts of unoccupied land and largely accounts for the great mobility and continual migration in the peninsula.

All Malays were Muslims and the mosque drew male villagers together in daily prayer. Since Islam had been absorbed not enforced, it adapted to local traditions, accepting ancient rites to propitiate spirits and the practice of animist ritual for planting and harvest. But it modified some *adat* customs, especially those relating to marriage, and it lowered the status of women which had been high in pre-Islamic agricultural society. While there was no seclusion or purdah, women now played a minor part in village affairs and the matriarchal system survived only among a few groups, notably the Minangkabaus.

While the mosque was the centre of religious life in the village, it had no organization, nor was formal training required for entry into the priesthood, since mosque officials were chosen by the villagers themselves. The mosque did not provide a focus of education as did the Buddhist temples in mainland states. The *imam,* or leading mosque official, gave instruction to village boys but this was normally confined to chanting the Koran in Arabic. There was little practical demand for literacy which provided no avenues for political, bureaucratic, clerical or commercial advancement, and education remained at a low ebb.

Nor was there incentive for commercial expansion. The peasantry had no inducement to produce a surplus, and economic initiative lay with the royal house and aristocracy. The export of products such as rice from Kedah, tin from Perak and Selangor, or gutta-percha from Johor, were royal monopolies, and the marketing in coastal ports was often handled by Chinese or Indian merchants. In their attempts to re-create the Melaka port economy in Johor, in Riau and briefly in early Singapore, Malay chiefs continued to encourage foreign merchants to develop commerce under the ruler's administrative control. Within their own states rulers discouraged the peasantry from abandoning their traditional way of life and brought in immigrant workers for new enterprises such as tin mining. Thus Malays became involved in commercial enterprise only at the top and in an administrative capacity. No commercial institutions or middle class evolved, nor was the lifestyle of the mass of the population affected by the developments in the economy.

While seemingly an unordered polity, the form of the Malay state made for a fairly stable yet flexible society, which imposed rights and obligations on all classes but provided an outlet for personal ambition and ability among the upper classes and some movement among the *rakyat.* Resilient in time of trouble, the system was suited to a fairly self-sufficient undeveloped economy but was not adapted for modernization. It precluded the organization of capital and the emergence of centralized states or powerful monarchies.

The East India Company and the Malay States

While the Anglo–Dutch treaty of 1824 implicitly marked out the peninsula as the East India Company's sphere of interest, fifty years elapsed before the British were actively drawn into the Malay states. The choice of island bases at Penang and Singapore stressed the Company's concern to insulate itself from local politics. On the mainland, Province Wellesley was acquired merely to protect Penang harbour and provide supplies for Georgetown, while in Melaka the Company aimed to steer clear of the confused politics of the adjoining Minangkabau states.

In all three settlements the British established themselves in a peaceful fashion by means of treaties, which they hoped would save them from further involvement in regional politics, and up to 1874 the government of India and subsequently the Colonial Office followed a consistent policy of trying to avoid entanglements in the peninsula.

The British determination to stay aloof was strengthened by an expensive and unnecessary war into which it was drawn by the folly of its own officials in Melaka. By longstanding treaty the inland state of Naning had been obliged to pay one-tenth of its produce in tribute to the Dutch authorities in Melaka, but the Dutch had commuted this to a small token payment in rice and other produce, and the British continued this practice during their wartime occupation of Melaka. After Melaka became a permanent part of the Straits Settlements the Company, wrongly advised by its officials on the spot concerning its rights over Naning, decided to extend the Melaka land system there and to enforce payment of the tenth. It took two military campaigns involving a force of more than 1200 men and expenditure of £stg100 000 to break Naning's resistance although by then the Company had realized its error. Naning was absorbed into Melaka in 1832, but it cost the Melaka treasury more to run than it provided in revenue, and this unjustified little war made the Company all the more wary of further involvement in local politics.

Despite this, the British presence in the Straits Settlements during these years proved in practice to be an instrument for positive change in the peninsula.

The immediate impact of the British presence was to confer a greater freedom of action on the Malay states by excluding external pressures: stemming Siamese expansion in the north, cutting the Malay states off from the Riau–Lingga empire and indirectly bringing Bugis and Minangkabau political interference to an end. For some years the Malay states were left to develop independently but, despite the rigid official policy of non-involvement, from the middle of the century the British authorities were in practice increasingly drawn into the affairs of the interior. The growth of capitalist enterprise in the Straits ports, the spread of commercial agriculture, the growing demand for tin in international trade and the influx of Chinese entrepreneurs and labourers to exploit these new opportunities created pressures for change.

The Bugis and Minangkabaus

Both the Bugis and the Minangkabaus, who had exerted a powerful influence in the peninsula in the previous century, found their power checked in the 1820s. The setback to their ambitions in Perak virtually confined the Bugis to their state of Selangor, and while Buginese traders continued to frequent peninsular ports, their numbers declined. In the early-1820s they constituted one-fifth of Singapore's population but by the middle of the century they no longer formed a distinct element either in the Straits Settlements or in the Malay states, but merged with the Malay population.

Ties with Sumatra also weakened. Raja Laboh, who came to Negri Sembilan in 1824 was the last Sumatran *yang di-pertuan besar*. He was powerless to stop civil strife, which persisted until 1832, after which the office passed into local hands.

Siam, Kedah and Perak

In the north, Kedah's internal troubles, continuing strife between Siam and Burma, and the expansionist policy of the first two Chakri kings of Siam threatened to engulf all northern Malaya.

The death of Sultan Abdullah of Kedah in 1798 sparked off a succession dispute. His half brother ruled the state until 1803 when Rama I of Siam ordered him to relinquish the throne to the late ruler's eldest son, who became Sultan Ahmad Tajuddin Halim Shah. Since the new sultan owed his throne to Bangkok, Kedah was reduced for the first time to the status of a Siamese tributary, and Ahmad Tajuddin's inability to assert his authority over his eight brothers increased his dependence on Siam. In 1808 the Siamese governor of Singora intervened to settle disputes between the sultan and the princes, and from that time both Bangkok and the provincial capitals of Singora and Nakhon Si Thammarat interfered repeatedly in Kedah's affairs.

The growth of Penang brought prosperity to Kedah, providing a market for its rice, cattle, poultry and other supplies, but its wealth encouraged the Siamese to make impossible demands.

In 1809 Bangkok ordered Kedah to help suppress a revolt in Patani and repel a new Burmese invasion, but the Burmese occupied Phuket, posing a direct threat to Kedah itself, and Ahmad Tajuddin's attempts to save his country by initially appeasing the Burmese were used by his brothers to stir up Siamese suspicions in the hope of gain for themselves. To prove his loyalty Sultan Ahmad helped the Siamese in recapturing Phuket, but in 1812 the governor of Nakhon Si Thammarat ordered Sultan Ahmad Tajuddin to prove his devotion by forcing Perak to pay tribute to Siam. Accordingly Kedah sent an embassy in 1813 to urge Perak's submission, but that state had never been a Siamese tributary and its Sultan Mansur, suspicious of Kedah's own intentions, sent evasive answers.

In the meantime both Kedah and Perak appealed in vain for British help. Sultan Mansur offered the East India Company a monopoly of Perak's tin in exchange for protection, while Sultan Ahmad Tajuddin sent a strong delegation of princes and ministers to Penang to call on the Company to ratify the 1786 agreement which promised support to Kedah. But the Company urged both states to submit to Siam's wishes.

Kedah then attacked Perak by land and sea in 1816 and subdued the state after a drawn-out two-year campaign. Sultan Mansur was deposed in favour of his son, and in 1819 Perak sent the *bunga mas* to Siam for the first time in its history.

Kedah's compliance brought only temporary respite. In the meantime King Bodawpaya of Burma had renewed his attack on Phuket. Again Siam demanded aid from Kedah, which was hard pressed in Perak and appealed once more in vain for the East India Company's backing. Its situation deteriorated when the aggressive King Bagyidaw, who succeeded Bodawpaya in 1819, launched a fresh campaign in south Thailand. Once more the *raja muda* of Kedah spread rumours in Nakhon Si Thammarat that Sultan Ahmad Tajuddin was collaborating with the Burmese. The sultan had delayed sending the customary *bunga mas* because of his financial burdens, which were compounded by a serious cholera epidemic, and in 1820 the governor of Nakhon Si Thammarat obtained permission from Rama II to invade Kedah and extend control over Perak and Selangor.

The appearance of a Siamese fleet off Kuala Kedah the following year came as a terrible surprise to the Kedah court. Its leaders resisted stoutly but were overwhelmed. The *laksamana* and *temenggong* fell in the battle, the *bendahara* died a prisoner soon afterwards, and Sultan Ahmad Tajuddin fled. A Siamese army from Nakhon Si Thammarat laid Kedah waste, putting down the population with brutal atrocities, and thousands of peasants fled south to the safety of Province Wellesley. The sultan finally took refuge in Penang, where the British authorities refused either to give him up to the Siamese or to support him in regaining his state by force.

In an attempt to establish friendly relations and open up trade with Siam, in 1821 the East India Company dispatched Dr John Crawfurd, a former Penang official, on a mission to Bangkok. His primary objective was to secure commercial concessions and a secondary aim was to apply for the sultan of Kedah to be restored. But Crawfurd's mission was a complete failure.

After installing a governor in Alor Star, the Siamese turned on Perak, ordering the new sultan to send the *bunga mas*. At first Perak sought Selangor's help, but hesitated to put itself in the hands of the Bugis regime, which had previously treated it so badly.

It was at this stage, in 1824, that Robert Fullerton was appointed in charge of Penang. Supported by many Penang officials and merchants who feared Siamese expansionist policy and nursed a guilty conscience about the British treatment of Kedah, the new governor resolved to check Siamese ambitions. Learning that the Siamese were fitting out a fleet to invade Perak and Selangor, Fullerton sent British ships in 1825 to warn Nakhon Si Thammarat that Penang would regard the dispatch of this fleet as an act of war. The bluff worked, and Fullerton then sent Captain Henry Burney, military secretary at Penang, to Nakhon Si

Thammarat, where he negotiated an interim agreement with the governor by which both the Siamese and the British undertook to respect the independence of Perak and Selangor. At the same time John Anderson, secretary to the Penang government, made a treaty with Sultan Ibrahim of Selangor in 1825 fixing the Perak–Selangor boundary.

Fullerton then persuaded Calcutta to send Burney to re-open negotiations in Bangkok. The Company's interest was still primarily commercial, but Fullerton impressed on Burney the need to curb Siamese expansion in north Malaya. The mission was only partially successful. Under the terms of a treaty signed in 1826 Siam refused to give up Kedah, but agreed that Perak should send the *bunga mas* only if it wished. Kelantan and Trengganu were expected to continue paying tribute, but Bangkok promised not to obstruct their trade with Singapore.

While Fullerton was disappointed, he ensured that the concessions made by the Siamese were enforced to the full. Another Penang official, Captain James Low, went to Perak, where the Siamese were still strongly entrenched at court, and signed a treaty in 1826, by which the Company acknowledged Perak's independence and promised support if Siam or any other state threatened it.

Since Low had exceeded his authority, Calcutta refused to ratify his treaty. But neither Siam, Perak nor Selangor were aware of this, and in the fullness of time Low's treaty came to be considered a binding agreement. Fullerton's active policy was effective. Both Siam and Selangor stopped interfering in Perak, and for almost the first time in its history this unfortunate buffer state enjoyed a brief respite from outside pressures.

Sultan Ahmad Tajuddin of Kedah lived in exile in the Straits Settlements for more than twenty years, the centre of intrigues to restore his regime. A half-Arab nephew, Tunku Kudin, stirred up a holy war against the Siamese in Kedah in 1831, recruiting about 5000 supporters from Penang and Province Wellesley, and with help from Trengganu and Kelantan, succeeded in temporarily driving the Siamese out. They soon returned to put down the revolt with customary cruelty. The British then transferred the ex-sultan to Melaka in a vain attempt to avoid further trouble. In 1838 another nephew, Tunku Muhammad Said, raised a fresh revolt in the form of a Muslim holy war. With a force of some 10 000 men, he expelled the small Siamese garrison from Alor Star, overran Kedah, Perlis, Trang and much of Patani, and laid siege to Singora, looting, burning and sacking Buddhist temples. Within a few months the Siamese counter-attacked, drove the rebels back and laid Kedah waste once more with terrible slaughter.

In both the 1831 and 1838–9 revolts the British helped Siam by blockading the Kedah coast to cut off the rebels' supply route. But the Company wanted to see peace restored in Kedah, and after the bellicose governor of Nakhon Si Thammarat died in 1841, the British authorities encouraged negotiations which led to Sultan Ahmad Tajuddin's restoration the following year. Perlis was detached from Kedah and given to Nakhon Si Thammarat, and Kedah continued to be a vassal of Siam until the early-twentieth century, sending the *bunga mas* regularly to Bangkok.

Sultan Ahmad Tajuddin returned to a desolate Kedah, devastated by the series of rebellions and subsequent fierce repression. Its agriculture was in ruins, its population depleted and Alor Star was destroyed, so that initially the sultan had to make Kota Kuala Muda his head-quarters.

Despite the state's natural fertility, recovery was slow. Refugees were reluctant to return from Province Wellesley, because their chiefs demanded so much forced labour for rehabilitation work, and Kedah was hurt further by natural disasters, notably by widespread floods in 1859, which sparked off further emigration. But in the next decade it began to recover, and during the 1870s and early-1880s several thousand Kelantan Malays migrated to Kedah to escape a series of misfortunes: hurricanes, cattle plague and famine. These immigrants opened up new areas for rice farming, and by the 1880s Kedah's population had swelled to more than 70 000.

The Kedah aristocracy led the way in encouraging agricultural pioneering and the first irrigation works: notably the minister, Wan Muhammad Saman, who in 1885 began work on a canal to link Alor Star with the Kedah Peak region, thus helping to open up the fertile southern plains. By the end of the century Kedah supported a flourishing export rice economy.

Kelantan and Trengganu

Siam's relations with Kelantan and Trengganu remained close throughout the nineteenth century, and the strong centralizing policy of the Chakri kings in extending their power to the limits of their frontiers and beyond left a distinctive stamp on the character of the two states. But, unlike Kedah, they escaped coming under Bangkok's direct yoke. For the first thirty years of the century they enjoyed peace, although Kelantan still feared Trengganu might try to subjugate it once more, and in order to maintain their separate identities Rama I made Kelantan the responsibility of Nakhon Si Thammarat and Trengganu that of Singora.

Siam's tutelage was light. When Kelantan sent help to Tunku Kudin's revolt in Kedah in 1831 and gave shelter to the fugitive raja of Patani, Bangkok imposed a heavy fine, but Kelantan's economy recovered within a few years.

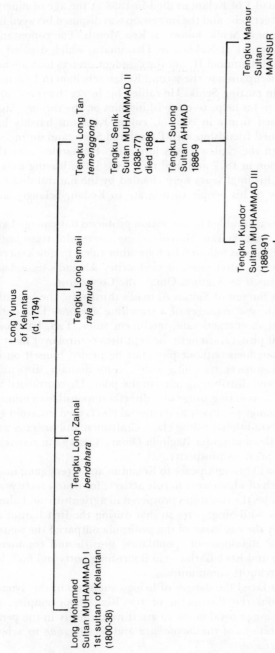

Table 11.1 The Kelantan royal house

Long Yunus
of Kelantan
(d. 1794)

Long Mohamed
Sultan MUHAMMAD I
1st sultan of Kelantan
(1800-38)

Tengku Long Zainal
bendahara

Tengku Long Ismail
raja muda

Tengku Long Tan
temenggong

Tengku Senik
Sultan MUHAMMAD II
(1838-77)
died 1886

Tengku Sulong
Sultan AHMAD
1886-9

Tengku Mansur
Sultan
MANSUR
(1891-99)

Tengku Kundor
Sultan MUHAMMAD III
(1889-91)

Tengku Senik
Sultan MUHAMMAD IV
(1900-20)

Tengku Ismail
Sultan ISMAIL
(1920-44)

Sultan Muhammad I of Kelantan died in 1838 at the age of ninety-three leaving no direct heir, and the succession was disputed between his brothers and a nephew, Senik, known as Red Mouth. The contestants intrigued for the support of Nakhon Si Thammarat which decided to recognize Senik as Muhammad II, but the dissident princes took advantage of Siam's preoccupation in the second Kedah rebellion in 1839 and nearly succeeded in ousting Senik. He rallied his forces, however, and the Siamese came to his help, re-establishing him on the throne. After that Senik remained firmly in control, ruling Kelantan harshly but fairly. He maintained friendship with Patani and Siam, and during his long peaceful reign the civil war was forgotten. He handed over the state's administration in 1877 and died nine years later, leaving Kelantan at peace. But his final years were clouded by the natural disasters which drove many of his people to migrate to Kedah, Selangor and other states.

Trengganu too was troubled by succession problems but emerged as a secure and stable state. Sultan Ahmad, whose uneventful reign lasted from 1808 until 1826, was followed by four other rulers in quick succession, until 1839 when, after years of civil strife, Ahmad's second son Omar installed himself as Baginda Omar, the Conqueror.

Omar, who was the son of Sultan Ahmad's third wife, the beautiful daughter of the Chinese manager of a travelling *manora,* Thai-dance drama group, was an energetic and intelligent ruler. Tall, handsome and a man of great physical strength, he kept firm control over his state and punished wrongdoers without pity. But he prided himself on his accessibility to his subjects, travelling widely in his domain, dispensing justice in person, and distributing alms to the poor. He centralized the administration by appointing *penghulus* directly responsible to himself, introducing the change gradually as territorial chiefs died, to avoid giving offence to the traditional ruling class. Craftsmen and artisans were encouraged to settle, and under Baginda Omar, Trengganu recovered and surpassed its previous prosperity.

Thus the year 1839 brought peace to Kelantan and Trengganu under strong sultans, both of whom were to rule actively for nearly forty years. During those decades the two states prospered in agriculture and also in trade, particularly with Singapore, so that during the first half of the nineteenth century the east coast of the peninsula outpaced the western states in economic development, population growth and commerce. Kuala Trengganu and Kota Barhu were flourishing ports and both had large Chinese mercantile communities.

But Trengganu faced the danger of being caught up in the dynastic upsets arising from the disruption of the Riau-Johor empire, the attempts by the Lingga royal house to assert its authority in the peninsula, and the ambitions of the *bendahara* and *temenggong* to achieve their independence.

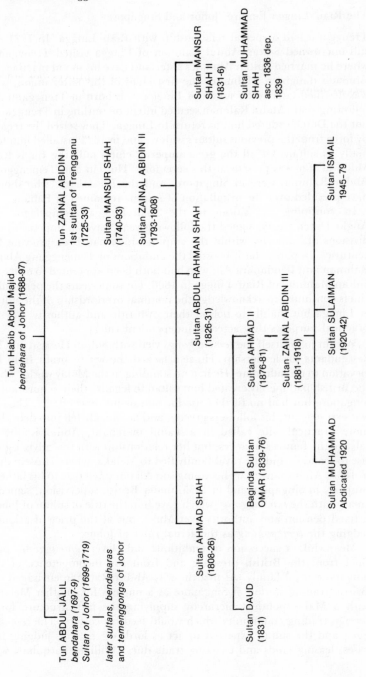

Table 11.2 The Trengganu royal house

Tun Habib Abdul Majid
bendahara of Johor (1688–97)

Tun ABDUL JALIL
bendahara (1697–9)
Sultan of Johor (1699–1719)

*later sultans, bendaharas
and temenggongs* of Johor

Tun ZAINAL ABIDIN I
1st sultan of Trengganu
(1725–33)

Sultan MANSUR SHAH
(1740–93)

Sultan ZAINAL ABIDIN II
(1793–1808)

Sultan AHMAD SHAH
(1808–26)

Sultan ABDUL RAHMAN SHAH
(1826–31)

Sultan MANSUR
SHAH II
(1831–6)

Sultan MUHAMMAD
SHAH
asc. 1836 dep.
1839

Sultan DAUD
(1831)

Baginda Sultan
OMAR (1839–76)

Sultan AHMAD II
(1876–81)

Sultan ZAINAL ABIDIN III
(1881–1918)

Sultan MUHAMMAD
Abdicated 1920

Sultan SULAIMAN
(1920–42)

Sultan ISMAIL
1945–79

The Riau-Lingga Empire, Johor and Singapore

Trengganu had a special relationship with Riau-Lingga. In 1821 the still-uncrowned Sultan Abdul Rahman of Lingga visited Trengganu, where he married Sultan Ahmad's sister and gave his son in marriage to Ahmad's daughter. Mahmud, the first child of this latter union, who was destined later to be sultan of Lingga, was born in Trengganu the following year. Abdul Rahman seemed intent on settling in Trengganu, but the Dutch ordered him to return to Lingga. They seized the regalia by force from the previous sultan's widow, and in 1823 installed him formally as sultan. Of all the great imperial chiefs only the Bugis Raja Muda Ja'afar was present at this ceremony. Hussein and Temenggong Abdur Rahman were in Singapore, and the *bendahara,* who should have presided over the installation of sultan, remained in Pahang.

In confining the sultan to the Riau-Lingga archipelago, the Anglo-Dutch treaty, signed the following year, gave an impetus to the divisions of authority within the empire which had been growing for centuries. In particular it boosted the ambitions of Temenggong Abdur Rahman and Bendahara Ali, who had both been appointed to office by Sultan Mahmud of Riau-Lingga in 1806. For some years the peninsular chiefs continued to acknowledge the nominal overlordship of the sultan at Lingga but mainly to bolster their own title and authority. For all practical purposes they acted as independent rulers.

Within Johor itself the *temenggongs* vied with Sultan Hussein and his descendants for leadership. Hussein lacked the wit to profit from his elevation to the sultanate. He had no standing in the Malay world, while the British had merely created him sultan to legalize their acquisition of Singapore but had no further use for him or his descendants. Hussein was extravagant, his followers greedy, and he quickly fell into debt. His more practical wife called in a Tamil merchant, Abdul Kadir, to salvage the family's finances, but her relationship with this adviser gave rise to scandal, and the royal family fled to Melaka, where Hussein died in 1835. After many years his young son Ali obtained title to his father's property in Singapore and in 1855, under British supervision, signed a treaty with the *temenggong,* which gave him the title of sultan of Johor, a fixed pension and authority over Muar, but at the price of acknowledging the *temenggong* as the actual ruler of Johor.

Meanwhile a succession of ambitious and clever *temenggongs* profited from the British presence and from the incompetence of the Singapore royal family. At first the wily Abdur Rahman envisaged the British trading station at Singapore as a nucleus for another Melaka, with a Malay political hierarchy supplying the infrastructure for a foreign trading community which would feed his coffers. The *temenggong* and the sultan expected to act as lords of the soil; judging law cases, leasing lands and exacting trade dues. William Farquhar, who was appointed first resident of Singapore by Raffles in 1819, was prepared to acknowledge this traditional role, but Raffles, who returned to spend eight months in Singapore in 1822–3, would not brook such interference in his plans. He eased the chiefs gently from public life and bought out their judicial powers, revenue claims and rights over land.

The eclipse of the chiefs was taken a stage further by John Crawfurd, resident of Singapore from 1823 to 1826, who regarded them as a tiresome and expensive obstruction. By withholding their allowances, he forced them to sign a Treaty of Friendship and Alliance in 1824, under which, in exchange for a cash payment and increased pensions, they ceded the whole of Singapore and its offshore islands to the East India Company and its successors in perpetuity.

While Abdur Rahman had failed in his attempt to develop Singapore as a latter-day Melaka, he and his successors turned the port's growing prosperity to their own advantage. Abdur Rahman's son, Ibrahim, who was installed as *temenggong* in 1841, threw in his lot with the British, helping the colonial authorities to suppress local piracy, cultivating the partnership of British and Chinese merchants and seizing the opportunities which Singapore offered to exploit Johor's economy. In the 1840s he organized the collection of gutta-percha throughout Johor and encouraged Chinese gambier and pepper planters to move into the hitherto uninhabited valleys of south Johor.

Ibrahim's son, Abu Bakar, who became *temenggong* in 1862, inherited his father's commercial acumen and strengthened links with the British, who valued his co-operation. He modernized his state, at least superficially, introducing a Western code of laws, organizing separate departments of administration and establishing schools. In 1866 the *temenggong* moved his headquarters from Singapore to Tanjong Putri in Johor, which Ibrahim had founded in 1855 and which Abu Bakar renamed Johor Bahru. He took the title of maharaja in 1868, and when Sultan Ali died in 1877, heavily in debt, his descendants were passed over and in 1885 the title was given to Abu Bakar.

The Pahang Civil War

Temenggong Ibrahim maintained a friendly relationship with Bendahara Ali of Pahang and the two families were linked by close marriage ties. During Ali's long reign Pahang consolidated its independence and profited from the proximity of Singapore by developing its trade in gold and tin.

But the death of Bendahara Ali in 1857 provoked a dispute between his eldest son, Mutahir, who succeeded him as *bendahara,* and a younger son, Wan Ahmad. A quarrel over revenue escalated into a struggle for the leadership itself, which plunged Pahang into a protracted civil war lasting from 1858 until 1863.

The war was aggravated by the intervention of Mahmud, former sultan of Riau–Lingga who was deposed by the Dutch in 1857, after which he took refuge with his nephew, Omar of Trengganu, and sought to carve out a new role for himself in the peninsula. At first Mahmud tried to claim overlordship of Johor and Pahang, but neither the British, Temenggong Ibrahim nor Bendahara Mutahir would admit the claim. Mahmud then gave his backing to Wan Ahmad's rebellion. Omar allowed his uncle to use Kemaman in southern Trengganu as a base for his ventures against Pahang, but became alarmed when Mahmud went to Bangkok in 1861, since he feared that the ex-sultan might be angling for Siamese backing to set him on Omar's own throne. The following year Mahmud returned to Trengganu in a Siamese ship, accompanied by Wan Ahmad, and the British, apprehensive that this indicated a resurgence of Siamese expansion in the Malay states, asked Bangkok to remove him. Six months later, while Bangkok continued to prevaricate, the anxious governor of Singapore sent a gunboat with an ultimatum to Omar, demanding that he surrender his guest to be escorted back to Bangkok. When Mahmud refused to go the British shelled Kuala Trengganu fort and the ex-sultan fled inland, making his own way back to Siam.

Meanwhile the British, trying to keep the Pahang civil war a domestic issue, at first prohibited Temenggong Ibrahim from going to Bendahara Mutahir's aid. By the time British objections were withdrawn in 1862, Johor's intervention was too late to stop the decline in morale among the *bendahara's* forces. The incompetence of Mutahir and his opium-addict son, Koris, contrasted with the determination of Wan Ahmad, who was backed by Omar of Trengganu and succeeded in building up a loyal following among many influential upriver Pahang chiefs. Making a final push from Trengganu over the mountains and down the Pahang river, Wan Ahmad won the day, and declared himself *bendahara* in 1863. Mutahir and Koris both died that same year and ex-sultan Mahmud a few months later, after which Wan Ahmad was left undisputed master of Pahang and eventually in 1887 became sultan.

After the Pahang civil war the Malay chiefs ceased to acknowledge the suzerainty of Riau–Lingga even formally. While the royal house of Lingga lasted until 1911, neither Bendahara Wan Ahmad nor his rival Temenggong Abu Bakar, applied to the sultan to confirm their titles.

The civil war episode halted any ambitions which Siam may have harboured of reviving its forward movement in the Malay states, but the now-ailing Omar still did not feel secure and in 1869 sent envoys to sound out the possibility of putting Trengganu under British protection. This evoked no response, and Omar continued to rule Trengganu until 1874, when, having no direct heirs, he appointed a nephew, Ahmad as ruler on his behalf and died paralysed two years later.

Straits Settlements, Economic Expansion and the Malay States

For many years British rule in the Straits Settlements acted merely as a negative force, keeping others out of the peninsula, but by the middle of the nineteenth century their impact was more positive. European governments had held sway in Melaka for centuries, but the Portuguese and Dutch had merely kept a foothold, having little influence in the interior. In contrast the British settlements brought significant economic change and also altered the character of Chinese activity. While Chinese had traded and lived in the Nanyang for centuries and many Melaka Chinese could trace their Straits-born ancestry back several generations, the Straits Settlements provided a new role for the Nanyang Chinese. In these predominantly Chinese ports they were no longer a small middleman minority and they adapted their entrepreneurial skills to lead the way in organizing agricultural enterprise and tin mining in the settlements themselves and later in neighbouring Malay territories: enterprise which was based entirely on Chinese labour and on a mixture of Chinese and British capital.

Chinese Hokkien and Teochew financiers in the Straits Settlements hired Cantonese or Hakka labourers advancing money and retaining a monopoly of the right to supply labourers' needs and to buy their produce.

The system was harsh on immigrants, particularly those who lived in appalling conditions in the mining camps. Even in times of peace half the *sinkhehs* employed in the interior died of disease and deprivation within a year, and the survivors were trapped in perpetual debt. Some were paid monthly wages and others received a share of the profits but in either event it was a mere pittance. The Chinese entrepreneurs took the financial risks but also pocketed the major share of the profits, and by selling supplies at inflated prices and buying produce cheaply these financiers managed to accumulate considerable capital.

Economically the system was suited to developing enterprises with a minimum of capital outlay and using an unskilled but swiftly replenished work force. Independent, hard-working, able to organize themselves and prepared to tolerate hardship in the hopes of material gain, Chinese labourers were ideal pioneers.

This type of capitalist enterprise was already well developed in financing gambier and pepper cultivation and tin mining in the Straits Settlements and was later extended to the Malay states, where it fitted in with traditional Malay practice. In trading, as in Melaka, Johor or Kedah, rulers had encouraged foreign merchants to organize their own enterprise and administer their own communities, providing revenue for the ruler without disturbing his Malay subjects. Similarly in developing tin mining, Malay rulers did not wish to divert their own peasants from the land and preferred to bring in outsiders. In previous centuries they had imported Batak and Rawa serfs from Sumatra for this purpose and from the early years of the nineteenth century welcomed Chinese. In general they left Chinese communities to govern their own day-to-day affairs, acknowledging a *kapitan* chosen by the Chinese themselves, but levying poll taxes, collecting tolls on the transport of tin and making profits from supplying opium and other needs.

This worked well with small immigrant groups and in districts where local rulers acted firmly but fairly and were in undisputed control of their territory. But the influx of increasing numbers of Chinese labourers from the middle of the nineteenth century, bringing with them their secret-society feuds, and the uneven development of economic wealth, put an intolerable strain on the fragile fabric of Malay politicial structure, leading to disputes over tin-rich territory and river tolls. Enterprising subordinate chiefs and adventurers, who were favourably placed, seized the opportunity to enrich themselves, to acquire disproportionate power in the state and sometimes to challenge the ruler's authority. Greed and political ambition combined and spilt over into violence. The tin states were plunged into civil war, endangering the lives of Chinese labourers and threatening the investment of Straits Settlements financiers, who appealed to the British colonial authorities for help. With the growing involvement of European merchants from the Straits Settlements in backing Chinese enterprise in the interior, the demand grew for British intervention to protect their interests.

Agricultural enterprise caused little friction. From the mid-1840s Singapore Chinese merchants encouraged gambier and pepper planters to move from exhausted plantations on the island to Johor. In 1844 Temenggong Ibrahim granted the first permit to clear land on the Scudai river, and by the middle of the century there were about 200 gambier and pepper plantations, each occupying specified areas in river valleys with the *temenggong*'s authority. They were self-contained communities, supervised by their own *kangchu* or master of the river. They paid taxes to the *temenggong* but otherwise had little contact with the Malay authorities, and in the mid-1860s Singapore financiers combined to thwart an attempt by Temenggong Abu Bakar to divert financial control of gambier and pepper production to his own hands. Chinese settlers caused little trouble in Johor, since they all belonged to one secret society and the *temenggong*'s territorial authority was undisputed.

In the 1860s Hokkien merchants from Melaka opened up the interior of that state to tapioca planting, using predominantly Hainanese labour, and this too was a peaceful development. The lifestyle of gambier, pepper and tapioca planters, living in isolated communities in formerly unoccupied lands, kept immigrant farming communities out of conflict with each other or with the indigenous population.

Tin mining caused much more trouble, bringing increasing difficulties to Sungei Ujong, Selangor and Perak. Tin had been mined and exported in small quantities for centuries, using the simple *lampan* method in which tin-bearing soil near river banks was loosened into the stream and the earth washed away to leave tin ore. The Chinese brought a system of open-cast or *lombong* mining, in which they dug down to tin-bearing levels, brought the earth up and washed away the soil to separate the tin ore.

Chinese miners were first invited into Sungei Ujong and into the neighbouring coastal belt of Lukut, which was then part of Selangor. By the late-1820s there were about 1000 Chinese miners in Sungei Ujong and some 200 in Lukut, but trouble between the Chinese and the Malay authorities led to the massacre of many Chinese in Sungei Ujong in 1828 and to a Chinese rising against Raja Busu of Lukut six years later, in which the Malay chieftain was killed and the surviving Chinese miners fled to Melaka.

Raja Busu was succeeded by Raja Juma'at, a very able Bugis chief of the Riau branch of the Selangor royal house, who worked in partnership with Chinese merchants in Melaka to bring the labourers back to the mines. Juma'at provided orderly and enlightened administration for his small compact state, guaranteeing security for the lives and property of immigrants and their financial backers, and he maintained a friendly relationship with the British authorities, who considered him a model ruler. His success encouraged other Malay rulers to invite in Chinese to exploit tin resources, and Chinese immigration became a flood in the second half of the century. New tin deposits were discovered, duties on tin were finally abolished in Britain in 1853, and the development of the canning industry in the 1860s stimulated a great international demand for the metal. But nowhere else could indigenous rulers provide the same efficient infrastructure as in Lukut.

Sungei Ujong

In Sungei Ujong the tin trade continued to be beset with troubles and violence. From about 1830 Chinese miners began to drift back to the mines and by the 1840s the Sungei Ujong tin trade brought considerable profit to Melaka merchants. But life was precarious and the tin trade was plagued with problems, particularly over control of the Linggi river, which was the main highway for transport, and which, in its lower stretch, marked the boundary between Melaka and the Malay states, reaching the sea about forty kilometres west of Melaka town.

While the Linggi was the gateway to the sea, the *dato klana*, ruler of

Sungei Ujong, had never attempted to extend his sway to the river mouth, and this left the field open for the rise of subordinate chiefs, notably the *dato bandar,* who controlled the middle reaches of the river, and the downriver chief, the *dato muda Linggi.*

The *dato klana* was the *undang,* or territorial chief, of Sungei Ujong and leader of the four *undang* of Negri Sembilan, lawmaker and head of the government, which he conducted in consultation with a council of the leading chiefs. The office of *dato shahbandar,* or *dato bandar,* dated only from 1715, when the sultan of Johor created a customs officer to collect dues along the Linggi river. He had no constitutional position within the Malay hierarchy, but in the middle of the nineteenth century he came increasingly to flout the position of the *dato klana,* taking on the functions of an *undang* to become virtually an independent ruler.

Normally the *dato klana* collected poll taxes, gambling taxes and court fines, while the *dato bandar* was entitled to river and port dues, although the *dato klana* also had the right to share in these. With the growth of the tin trade, the *dato bandar* came to control more wealth than the *dato klana,* and the different clans and chiefs divided into supporters of one or the other.

The office of *dato muda Linggi* was of very recent origin, dating only from the 1830s, and Linggi's relationship to Sungei Ujong was undefined, but the chief exploited his position over the vital lower reaches of the Linggi river to exact tolls.

All three chiefs made considerable profits but mounting rivalry reached a peak after the election in 1846 of a new *dato klana,* Sending, and a new *dato bandar,* Kulop Tunggal. In 1849 the *yang di-pertuan besar* presided over an agreement between the chiefs. The tolls on the Linggi river were to be regulated and the *dato klana* was to receive a share, in exchange for admitting the *dato bandar* as his equal. But the *dato klana* was powerless to enforce this pact and a tense situation arose in which the two chiefs intrigued and sometimes fought one another for nearly twenty-five years.

The ambitions of Kulop Tunggal, who was a shrewd businessman and owned a number of tin mines, brought him into conflict with the British authorities in the Straits Settlements, who from the middle of the century were drawn in to protect the interests of Melaka merchants. The British constantly urged the *dato klana* to enforce the 1849 pact and to close down illegal toll stations put up by subordinate chiefs, but without success. In 1857 Governor Blundell sent a naval expedition to destroy forts which exacted irregular tolls on the river, but this provided only temporary relief.

Meanwhile Chinese miners in Sungei Ujong became restive and in 1860 rebelled against the *dato klana*'s exactions, as a result of which hundreds of Chinese were killed and the rest fled. Chinese merchants in

Melaka urged Governor Cavenagh to take over Sungei Ujong but, restrained by Calcutta's policy of non-intervention, Cavenagh could do nothing beyond issuing vague warnings. After a short absence Chinese miners drifted back to Sungei Ujong but continued to live a precarious existence.

Selangor

In the 1820s Selangor's scattered population lived in the lower reaches of the five main rivers. Sultan Muhammad resided at Langat and granted the rest of the state to relatives and subordinate chiefs, notably to his nephew, Abdul Samad, and two brothers, Juma'at and Abdullah, all of whom were the sultan's sons-in-law.

Up to the middle of the century the most flourishing tin district was Lukut, which was developed by Raja Juma'at. Other Selangor chiefs tried to emulate him, including Raja Abdul Samad, who opened up mines at Kanching in the upper Selangor valley in the late 1840s. However Sulaiman, the sultan's eldest son, who tried to exploit tin mining in the Klang valley, where it had been carried on in a small way

Yap Ah Loy *(By courtesy of the Arkib Negara Malaysia)*.

for many years, failed in his enterprise, and in 1853 Sultan Muhammad, passing over Sulaiman's son, Raja Mahdi, transferred Klang to Juma'at's brother, Abdullah. Abdullah and Juma'at then went into partnership with two Chinese merchants from Melaka and in 1857 brought in miners from Lukut to open up mines at Ampang, near the present Kuala Lumpur. Of the original eighty-seven miners only eighteen survived the first month's rigours, but replacements were quickly found, and the success of the Ampang mines led to a steady influx of Hakka miners and traders, who established themselves at Kuala Lumpur. In 1868 they chose as their *kapitan* Yap Ah Loy, a ruthless and energetic Kwangtung-born Hakka, who had come to Melaka as a penniless immigrant in 1854, worked as a pig trader, miner and shop assistant in Lukut, made his reputation as a fighting man in the Sungei Ujong troubles in 1860 and came to Kuala Lumpur two years later. The downriver Malay chiefs acknowledged the *kapitans* whom the Chinese miners themselves chose and at first left the mining communities to organize themselves, but the rapid success of tin mining at Kuala Lumpur and Kanching led to jealousies and dissensions among the Malay chiefs and between the miners themselves. A scheme proposed by Juma'at and Abdullah to regulate tin revenues was never brought into effect because of the death of Sultan Muhammad and disputes about the succession which followed.

Muhammad, who ruled Selangor for thirty-one years, died in 1857, and the chiefs decided, after considerable wrangling, to pass over Muhammad's sons in favour of his nephew and son-in-law, Abdul Samad, who became sultan in 1859. At first this seemed a sensible choice and was supported by Abdullah of Klang and Juma'at of Lukut. But Abdul Samad, though an active and formidable fighter in his youth, had become a tired middle-aged opium addict, who went into retreat in Langat and was content to let affairs of state drift.

The able Raja Juma'at died in 1864, leaving Lukut to decline under two incompetent sons, and two years later the rejected Raja Mahdi seized Klang from Abdullah starting a war which was to last for seven years.

Raja Mahdi recognized Yap Ah Loy as *kapitan China* of Kuala Lumpur, and the change of leadership did not at first threaten to disrupt the tin trade. But Raja Mahdi lost favour with Sultan Abdul Samad, who in 1868 married his daughter to an outsider, Tunku Ziauddin (Kudin), younger brother of the sultan of Kedah, instead of to Raja Mahdi as he had promised. He then virtually abdicated control to his new son-in-law, Tunku Kudin, who threw in his lot with Ismail, son of the dispossessed Abdullah of Klang. In 1869 Ismail borrowed money from Chinese merchants in Melaka, recruited Illanuns from Riau together with men from Siak and blockaded the Klang river mouth.

Table 11.3 The Selangor royal house in the mid-nineteenth century

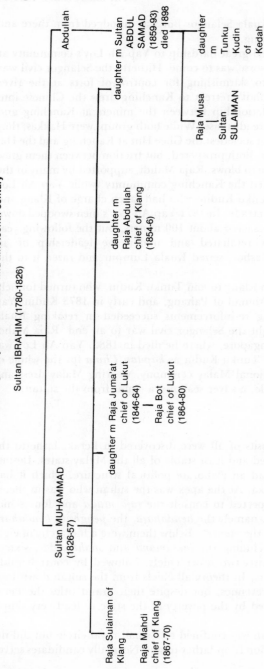

Raja Mahdi fled to Kuala Selangor but was dislodged from there and fled upriver to Kanching.

The blockade caused great hardship to Yap Ah Loy's community at Kuala Lumpur, but worse was to come. Hitherto the Selangor civil war had been confined to skirmishing for control of forts at the river mouths, but Raja Mahdi's retreat to Kanching drew the Chinese into the fighting. The relationship between the miners at Kanching and Kuala Lumpur was already tense. While both groups were Hakkas, they belonged to rival secret societies: the Ghee Hin at Kanching and the Hai San at Kuala Lumpur. Both prospered, but friction between them grew and in 1869 they came to blows. Raja Mahdi, supported by many of the Selangor chiefs, backed the Kanching community, while Yap Ah Loy allied himself with Tunku Kudin, who had taken charge of Klang and was trying to revive its trade. In 1871 Yap Ah Loy's men swooped down on Kanching and massacred about 100 miners, but the following year Raja Mahdi's forces retaliated and under the leadership of an Arab–Malay, Syed Mashor, seized Kuala Lumpur and razed it to the ground.

Yap Ah Loy fled to Klang to join Tunku Kudin, who turned for help to Bendahara Wan Ahmad of Pahang, and early in 1873 Kudin, Yap Ah Loy and Pahang re-inforcements succeeded in retaking Kuala Lumpur. This brought the Selangor civil war to an end. Raja Mahdi went into exile in Singapore, where he died in 1882. Yap Ah Loy was formally installed by Tunku Kudin as *kapitan China* for the whole of Selangor, in a traditional Malay ceremony, wearing Malay dress and receiving a Malay title, a silver seal and a drum from the sultan.

Perak

The richest tin deposits of all were discovered in Perak, hitherto the poorest, most troubled and least stable of all the Malay states. Despite its poverty, Perak had an elaborate political structure, which it had inherited from Melaka. At the apex was the sultan who was in theory absolute but was expected to consult the *raja muda* and four senior chiefs or *orang kaya*, namely the *bendahara*, the *penghulu bendahari*, the *temenggong* and the *mantri*. Below them were a hierarchy of eight *orang kaya-kaya*, including the *laksamana* and *shahbandar*, sixteen minor chiefs and thirty-two lesser chiefs, followed by court heralds, courtiers and warriors. In theory all chiefs from the sultan down were entitled to specific revenues, but despite their grand titles the Perak nobles were compelled by the poverty of the state to lead very simple lives.

The office of sultan was confined to a small royal circle but did not pass in direct succession from father to son. Normally candidates served

Table 11.4 The Perak succession

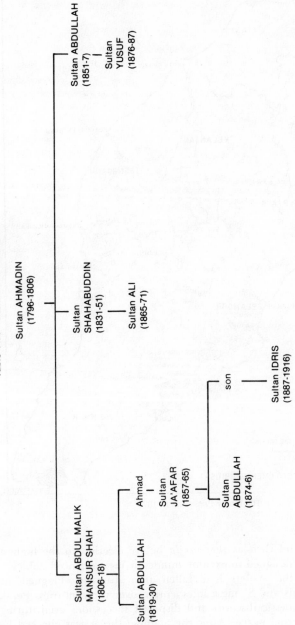

Sultan ISMAIL (1871-74) was not a member of the immediate royal family but descended on his mother's side from eighteenth century sultans of Selangor.

PATANI

PERLIS

KEDAH

KUALA
KEDAH

ALOR
STAR

K. MUDA
GEORGE
TOWN
PENANG I.

KOTA

PROVINCE
WELLESLEY

KOTA BHARU

KELANTAN

KUALA TRENGGANU

TRENGGANU

KUALA LARUT   TAIPING   KUALA KANGSAR

P E R A K

DINDINGS
PANGKOR I.
LUMUT

PASIR
SALAK

KUALA
LIPIS

KEMAMAN (CHUKAI)

P A H A N G

JERANTUT

RAUB

KUANTAN

KUALA SELANGOR

SELANGOR

JERAM

KLANG

LANGAT

TEMERLOH

PAHANG
(PEKAN)

SUNGEI
UJONG

(SEREMBAN)
SRI
MENANTI

REMBAU

LUKUT

CAPE RACHADO
KUALA LINGGI

NANING   SEGAMAT

MELAKA

MELAKA

MUAR

J O H O R

BATU PAHAT

JOHOR BAHRU

JOHOR
LAMA

SINGAPORE

0   20 40 60 80 100 120 km

▨ STRAITS SETTLEMENTS (BRITISH)

The Malay Peninsula in 1873

as *bendahara* and then as *raja muda* before election to the highest
office, a system designed to exclude minors or inexperienced nobles.

In practice the system had fallen into disarray. Plagued by
Achehnese, Bugis and Siamese intervention over the centuries, Perak
was rent by domestic discords and disputed successions even during
intervals of external peace. After the Siamese threat was checked by
James Low's treaty in 1826, the sultan found it difficult to impose his

will, and by the time Sultan Abdullah Muhammed died in 1857, he and his son, Yusuf, were quarrelling with most of the chiefs.

At that time the office of *bendahara* was held by Raja Ismail, of mixed Siak-Perak descent, who was created *bendahara* in 1851 in the absence of suitable royal candidates but was not entitled to succeed to the office of *raja muda* or sultan. When Ngah Ja'afar was elected sultan in 1857, Ismail remained as *bendahara* and Yusuf was passed over completely. Sultan Ja'afar died in 1865, and was succeeded by Raja Muda Ali, Ismail still retaining the office of *bendahara*, while Abdullah, the late Sultan Ja'afar's son, became *raja muda*.

About the middle of the century rich tin deposits were discovered at Kamunting and Taiping in the hitherto almost uninhabited Larut district, which was under the control of a minor chief, Long Ja'afar. In 1858 he was succeeded by his son, Ngah Ibrahim, then a young man in his early twenties, who encouraged Chinese immigrants to work the tin mines.

Undeterred by the appalling conditions in the fever-ridden mining camps, Chinese labourers flocked into Larut in thousands, and Ngah Ibrahim soon became the richest chief in Perak. But disputes broke out between rival secret societies, which in Perak were divided along dialect lines: the Hai San being largely Hakka in membership and the Ghee Hin Cantonese. In 1861 quarrels between the Ghee Hin miners of Kamunting and the Hai San miners of Taiping flared into open warfare. Ngah Ibrahim supported the more numerous Hai San, who drove the Ghee Hin out with heavy losses. The survivors fled to Penang, where the society leaders, as British subjects, appealed to the colonial authorities for redress.

The governor of the Straits Settlements ordered a blockade of the Perak coast, demanding that the sultan force Ngah Ibrahim to pay compensation. The Larut chief agreed on condition the sultan rewarded him, and in 1862 the sultan created Ngah Ibrahim *orang kaya mantri,* making him one of the four great officers of state and virtually the independent ruler of Larut.

Peace returned to the mines and the Ghee Hin were re-instated, but still nursed grievances against the Hai San, and in August 1867 they turned on their rivals in Penang, where fighting went on for ten days before the British authorities were able to control the situation.

The death of Sultan Ali of Perak in 1871 plunged the state into a succession quarrel. Abdullah's claims as *raja muda,* as son of Sultan Ja'afar, and as brother-in-law of Sultan Ali, were impeccable, but he was on bad terms with the *mantri*. Ngah Ibrahim preferred to see the throne pass to the ageing Bendahara Ismail, who lived far inland and was no obstacle to the *mantri's* plans. Abdullah damaged his case by being frightened to go upriver for Ali's funeral and for his own installation as sultan and he lost more respect when his wife ran off with a

Selangor chieftain and he took no steps to avenge the insult. Having waited in vain for Abdullah's arrival, the chiefs finally branded him a coward and installed Ismail as sultan instead.

With the exception of the *laksamana,* the Perak leadership was willing to accept Ismail, by now an experienced old man who had held senior office for twenty years. But Abdullah continued to claim the sultanate and named Raja Yusuf as *raja muda.* He enlisted the backing of merchants in the Straits Settlements, notably a wealthy Singapore merchant, Tan Kim Ching, to whom he offered concessions, and involved himself in the Chinese disputes over the Larut tin fields. While Abdullah made promises to the Ghee Hin, the *mantri* gave his support to the Hai San, who marshalled a force of professional fighting men in Penang in 1872 and once more attacked their Ghee Hin rivals in Larut. Hundreds of Ghee Hin men were killed and 2000 fled to Penang. The Ghee Hin society then organized a blockade of the Larut coast to starve the Hai San out.

The tin trade came to a halt, the waters between Larut and Penang became unsafe for shipping, and the quarrel threatened to spill over into Penang itself. In August 1873 the lieutenant-governor of Penang called together the rival leaders, the heads of the Ghee Hin and Hai San, Raja Abdullah and the *mantri.* They all accepted his arbitration, but could not, or would not, put agreement into practice. Raja Abdullah declared the *mantri* deposed, while Ngah Ibrahim recruited Captain Speedy of the Penang police to raise a force of Indian sepoys to put down Ghee Hin resistance in Larut.

Faced with the dangers of large-scale violence in Penang, but precluded from pledging any active British backing for a settlement, Governor Ord decided in August 1873 to support the *mantri's* efforts to produce peace. He recognized Ngah Ibrahim's claim to be independent ruler of Larut and raised no objections to Speedy's activities. This provoked the Ghee Hin to try to murder the *mantri* by blowing up his Penang house, but the plan miscarried as Ngah Ibrahim was not there.

While the troubles in Sungei Ujong and Selangor did not impinge directly on the Straits Settlements, the turmoil in Perak which was disrupting peace in Penang could not be ignored. For the moment the British governor's hands were tied but he realized the official policy of non-involvement was no longer realistic. For half a century the Straits authorities had been endeavouring to cope on a piecemeal, *ad hoc* basis with problems arising in the Malay states. This was no longer adequate. By the early-1870s order had broken down in the three major tin-producing states under the pressures of economic activity and immigration, and merchants in the Straits Settlements, who had tasted the fruit of the tin trade and found it sweet, clamoured for change.

CHAPTER 12

The Spread of British Rule in the Malay Peninsula, 1874-96

The transfer of the Straits Settlements to colonial rule in 1867 brought no immediate change in the official British policy to stand clear of entanglements in the Malay states. British opinion was still swayed by the experience of the revolt of the American colonies almost a century before and the lessons it had taught: that colonial rule incurred expense in administration and defence, breeding friction which would inevitably lead to bitter separation, and that the 'old colonial' trading system was unprofitable to colony and mother country alike. Britain's trade had increased substantially after the American colonies won their independence, and 'free traders' in mid-nineteenth century Britain argued that the colonial empire should be run down rather than expanded. Where possible they favoured loosening ties by granting self government, such as that achieved by Canada in 1854 and consolidated in 1867 by confederating the British North American provinces to form the Dominion of Canada. Generally liberal and conservative politicians and senior officials, including those in the Colonial Office itself, were committed to cutting the financial burdens of empire, believing that a strong navy and a chain of naval stations would suffice to protect overseas trade. Territorial commitments were avoided, and in 1861 the secretary of state for the colonies promised parliament that no colonies would be acquired in future unless they could pay their own way and put no burden on the British exchequer.

In the early-1870s the climate of opinion in London began to change. The increased pace of industrial development whetted the appetite for foreign markets and raw materials but with attendant fears of competition from other European powers. British business in Southeast Asia flourished in the trade boom which followed the opening of the Suez Canal in 1869 but was hampered by the coincidental disruption of the Malayan tin trade. Further, British firms and government became increasingly concerned about the possible checks and tariff barriers which might result from the expansion of French interests in Indo-China, the Dutch advance in Sumatra and the vague ambitions of recently-unified imperial Germany in the Malay peninsula. While British political leaders still did not favour annexation of territory or the

Sultan Abdullah of Perak (sitting). Deposed in 1875.
(By courtesy of the Arkib Negara Malaysia).

imposition of direct rule, they veered towards gaining more influence
with local rulers.

In view of Ord's strained relationship with the Straits Settlements
merchants, the Colonial Office had no confidence in entrusting him
with delicate matters of policy in the Malay states and continued to
reject his repeated requests to be allowed to take a stronger line. But at
the end of Ord's term of office they briefed his successor, Sir Andrew
Clarke, to inquire into and report on the situation in the Malay states
and to advise on measures to restore and maintain peace, possibly
through the appointment of British officials as advisers to Malay rulers.

British Intervention in the West Malay States, 1874

By the time Clarke arrived in Singapore late in 1873 the once profitable
tin trade had dwindled to a trickle at a time when the demand for tin in
the international market had reached a tantalizing peak, and the new
governor was greeted with demands for intervention from leading

officials, including Archibald Anson, the lieutenant-governor of Penang, and Thomas Braddell, the attorney-general, and from a vocal element among the Singapore business community, led by William Henry Read, senior non-official in the legislative council. Finding Clarke sympathetic, Read provided him with the excuse to intervene, in the form of an invitation from Raja Abdullah of Perak, who was then staying in Singapore with Read's business associate, Tan Kim Ching. Provided he could obtain title to the sultanate, Abdullah promised to make over the Larut revenues for ten years to Tan in exchange for payment of his debts. Read now induced Abdullah to appeal to Clarke to arbitrate in Perak.

Clarke was a man of action and immediately proceeded to make a settlement. He sent William Pickering, Chinese interpreter to the Straits Settlements' government, to negotiate peace between the warring Ghee Hin and Hai San and followed this by inviting the rival claimants to the Perak throne, together with most of the leading Perak chiefs and Chinese society leaders, to meet him at Pangkor. Clarke arrived there with an open mind, apparently prepared to confirm Ismail as sultan and to pension off Abdullah, but the meeting changed his views. Ismail and the upcountry chiefs boycotted the conference, and of the Lower Perak leaders only the *mantri* opposed Abdullah's claims. Clarke was impressed with Abdullah, who was a personable, pliant young man of charm and grace, accustomed to dealing with Europeans and adaptable to their ways. Accordingly Clarke and those Perak chiefs who were present signed the Pangkor Engagement in January 1874, by which Abdullah was recognized as sultan of Perak and was to accept a British resident, whose advice must be taken on all matters other than Malay custom and the Muslim religion. The *mantri* was demoted, from the independent status which Ord had recognized, to be governor only of the Larut district, subject to the sultan and to the advice of a British assistant resident.

The following month Clarke proceeded to Selangor, where he used the issue of a recent pirate attack by some of the sultan's men on a Melaka trading ship at Kuala Langat to force an agreement on Sultan Abdul Samad. The sultan agreed to accept a British assistant resident at his Kuala Langat court and a British resident at Klang to advise the viceroy, Tunku Kudin, whom the British recognized as the executive head of government.

Shortly afterwards Clarke intervened in Sungei Ujong to support the authority of the newly appointed *dato klana*, Syed Abdul Rahman. His succession was not popular among the Negri chiefs, who regarded him as an outsider since, although he was the late *dato klana*'s nephew on his mother's side, his father was an Achehnese Arab.

The *dato bandar*, Kulop Tunggal, continued to bid for power, renewing the discord which impeded tin traffic on the Linggi river, and in April 1874 the *dato klana* and the *dato muda Linggi* came to Singapore at Clarke's invitation to make a treaty in which they promised freedom of trade on the Linggi in exchange for British protection. When the *dato bandar* continued to make trouble, the Singapore authorities sent troops to the *klana's* aid, and in November 1874 defeated, deposed and exiled Kulop Tunggal to Singapore. The *klana* and *bandar* then made a pact, witnessed by the chiefs and Pickering, which recognized Dato Klana Syed Abdul Rahman as *undang* of all Sungei Ujong but bound him to act in consultation with the *dato bandar*.

Though initially startled at the extent to which Clarke had exceeded his instructions, the British government did not repudiate his actions. They confirmed the junior appointments of British officials in Larut, Kuala Langat and Sungei Ujong and agreed rather more reluctantly to the appointment of British residents in Perak and Selangor.

James Woodford Wheeler Birch, colonial secretary of Singapore, was appointed first resident of Perak, with Captain Speedy as assistant resident in Larut. James Guthrie Davidson, a prominent Singapore lawyer, became resident of Selangor, with Frank Swettenham, a young cadet official, as assistant resident at the Kuala Langat court.

The governor, merchants and officials were well pleased with these arrangements, which apparently had been made with so little opposition. In each state the colonial authorities had put themselves in alliance with seemingly co-operative rulers. Sultan Abdullah in Perak had close associations with Chinese and European merchants in Penang and Singapore. Tunku Kudin, viceroy of Selangor, was on friendly terms with Davidson, his former legal and financial adviser. Syed Abdul Rahman, *dato klana* of Sungei Ujong, had spent many years in Melaka where he was on cordial terms with both officials and Chinese merchants.

The Murder of Birch

For a time all went well. The fighting between rival Chinese factions subsided, peace came to the mining districts of Selangor and Perak, and traffic returned to normal on the Linggi river. But the calm was deceptive.

The first trouble exploded in Perak in a protest against the activities of the British resident. Birch, who took up the office in November 1874, was a middle-aged official with impressive administrative experience. After service in the Royal Navy in his youth, followed by twenty-four years as an official in Ceylon, he was appointed colonial secretary for the Straits Settlements in 1870 and performed with distinction during the difficult years of adaptation to colonial rule. While he was an honourable, respected and energetic officer, Birch was not versed in Malay language or custom. He was contemptuous of the Malay regime in Perak, assuming the confusion and chaos of that time to be the norm of Malay organization. 'A man in a hurry to carry Victorian light to Perak',[1] he set out with crusading zeal on a mission of radical reform, to modernize the revenue system, abolish slavery and debt bondage.

Birch aimed to transfer responsibility for revenue collection from local chieftains to government officials, to impose regular port dues, and organize one opium, spirits and gambling excise farm for the whole state. He also wanted to stop the personal extravagance of Sultan Abdullah, who on assuming power had leased the collection of Perak's trade dues to Tan Kim Ching as promised and squandered most of the proceeds on his own pleasures.

The upriver chiefs were reluctant to acknowledge the Pangkor Engagement and ex-sultan Ismail was furious at his supersession. Soon Birch's high handedness came to alienate Abdullah and the downriver chiefs too, drawing the former rivals together. In May 1875 Abdullah sent a secret deputation to complain to the British governor about Birch's behaviour, but the embassy arrived in Singapore as Clarke was handing over to his successor, Sir William Jervois, who refused to accept any petition except through Birch himself.

Tension mounted in the ensuing weeks as Birch ordered the abolition of former river tolls without offering compensation and gave refuge to runaway slaves. In July 1875 Abdullah summoned all the leading chiefs to a meeting. Angry at the interference with their customs and the indignities thrust upon them, they resolved that Birch must go. If all peaceful means failed, the *Maharaja Lela,* most senior of the eight *orang kaya-kaya,* whose traditional duties dating from the Melaka sultanate included the summary execution of anyone who infringed loyalty or court etiquette, volunteered in the last resort to kill Birch. With the exception of Raja Yusuf, the senior chiefs present were amenable to this proposal, to which Ismail gave his blessing.

Meanwhile Governor Jervois wanted to strengthen British authority and in October 1875 browbeat Abdullah with threats of deposition into agreeing to put administration into the hands of British officials. Birch, ignoring warnings about unrest and animosity towards himself, brought the chiefs to breaking point in November 1875, when he humiliated Abdullah into signing proclamations enforcing the new revenue system and went upriver in person to post the announcements. When he arrived at the *Maharaja Lela's* village at Pasir Salak, he was hacked to death.

Birch's murder shocked the Straits authorities, who were alarmed also by restlessness in Selangor and trouble in Sungei Ujong. Fearing a general uprising, the governor sent for reinforcements from Hong Kong and India and dispatched an armed force to Perak to put down trouble, but it met with little resistance since the violence had been directed solely at removing one objectionable official. The conspirators were rounded up and arrested. The *Maharaja Lela* and two followers who had done the killing were hanged and his title and office abolished. Sultan Abdullah, the *mantri, laksamana* and *shahbandar* were exiled to the Seychelles and ex-sultan Ismail to Johor, but the other chiefs implicated in the plot were pardoned, since the Straits executive council admitted Birch had been largely responsible in personally provoking attack. No further punitive measures were taken and the Straits authorities sought to restore peace and harmony. Raja Yusuf, who had not been invited to the Pangkor conference but was now indisputably the strongest legal claimant to the Perak throne and untainted by complicity in Birch's murder,was appointed regent, and subsequently, in 1876, sultan of Perak.

Meanwhile in November 1875 the British intervened once more in Negri Sembilan to settle a dispute between the *dato klana* and Tunku Antah, newly elected to the office of *yang di-pertuan besar*. When the Colonial Office over-ruled Jervois's proposal to take Sri Menanti, Terachi and Ulu Muar under British protection, he used the Maharaja Abu Bakar of Johor as a go-between to form the minor states into the Sri Menanti confederacy under Tunku Antah. The new confederacy, together with the independent states of Rembau, Jelebu, Tampin and Kesang, still looked to Johor rather than to Singapore to settle their disputes.

Perak

The British government, horrified at the developments in the Malay states and attributing the disaster in Perak to Jervois's attempts to enforce direct government, called a halt to further expansion and set its face firmly against annexation or any form of direct rule. While it could not withdraw the appointed residents it insisted that they should interfere as little as possible in Perak, Selangor and Sungei Ujong and refrain from extending British responsibilities beyond these boundaries.

This left a nebulous situation in which the residents were required to give 'influential advice' to the Malay rulers but the scope of their powers was undefined. In practice they came to assume increasing executive power and drew the colonial government deeper into the affairs of the interior, whatever official policy might be.

By the end of 1876 British authority was established in the Protected Malay States and steadily consolidated over the next twenty years. Consultative state councils, comprising the Malay ruler, the British resident, leading Malay chiefs and Chinese *kapitans*, were established under Jervois's direction in all the Protected States: in Selangor and Perak in 1877 and in Sungei Ujong the following year.

In Perak the collapse of the traditional ruling structure following Birch's death left the British resident as the sole executive power in the state and opened the way for introducing the type of reform which Birch himself had sought so clumsily to enforce. Davidson was transferred to Perak as acting resident immediately after Birch's assassination but resigned early in 1877 to return to his law practice in Singapore, and the reconstruction of Perak fell to Hugh Low, who held the office of resident of Perak from 1877 until his retirement ten years later.

At first sight Low seemed an inauspicious choice, since he was Birch's contemporary, fifty-three years old at the time of his posting, and had spent nearly thirty years of undistinguished service in Borneo, mostly as colonial secretary of the insignificant island of Labuan. In fact Low's appointment proved to be a great success, for he was the antithesis of Birch in his attitudes and methods, approachable, gracious and patient, a fluent Malay speaker who respected local custom. Courteous to chiefs and peasants alike, Low lived simply among the people, travelling unarmed throughout the state and making informality the hallmark of his administration.

The Perak ruling class, now frightened and depleted by executions and exile, was prepared to accept changes which had seemed intolerable in Birch's day. But despite the fact that the removal of most of the great chiefs of state gave him a clear hand, Low believed in winning confidence and carrying local opinion with him in his reform programme. He was particularly concerned to reconstruct the sultanate, which became in Perak and the other Protected states the basis on which British influence was founded.

Low worked closely with the regent (later sultan) Yusuf and with Raja Idris, who himself succeeded as sultan in 1887. While Yusuf was a difficult man, grasping, and unpopular among the Malays, old-fashioned in his thinking and with little understanding of the outside world or Western ways, the younger Idris was intelligent and adaptable, appreciating the need for change and modernization.

The most pressing, immediate problem was financial, since Perak was deeply in debt. Low organized efficient revenue collection under direct central control, transforming the chiefs into government officials who were responsible for collecting revenue and in return received a salary. At the same time, partly in the interests of economy, the resident left local administration and the preservation of law and order in the hands of Malay headmen.

Within six years Low managed to pay off the Perak debt. From that time most surplus revenue was spent on developing communications to open up the state, particularly the immense tin resources of the Kinta valley. Perak derived the bulk of its revenue from the tin trade and excise farms, but in 1879 Low promulgated land regulations, which

Sultan Idris of Perak *(By courtesy of the Arkib Negara Malaysia).*

fixed tenure and registration, to encourage agricultural development and lay the foundations for a land revenue.

At the same time the resident successfully mastered the thorny problem of slavery by encouraging the practice to atrophy. In 1877 there were about 3000 slaves and debt bondsmen in Perak, but from that time everyone born in the state was free, no slaves could be imported into Perak, and provision was made for existing slaves to buy their freedom. By 1883 the number of bondsmen had dwindled to the point where the state council agreed, with comparatively little opposition, to buy their freedom.

During his ten years as resident of Perak, Low gradually smoothed away discontent, brought in Malay and Chinese leaders for consultation, and succeeded in setting Perak on the path of modernization without antagonizing the traditional ruling class, while at the same time being approachable by the humblest peasant. By the time he retired in

1887 Perak was at peace, the economy thriving and attracting an inflow of immigrants, so that the population rose from 81 000 in 1879 to 214 000 in 1891. While no other resident enjoyed the same pre-eminent position or had such a clean slate on which to write, Low's administration in Perak provided a model, and his personality shaped the character of British rule in all the Protected Malay States during the 1880s.

Selangor

In Selangor Davidson's close partnership with Tunku Kudin came to an end in 1876 when he was posted to Perak. He was succeeded by Captain Bloomfield Douglas, who had little local experience. A retired naval officer, fifty years of age, he had served in South Australia prior to his appointment as magistrate in Singapore in 1874 and assistant resident in Selangor the following year. Brusque, difficult and aloof, he kept apart from the Malay population in his heavily-guarded residency, so that the residential system in Selangor took on a different character from Low's open accessibility in Perak.

Douglas's relationship with Tunku Kudin was amicable but not as intimate as in Davidson's time, and the creation of the Selangor state council in 1877 put administration on a more formal basis. Kudin was first president of the Selangor state council but retired on pension to Penang after a few months, handing over the presidency to Sultan Abdul Samad's heir, Raja Muda Musa.

Klang gradually declined as traders moved upriver to Kuala Lumpur, which Yap Ah Loy had painfully resurrected from the devastation of the civil war. After several years of slow reconstruction a sudden boom in tin prices in 1879 brought an influx of immigrants, and in 1880 Douglas decided to transfer the headquarters of government to Kuala Lumpur.

While Yap Ah Loy had managed to keep rough law and order in the early days in Kuala Lumpur, the town was in a disgraceful condition, a filthy, disease-ridden mining camp, with a squalid brothel area and a mammoth gambling establishment which remained open round the clock. Hitherto the undisputed master of Kuala Lumpur, Yap Ah Loy accepted the British resident's move with some reluctance. He continued to participate in administration as state councillor, magistrate and *kapitan China* until his death in 1885 but became increasingly absorbed in his considerable business interests as mine owner, property magnate and state tax farmer.

Douglas did little to improve Kuala Lumpur and in 1882 was forced to resign to avoid an investigation into incompetence and financial mismanagement. He was succeeded by the assistant resident of Langat, Frank Swettenham, who held the post of resident of Selangor for the next seven years. During that time he rebuilt Kuala Lumpur, put the state's administration on a sound footing and helped to promote the economy by developing communications, raising a loan to build a railway from Kuala Lumpur to Klang.

Europeans who attempted to break into tin mining in Selangor in the early-1880s failed, largely owing to the heavy overheads of their type of operation. They brought with them modern machinery, particularly the steam engine and centrifugal pump, which were used to pump out mines and prevent flooding, hitherto the problem which had inhibited most the expansion of tin mining. Yap Ah Loy and other Chinese bought up European mines and machinery, and tin mining spread to other parts of Selangor on the crest of a new tin boom. In the early-1890s Chinese miners flocked into the state and Kuala Lumpur became a relatively well-kept and orderly town with hospitals and schools.

Sir Frederick Weld

By the end of the 1870s the British residential system was well established, and in the time of Sir Frederick Weld, who was governor of the Straits Settlements from 1880 to 1887, British influence spread even

Sir Frederick Weld *(By courtesy of the Arkib Negara Malaysia).*

more firmly. Weld, who was fifty-seven when he became governor, had spent his adult life in New Zealand and Australia, first as a New Zealand sheep farmer and subsequently as governor of Western Australia and later of Tasmania. He was a strong supporter of responsible government in New Zealand and Australia, but in the Malay states favoured extending British influence, not by annexation, but by working through the existing rulers. Leaving the administration of the Straits Settlements colony to his subordinates, he concentrated on the peninsular states which he visited frequently.

Weld wanted to make Britain the unchallenged paramount power in the peninsula and to protect British commercial interests by strengthening the position of the existing residents, by extending protection to Pahang, and by putting a check on the independent and influential power of Johor.

In the Protected States, Weld gave strong support to Low in Perak, insisted on appointing the vigorous and like-minded Swettenham as resident of Selangor, despite Colonial Office objections to his youth, and set out to build up British influence in Negri Sembilan at the expense of Johor. He made agreements with Rembau in 1883, with Jelebu in 1886 and with the Sri Menanti confederacy in 1887, appointing British officers to each state. Two years later Weld's successor, Sir Cecil Clementi Smith, united Sri Menanti with Jelebu, Tampin and Rembau in a Negri Sembilan confederacy with a British resident, and in 1895 Sungei Ujong was merged in this confederacy to form the present state of Negri Sembilan. The four *undang* installed a *yang dipertuan besar* in 1898. British district officers took over executive powers, and the former revenues of the *dato klana, dato bandar* and other chiefs were replaced by fixed pensions.

In the years immediately following British intervention in the mid-1870s Johor was on very friendly terms with the Straits authorities, who considered the Maharaja Abu Bakar to be a model ruler, enlightened in the administration of his own state, and a co-operative and helpful intermediary in the other states at times of trouble. Jervois relied a good deal on Abu Bakar, permitting him to annex Muar after the death of Sultan Ali in 1877 and seeking his advice in negotiating the Sri Menanti confederation settlement. Under the cover of British friendship, Abu Bakar attempted to resurrect the Johor sultanate's authority in Negri Sembilan, exerting much influence over Tunku Antah, head of the Sri Menanti confederacy. He also tried to bring his erstwhile enemy, Bendahara Wan Ahmad of Pahang, into his fold, exchanging state visits in 1880.

Weld was alarmed at Abu Bakar's ambitions and did not share his predecessor's personal admiration for the Maharaja, whose 'modernization' in Johor began to look superficial as the residential system brought

Sultan Abu Bakar of Johor *(By courtesy of the Arkib
Negara Malaysia).*

peace and progress to the west coast states. When Weld tried to persuade the Colonial Office to bring Johor under British protection too,
Abu Bakar, alarmed at the threat to his independence, went to London, where he signed a treaty in 1885. This agreement guaranteed
Johor British protection against external attack but constituted an
alliance rather than a normal treaty of protection. Abu Bakar signed it
as an equal with the secretary of state and agreed only to accept a consular official not a British resident, while the British government
guaranteed Johor's internal sovereignty and recognized Abu Bakar as
sultan of Johor. But he was sultan only of the state of Johor, not of the
old Johor empire, and was prohibited from reviving the former
sultanate's powers over other peninsular states.

Pahang

The British discovered they still needed Abu Bakar's help in exerting
their will in Pahang. For some years after Wan Ahmad's victory the

colonial authorities took little interest in the state, despite appeals from European merchants in Singapore when Wan Ahmad repudiated contracts which they had made with the previous *bendahara* for control of the Kuantan mines and tin trade. Chinese miners and Singapore investors had suffered during the civil war in Pahang, but Straits Settlements' involvement in the state was small compared with the west coast. Over the years personal insecurity, arbitrary taxation and exorbitant river tolls deterred outside investment and settlement, so that by the mid-1880s there were probably little more than 100 Chinese in the whole state of Pahang, most of them traders in the capital of Pekan or miners in the Raub district. Pahang was the largest but least populous of the peninsular states, with the longest river, but no roads, apart from a couple of tracks over the mountains to Selangor. The vast majority of its 40 000 population were Malays, scattered mainly along the Pahang, Tembeling, Jelai and Lipis rivers.

The *bendahara* wielded more power in Pahang than the sultans in the west coast states, his authority resting on a close relationship with

Sultan Ahmad of Pahang *(By courtesy of the Arkib Negara Malaysia)*.

the chiefs in council, based upon the four *orang besar,* eight *orang kaya* and traditional hierarchy of lesser chiefs. But Bendahara Wan Ahmad defied the customary checks on a Malay ruler's power, and the toughness and determination which had brought him through adversity to triumph in the civil war shaped him into a cruel, arbitrary and autocratic ruler. Ignoring the hereditary senior chieftains, he surrounded himself by favourites, often men of humble birth who had helped him win the war, and by the *budak raja,* his personal bodyguard of young warriors, who wielded power over life and property at will.

The great inland chiefs, notably the Maharaja Perba, whose family had held sway over Jelai since the early-seventeenth century, and Orang Kaya Setia Wangsa of Lipis, resented the favours heaped on newcomers such as: Bahaman, a part-Jakun warrior of lowly origin who had been raised to the office of *orang kaya* of Semantan as a reward for distinguished service during the Pahang and Selangor civil wars; Dato Gajah, the son of an obscure Sumatran immigrant, whom Wan Ahmad made district chief in Lipis, his right-hand man and one of the Council of Four; Tuan Itam of Achehnese extraction, who as secretary to Wan Ahmad wielded great influence over the illiterate *bendahara;* Orang Kaya Bakti, a Tamil who was appointed chief financial officer.

In their disaffection the inland chiefs rallied behind Wan Mansur, the *bendahara's* half brother and heir presumptive, who was aggrieved when Wan Ahmad claimed the title of sultan and declared his own son, Mahmud, as heir. Wan Mansur for a time retired to Singapore, where in 1884 he petitioned the British authorities through W. H. Read to intervene in Pahang to put an end to Wan Ahmad's misgovernment. But neither the Colonial Office nor Sir Cecil Clementi Smith, who was acting governor in Weld's absence, was willing to use Wan Mansur in the way Clarke had employed Raja Abdullah of Perak as the key to open the door of Pahang.

But by that stage British intervention was almost inevitable. The tin boom brought a new wave of speculators to the Malay peninsula in the mid-1880s and Wan Ahmad, through Tuan Itam and Orang Kaya Bakti, who profited greatly from the transactions, sold large concessions to Chinese, European and Arab prospectors from the Straits Settlements and Johor without regard to the existing rights of chiefs and *rakyat* and without any guarantees of protection to immigrants. This was unsettling enough, but Governor Weld feared the *bendahara* might plunge Pahang into the chaos which had plagued Perak prior to 1874 and might also extend concessions to French or German speculators. Weld believed that Pahang had enormous economic potential which he wished to bring under British control, and he used various instances of atrocities and misgovernment to try to persuade London to permit intervention.

At first the Colonial Office was lukewarm, but in view of the upsurge

Hugh Clifford (as a young man aged 29, in Pahang in
1895) *(By courtesy of the Arkib Negara Malaysia)*.

of French and German imperialism in the mid-1880s, they acquiesced
in Weld's proposals to put pressure on Pahang. First of all the governor
dispatched Swettenham to make a pact, but without success. In 1886
Weld visited Pahang in person to offer Wan Ahmad a treaty along the
same lines as Johor, but the *bendahara* received his visitor coldly and
again rejected the advances. Finally Weld sent his nephew, Hugh Clifford, and Wan Ahmad, apparently prompted by Sultan Abu Bakar,
reluctantly agreed in 1887 to sign a treaty similar to the Johor agreement, recognizing him as sultan of Pahang, bringing the state under
British protection, and providing for a British agent.

Wan Ahmad continued to exert his independence, but by that stage
the Pahang Corporation, a company backed by influential London
financial interests, wanted to acquire large-scale concessions in Pahang
and persuaded the Colonial Office to give vigorous support to British
enterprise in the state. Urged on by London, Clementi Smith, now
governor of the Straits Settlements, used the pretext of the murder of a

Chinese shopkeeper, allegedly a British subject, at the hands of Wan Ahmad's men, to insist on the sultan accepting a British resident.

The first British resident, John Pickersgill Rodger, a fluent Malay speaker, was appointed in 1888 and held the office for eight years. The sultan went into virtual seclusion, but Rodger met with considerable opposition not only from the sultan's favourites but also from the inland chiefs who had initially welcomed the British as a means of regaining their lost authority. Instead they discovered that power now lay with the resident and state council, their judicial functions transferred to courts of law, their powers to raise revenue commuted to fixed allowances, their control over their people whittled away by the abolition of slavery and forced labour.

The standard of revolt was raised in the interior in 1891. The resistance was led by Bahaman of Semantan, Dato Gajah and his spirited son, Mat Kilau, with the tacit support of Sultan Ahmad. English prospectors were murdered, and the British, convinced that the sultan was in league with the rebels, forced him to help suppress the rising. The rebellion dragged on for several years but petered out when Sultan Ahmad and the Maharaja Perba of Jelai negotiated with the British an amnesty for all the chiefs except Bahaman and Dato Gajah, who fled with the remnants of their supporters to Trengganu and Kelantan. Bahaman surrendered in 1895, while Dato Gajah and his son vanished, although an old man claiming to be Mat Kilau reappeared in 1969.

The Semantan revolt was a shock to the British, who questioned whether it was worth keeping a resident in Pahang, but the state's future was settled by bringing it into closer association with the other protected states. The administrative capital was transferred from Pekan, which had been the royal capital for 600 years, to Kuala Lipis, 300 kilometres up river, and that same year Ahmad's son, Mahmud, was appointed *tengku besar*. While Mahmud co-operated with the British in restoring stability to Pahang, Sultan Ahmad withdrew into the background, eventually dying in 1914 at the age of eighty-three.

Johor

Peace in Pahang was bought at the price of delaying the extension of control over Johor, since the British were indebted to Abu Bakar for his help. In return the Johor sultan used his links with the British crown, contacts with London politicians, and connections with European and Chinese merchants in Singapore to keep the colonial authorities at arm's length, and put off accepting a British agent or consul in his lifetime.
'   In Johor itself, Abu Bakar developed up-to-date institutions, modernized the administration and judiciary, built schools and hospitals. In

1895 he promulgated a constitution for Johor, providing for a council of ministers and a state council, similar to the colonial executive and legislative councils.

He encouraged economic development but refused to grant large land concessions to outsiders. While Johor did not enjoy the tin resources of other states, Abu Bakar encouraged immigrants, particularly Chinese, to develop agriculture and to open up the deserted river valleys of the east coast. By the mid-1890s Johor had a population of 300 000 of whom two-thirds were Chinese. Johor Bahru was a flourishing and cosmopolitan town of some 15 000 inhabitants, surrounded by coffee, tea, cloves, gambier and pepper plantations, and vegetable gardens which catered for the Singapore market. The state claimed to be the world's leading gambier producer, at a time when gambier reached the peak of international demand.

Formation of the Federation

By 1895 British influence was firmly established in all the peninsular states south of the Siamese sphere. The Straits authorities had achieved peace and stability in Perak, Selangor and Negri Sembilan, they had brought Pahang into the residential system and put Johor under protection. Malay wars of succession, Chinese secret-society fights, and disputes over tin rights had come to an end in the protected states. Slavery had disappeared, except in parts of Pahang.

River tolls were abolished, freeing trade within each state, and an efficient revenue system was enforced. Perak and Selangor prospered, while solvency was in sight in Negri Sembilan. The revenues of Perak, Selangor and Sungei Ujong increased more than ten fold in the first fifteen years of residential rule. While the bulk of the revenue came from tin export duties and the remainder chiefly from opium excise, new land regulations provided the basis for a future revenue from commercial agriculture. From 1879 virgin land in Perak and Selangor was sold or granted on long lease to encourage the development of coffee, sugar and tea estates.

Most of the early revenue was ploughed back into improving communications in the form of roads and railways, which in turn facilitated administration and opened up new areas to economic exploitation. The first step was to replace the primitive tracks which linked the tin mines with the coast and with each other across the hills separating the river valleys. A railway connected Taiping and Port Weld in 1885; Kuala Lumpur and Klang in 1886; Seremban and Port Dickson in 1887. The Klang–Kuala Lumpur railway line was extended north to Rawang in 1892 and Kuala Kubu in 1894, and south to Sungei Besi in 1895. By the early-1890s an inland trunk road ran from Melaka to Butterworth following the railway line, thus linking the interior in a radically different way from the days when the only form of access was upriver.

The *pax Britannica* put wealth in the hands of the sultans and served to expand their authority more effectively throughout their states beyond their own immediate districts. In turn the British used the sultanate to bolster their own position. The state councils, though providing the basis of consultation with the traditional Malay ruling class and Chinese leaders, were merely advisory bodies and did not put as great a check on the sultans or residents as the *orang kaya* in the past.

The success of the residential system in establishing law and order, centralizing revenue collection and developing the economy justified the British policy of working through the existing rulers. But the system of indirect rule also led to discrepancies, and comparative isolation from Singapore encouraged individual residents to develop their state administration along different lines.

Some overall authority was needed to ensure efficiency and uniformity in Perak, Selangor and Negri Sembilan and to develop a coherent communications system. Furthermore, funds were required to develop Pahang, which proved to be a constant drain upon Straits finances. While it was the largest of the protected states and presumed to have great wealth, Pahang proved a disappointment. The Semantan rising plunged the state deep into debt, and the only prospect of solvency seemed to lie in opening up communications with the west coast and deploying profits from the more prosperous states to exploit Pahang's resources.

In 1893 Governor Clementi Smith advocated a closer grouping of the Protected States. There was talk of drawing together all the British colonies and protectorates in the region, including the Borneo territories, but this was premature. William Maxwell, colonial secretary of the Straits Settlements, who had served in the Straits and the Malay states for nearly thirty years, argued for a confederation of the protected states and the Straits Settlements colony. His rival and contemporary, Swettenham, then resident of Perak, who had no wish to see more control exerted from Singapore, countered with a proposal for a federation of the protected states only. And the new governor, Sir Charles Mitchell, who arrived in 1893 gave his support to Swettenham's scheme, which was also favoured by the other residents.

Swettenham was commissioned to obtain the Malay rulers' sanction for the formation of the proposed federation, which they readily gave to this accomplished diplomat, whom Sultan Abdul Samad of Selangor had described to Clarke twenty years before as 'very clever in gaining the hearts of rajas and sons of rajas with soft words, delicate and sweet, so that all men rejoice in him as in the perfume of an opened flower'. Swettenham persuaded the sultans, and notably Sultan Idris of Perak, to see

Sir Frank Swettenham *(By courtesy of the Arkib Negara Malaysia).*

the federation as a means to curtail the power of their residents and thus enhance their own position.

The federation treaty was signed in 1895 and the Federation was formally inaugurated in July 1896, linking the protected states of Selangor, Pahang, Perak and the newly unified Negri Sembilan. A British resident-general co-ordinated policy from the federal capital of Kuala Lumpur, and the civil service was unified with federal heads for each department of government. The residents remained and state councils retained legislative powers and control of their own budgets, after paying a share of their revenues to the central government.

Maxwell left Malaya to be governor of the Gold Coast in 1895 and died two years later. The triumphant Swettenham became resident-general of the new Federation and subsequently rose to be governor of the Straits Settlements and high commissioner of the Federated Malay

States. The separation of colony and peninsular states which began largely as a tussle of private ambitions was to have important repercussions, since the Federation developed independently of the Straits Settlements Colony and was constantly on its guard to preserve its freedom from Singapore.

1. Winstedt. R. O. and Wilkinson. R. J. 'A history of Perak *, Journal of the Malaysian Branch, Royal Asiatic Society,* XXII (1). 1934. p. 102.

CHAPTER 13

Nineteenth-Century Borneo

Northern Borneo in the Early-Nineteenth Century

By the beginning of the nineteenth century Brunei had been in decline for 200 years. Its opposition to Spanish conquests in the Philippines in the seventeenth century involved it in wars, in which it lost control over its northern provinces so that the rulers of Sulu took the chance to cut free. They themselves were fervently Muslim and even more bitterly in conflict with the Spaniards, but after Spain gave up its attempts to sub-jugate the southern islands in the mid-seventeenth century, Sulu turned its attention to disputing Brunei claims to the northern part of Borneo. Sulu was an aggressive state, the homeland of the dreaded Balanini pirates, who, with the Illanuns of Mindanao, roamed the seas and ravaged the Borneo coast and as far afield as the Straits of Melaka and Riau archipelago.

By the early-nineteenth century Brunei could lay claim only to the district centring on Brunei town itself, the Sarawak river, and the western coast of northern Borneo, and even there exerted only a weak control along the coastal strip and the lower reaches of the main rivers. Brunei town was little more than a centre for pirates' loot and slaves, a shrunken shadow of its former self. In the mid-eighteenth century it could still boast some 40 000 inhabitants, including a community of Chinese pepper planters, and it traded regularly with China, but over the years this legitimate trade dwindled, so that by the 1830s its popula-tion had declined to about 10 000 people.

Brunei's government was still organized in principle as a typical Muslim–Hindu Malay sultanate, with four great chiefs and a hierarchy of lesser nobles, or *pangiran.* It was not a centralized polity but com-prised a group of individual river states ruled by *pangiran,* some holding a river valley by hereditary right, others by the sultan's gift. As in the Malay peninsula, some fortunately-placed and enterprising *pangiran* were wealthier than the sultan, commanding more labour or more revenue from river tolls or poll taxes.

The population was mixed. Of the coastal Muslims a few had migrated from Sumatra or the Malay peninsula, others were part-Arab adventurers, but most Borneo 'Malays' were indigenous Kedayans or

155

Melanaus living in the lower parts of the rivers, who were converted to the Muslim religion and had adopted the Malay language and way of life. The swidden farmers in the middle reaches of the rivers usually rejected both the religion and lifestyle of the coastal peoples.

Huge areas of Borneo were still uninhabited in the middle of the nineteenth century. The lower reaches of the Mukah and Oya rivers were peopled by Melanau 'Malays', who produced sago for the Singapore market. But apart from this thriving area, the vast region centring on the Rejang river, the present Third Division of Sarawak, was virgin jungle supporting only isolated communities of upriver Kayans and Kenyahs.

By the mid-nineteenth century Iban swidden farmers were the largest ethnic group in the territory which forms modern Sarawak. The Ibans originated from the Kapuas river basin of Indonesian Kalimantan, but in the early-sixteenth century families began to migrate across the low hills into the present-day Second Division of Sarawak. Settling first along the Batang Lupar river, new migrants spread to the Skrang, Bangat, Saribas and Rimbas rivers, and by the early-nineteenth century began to spill over into the Rejang valley.

The Ibans occupied the middle reaches of the rivers, practising a shifting cultivation based on dry rice, sago and roots. The deep peat of Sarawak's plain made it impossible to grow wet rice, so that Iban migrants could not develop permanent agriculture and had to move frequently to allow the nutrients in the soil to replace themselves. As swidden farmers, the Iban retained their pioneer social organization of nuclear family groups living together in longhouses and did not evolve more sophisticated political institutions. Long-settled families acquired prestige, but the Ibans did not merge into tribes and had no chiefs, no *rakyat* class nor slaves.

In the early years there was plenty of virgin land, so that Iban immigrant groups did not come into conflict with each other, but by the early nineteenth century the heavy influx of new Iban migrants led to skirmishing over land and to widespread head-hunting. Head-hunting was practised by other Borneo peoples but most widely by the Iban, who prized human heads as trophies in love and war.

Apart from Brunei town and the Mukah and Oya sago-exporting districts, economic development was confined to the Sarawak river basin, the present First Division of Sarawak, which was more favoured by nature both in fertility and in mineral deposits. The comparatively rich earth, which included pockets of volcanic soil, encouraged sedentary agriculture and settled village life among the Land Dyaks of the hilly interior. The district was also rich in minerals, notably gold and antimony. Hakka Chinese gold miners moved into the Bau district of the upper Sarawak river from western Borneo, which in the eighteenth century had developed into a thriving gold-mining area. High quality

Raja Sir James Brooke. Portrait by Sir Francis Grant, 1847 *(By permission of the Trustees of the National Portrait Gallery, London).*

antimony was also discovered in the Sarawak valley in 1824. Land Dyaks organized by Brunei chiefs worked the ore and the export trade was handled by Armenian merchants in Singapore.

Brunei chiefs, who came to the Sarawak valley to exploit its comparative wealth, established Kuching in the early-1830s, and the town soon grew to about 800 inhabitants. But the extortions of the young and vigorous but greedy governor Pangiran Makota, drove the Malay chiefs and Land Dyaks to rebel. The feeble-minded Sultan Omar Ali Saiffuddin of Brunei could not cope with this revolt. In 1837 he sent his uncle, Hasim, regent of Brunei, to quell the trouble, but Hasim, himself middle aged and indecisive, could make no headway. The province was still in a state of armed rebellion in 1839, when an Englishman, James Brooke, arrived unexpectedly on the scene and changed the course of Sarawak's history.

James Brooke becomes Raja of Sarawak

Brooke, who was born in India in 1803, the son of an East India Company official, became a cavalry officer in the Indian army and was commended for gallantry in the first Anglo-Burmese war. But he was seriously wounded in that campaign in 1825 and after five years of slow recuperation in England was forced to resign his military commission. Brooke first visited the Straits Settlements and China in 1830-1 and came to the East again in 1834 when he made a financially disastrous trading trip to China.

Returning to England, Brooke remained fascinated by the East, an admirer of Raffles and convinced of Britain's mission to rescue the archipelago, 'this Eden of the Eastern Wave', from anarchy and poverty. In 1838 he published a prospectus outlining the need for Britain to establish territorial possessions in the East Indies, to develop commerce and promote Christian missionary activity. He bought another schooner and set off to investigate the potential of Marudu Bay at the northern tip of Borneo and thence to sail to Celebes, New Guinea and the eastern islands to explore and to study plant and animal life.

When Brooke reached Singapore in 1839, the governor, George Bonham, asked him to call at Kuching in order to deliver a message of thanks to the Regent Hasim for saving some shipwrecked British sailors and returning them to Singapore. The relationship between the East India Company and Brunei had always been friendly, and Singapore merchants, who were keen to build up the Sarawak trade, welcomed Hasim's gesture as an opportunity to establish a profitable connection. For his part Hasim hoped for English support in coping with the troublesome rebellion in Sarawak, and he received Brooke with every courtesy.

A man of flair, courage, humanity and charm, Brooke was the ideal diplomat in these circumstances, and he found Sarawak exciting and intriguing. Returning for a second visit on his way home almost a year later, he found the country still in revolt, and Hasim promised to give him the Sarawak river district and the title of raja if he helped restore peace. Brooke succeeded in bringing the rebels to parley and after considerable pressure and argument induced Hasim to keep his part of the bargain. In November 1841 Brooke became raja and governor of Sarawak, an area roughly equivalent to the present First Division, and he obtained confirmation of his title the following year when he made a ceremonial visit to the sultan at Brunei and paid the customary tribute.

While the Singapore merchants were delighted with Brooke's accession, the Straits Settlements' and British governments were embarrassed, fearing it might provoke Dutch opposition. But the Netherlands authorities, though angry at the encroachment of an Englishman into what they held to be their own sphere of interest, took no immediate action.

Brooke had acquired a unique opportunity to fulfil his ambition to take on 'the white man's burden,' but as yet had no conception of the magnitude of the problems which faced him. He needed money to develop the country and official backing to cope with the head-hunting and piracy which plagued its northern borders.

Large numbers of Iban had migrated to the region drained by the Batang Lupar and Saribas rivers and their tributaries. Normally Iban shunned contact with the coastal people and resisted adopting the Muslim religion or adapting to a sedentary life. When they encountered Malay officials who tried to collect taxes or exert some control over them, the result was usually violence and fighting. But the Iban who moved into the lower stretches of the Saribas, Batang Lupar, and Skrang rivers in the late-eighteenth century struck up a profitable partnership with local Arab and Malay chiefs and took to the sea as pirates, the Ibans primarily in search of heads and the Muslims of booty. Piracy appealed to the adventurous spirit of these people, who roamed the shores of north and west Borneo as far south as Pontianak. Since Westerners first encountered the Ibans as pirates, they called them Sea Dyaks, to distinguish them from the Land Dyaks of the inland region of the Sarawak river, but in reality the Iban were also an inland people who had only recently taken to the sea.

The Sea Dyaks and Brunei Malays practised piracy on a different scale from the Illanun and Balanini, who sailed in three-storied galleys rowed by up to 150 men and were prepared to attack even heavily-armed European vessels. In contrast the Borneo pirates kept close to shore and confined their attacks to Chinese, Bugis and other Asian craft. But they terrorized the Sarawak coast, and the sultan of Brunei was powerless to restrain them.

Brooke's friend and admirer, the firebrand Captain (later Admiral Sir) Henry Keppel of the Royal Navy, joined Brooke in punitive expeditions against the Saribas and Skrang Dyaks in 1843 and 1844, bringing the danger under temporary control. But in 1846 Brooke's very survival was endangered when, with the sultan's connivance, Brooke's ally, Raja Hasim, and all his brothers were slaughtered in a Brunei palace plot. The British Navy came to Brooke's rescue, and the sultan was compelled to confirm tenure in Sarawak for Brooke and his successors in perpetuity, to cede the island of Labuan to Britain, and to sign a treaty in 1847 undertaking not to cede any further territory without British approval.

In order to obtain recognition and support, in 1847 Brooke visited Britain, where his exploits and charismatic charm made him a romantic national hero. Lionized in London society, Brooke received a knighthood and was appointed governor of the Labuan crown colony and consul-general for Brunei. But the British government still refused to recognize him as Raja of Sarawak and put to one side his requests to make Sarawak a British protectorate.

London would provide neither protection nor financial backing, but

Brooke was reluctant to open up Sarawak to private capitalist development. His concern to shield the Dyak population brought him into collision with his London agent, Henry Wise, an enterprising businessman, who wanted to capitalize on Brooke's popularity in England and in 1848 formed the Eastern Archipelago Company to exploit Sarawak and Labuan. This soured his relationship with Brooke, who broke the connection, leaving Wise bitter and angry.

Meanwhile Brooke returned to set the pattern for 'white raja' administration: a paternal informal government, based upon consultation with local community chiefs, which aimed to preserve the best in local custom and to protect the country from what Brooke considered to be undesirable outside influences, both Western and Chinese. He regarded the Christian mission, which was established in Kuching, with mixed feelings, and its activities were confined to ministering to the Dyak community, avoiding any friction with Muslims.

At the beginning, in 1842, James Brooke had written, 'I hate the idea of a Utopian government, with laws cut and dried ready for the natives, being introduced . . . I am going on slowly and surely basing everything on their own laws, consulting all the headmen at every stage, instilling what I think is right — separating the abuses from the customs'.

While James Brooke was a warm, approachable character, the justice which he administered in person was based on a stern morality, and he expected utter devotion to duty on the part of his British subordinates, notably his two nephews, Brooke and Charles Johnson. Brooke Johnson came to Sarawak in 1848 as James's heir, the *tuan besar*, and Charles Johnson as *tuan muda* in 1852.

James Brooke used his own wealth to finance administration in Sarawak, but his fortunes shrank quickly. He showed little ability as a financier and Sarawak was constantly in debt. At first Labuan's prospects looked brighter. The island's coal deposits and apparent favoured geographical position made the merchants of Singapore nervous lest the new crown colony should steal Singapore's trade and become the dominant emporium. Labuan was intended as a commercial centre and coaling station but from the start the island was a disappointment, the coal of poor quality and the climate unhealthy.

Meanwhile fresh trouble brewed among the Saribas Dyaks, who were pillaging Melanau villages along the coast. With the help of the Royal Navy and some Malay and Dyak allies, in 1849 Brooke destroyed the pirate fleet at Batang Maru, near the mouth of the Saribas river. Only eleven of the ninety-eight pirate boats escaped, nearly 500 men were killed and 2000 others fled, of whom hundreds died before reaching their home villages. Brooke's expedition went on to burn villages up the Saribas and its tributaries. The battle of Batang Maru effectively crushed Saribas Dyak piracy, which never revived except on a small local scale. Brooke's victory was consolidated in 1853 when the new sultan of Brunei, Abdul Mumin, agreed to cede the troublesome Saribas and Skrang districts, which came to constitute the present Second Division of Sarawak.

The country was soon peaceful, and the Skrang Dyaks decided to throw in their lot with the raja's regime, but Brooke's activities were misinterpreted in London. The Royal Navy's role in dealing with the Illanun and Balanini, who were a menace to international shipping far afield on the high seas, was accepted, but the diversion of its activities against Dyaks was open to question, and a group of liberal members of parliament, urged on by Henry Wise and supported by a newly-formed Aborigines Protection Society, accused the raja of using the Royal Navy to slaughter harmless primitive people. When Brooke went on to help the Royal Navy in suppressing pirates in Marudu Bay in North Borneo in 1853, the cry for an official inquiry into alleged atrocities was taken up by the editor of the *Straits Times* in Singapore and by various Singapore merchants, who resented Brooke's reluctance to ease the way of businessmen in Sarawak. In England the adulation formerly lavished on Brooke turned to bitterness against a fallen idol, and a commission of inquiry was set up in Singapore in 1854. The investigation cleared Brooke's name but damaged his prestige and made it more difficult for him in future to call for British protection.

Soon he had to face a fresh crisis, this time from the Hakka gold miners at Bau, upriver from Kuching. The Bau community dated back long before the founding of Kuching or the Brooke takeover and had no wish to submit to European government nor to exploitation by Cantonese, Hokkien and Teochew traders settled in Kuching. The Chinese in Kuching were administered by their own headmen and had created no problem for Brooke, but his interference in the Bau opium trade and vain attempts to suppress secret societies there drove the Chinese miners to revolt. One night in 1857 they made a surprise attack on Kuching. Some of the raja's officials and their familes were murdered and Brooke himself escaped only by swimming across the river. The Chinese rebels then burned and pillaged the Malay quarter of the town, but the raja rallied his men and drove the rebels out with the help of Skrang Dyak reinforcements under the leadership of his nephew, Charles. The whole Hakka community, probably some 4000 strong, fled from Bau over the border. Brooke was shattered by the uprising, and the episode implanted in him and his nephew, Charles, a strong distrust of Chinese and a reluctance to let them settle in Sarawak.

Weighed down with anxiety and illness, Brooke visited England again in 1857 but once more failed to win over the British government into taking Sarawak as a protectorate. After receiving a similar rebuff from the Netherlands, he made tentative approaches to France. His strongest supporter was the very wealthy Angela Burdett-Coutts, who lent him a substantial sum of money in 1859, gave him a steamer in 1860, and became Sarawak's chief creditor.

News of fresh piracy and trouble which threatened the profitable sago trade of the Mukah and Oya coastal region brought Brooke back briefly to Sarawak in 1861, when he persuaded the sultan to cede to him the present Third Division of Sarawak. This brought peace at last to the coastal regions and also marked the end of the scourge from the Il-lanun, who made their last raid on Sarawak in 1862.

But by that time Brooke was worn out with years of exertion. A severe bout of smallpox in 1853 which nearly killed him, the strain and the accusations which culminated in the Singapore commission of inquiry in 1854, and the Chinese rebellion three years later, all combined to crush his spirit and undermine his powers of leadership. Always an emotional man, in his last years Brooke became increasingly bitter, disillusioned, unpredictable and given to irrational fits of anger. His administration disintegrated with family and succession squabbles. When the raja visited Sarawak for the final time in 1863 he quarrelled with and disinherited his heir, Brooke Johnson, and, leaving Charles in charge of the government, he retired that same year to England, where he died in 1868.

Despite the troubles of his final years, James Brooke could look back upon a life of remarkable achievement. Through imagination and courage he had preserved Sarawak through its early crisis of survival, extended its boundaries and put an end to extremes of lawlessness and piracy. His influence went further than Sarawak itself, since the impact of his personality and the informal, consultative type of government which he sponsored were strongly reflected in the residential system of the Protected Malay States; particularly in the work of Hugh Low, Brooke's staunch admirer, who had spent three years in Sarawak as a botanist before being appointed colonial secretary at Labuan.

Raja Charles Brooke

Charles Johnson, who changed his surname to Brooke in 1862, was a great contrast to his uncle. Remote, reserved, and spartan in his tastes, he was a man of few words and little social grace. Where James had been the darling of London society, Charles preferred the solitude of Sarawak's rain forests, where he spent the first ten years of his service, and was ill at ease even in the small-town atmosphere of Kuching.

Despite these differences in personality, Charles believed essentially in the tradition founded by his predecessor and used his own strong qualities to consolidate and improve the character of Brooke rule. James had laid down the rudiments of a government by consultation, but he was a poor administrator and a hopeless financier, leaving the state in debt. Charles's primary task was to organize an efficient administration and ensure solvency, but to do so without creating an expensive and top-heavy bureaucracy or opening up Sarawak to European exploitation and heavy Chinese immigration.

Frugal by nature, Charles insisted on strict economy and simple informal administration with a very small establishment. He kept a tight rein, driving himself and his subordinates to the limits of their energy, and insisting on officials sending him lengthy reports down to the most detailed minutiae. Service for European staff was hard, salaries meagre, living conditions rugged, and officials were discouraged from marrying and expected to serve for many years at a stretch without returning to Europe. Yet rigid and demanding though he was, Raja Charles commanded deep respect and devotion among his officials.

The country was divided into three divisions, each administered by a European resident with assistant residents and district officers, who might be European or Malay. Disputes among Malays, Chinese or Dyaks were generally settled by their own headmen, but difficult or intercommunal cases were judged by the residents, their assistants or by the raja in person, acting in accordance with customary law and common sense.

While the raja's authority was supreme, Charles continued and extended his uncle's custom of consulting local opinion. Residents lived close to the Dyaks and held councils to which local chiefs were invited. At the central level a Supreme Council, founded in 1855 and comprising the raja, the resident of the First Division and three or four leading Malays, met each month; and a Council Negri, created by Charles Brooke in 1865, which included senior European and Malay officials and leading Dyak chiefs, was called every two to three years to confirm major changes and discuss future policy.

Keeping public expenditure to a minimum, Charles managed by 1877 to pay off the state debt. From that time until the Second World War Sarawak's revenues rose steadily but slowly. Most revenue came from excise farms in opium and arrack, from royalties on minerals, particularly antimony, and from poll taxes. The state kept out of debt, but real prosperity was beyond its grasp. The comparative wealth of the Sarawak river region encouraged the Brooke family to think the whole territory was potentially rich, but this proved to be false. The Second and Third Divisions were acquired for security reasons, and apart from the sago-producing district of the Oya and Mukah they had no export trade and were an economic drain. Few mineral deposits were discovered apart from the antimony of the First Division, the dense rain-forest terrain made communications difficult, most rivers were only navigable by small craft, and the peat-bog plains which comprised much of the territory were unsuitable for agriculture. Sarawak never became self sufficient in rice. It exported sago, pepper and gambier in small quantities, but plantation agriculture was dogged by failure throughout the nineteenth century, and attempts to grow tobacco, sugar-cane, coffee and tea all collapsed.

Private enterprise was discouraged, both European and Chinese. The British-owned Borneo Company, formed with James Brooke's blessing in 1855, was the only European concern permitted to operate in Sarawak in the nineteenth century. It led the way in agriculture and mining but made no profit until 1898. By the 1880s Charles no longer regarded the Chinese as a security risk and from that time provided some funds to subsidize Chinese immigration. He admitted the value of Chinese settlers in opening up the economy and providing a source of revenue but was determined that they should not dominate the economy, as they did the Malayan tin industry.

In his early days in Sarawak, Charles had been occupied chiefly in trying to suppress fighting and head-hunting among the Iban, and he created the Sarawak Rangers, a Dyak field force, to keep order in 1862. He adopted the dangerous practice of pitting one community against another, leading co-operative downriver Dyaks in head-hunting expeditions against warring inland groups. This use of violence to produce peace paid off, and by the late-1870s the interior was largely pacified. The only subsequent serious disturbance came in Ulu Ai in 1893 when Banting, a Dyak of humble origin, set himself up as leader of the Batang Lupar Dyaks and launched attacks on other longhouses. The trouble was not finally suppressed until 1907.

It took much longer to remove the underlying causes of Iban friction, to persuade them to settle down to a permanent way of life and to induce a sense of cohesion. Charles Brooke tried to do this by appointing new *penghulus* with responsibility for longhouses dispersed along whole stretches of rivers, but producing a sense of identity was a slow process.

Sarawak, Britain and Brunei

While James Brooke had persistently sought the formal protection of Britain or another friendly European power, by 1868 Sarawak's position was secure, it could count on British support, and Charles was eager to retain its independence and if possible to extend its authority. Border troubles had led the Brookes to expand into the Second and Third Divisions, and the problems of the 'turbulent frontier' impelled Sarawak into further pressures on Brunei. From 1868 Raja Charles tried to extend Sarawak's rule over the lawless upper Baram area, the scene of recurrent friction between Sarawak people and Brunei traders. But the raja's wish was opposed by London and by successive British governors of

Labuan, who saw Sarawak's expansion as a threat to the development of their own colony.

Despite the fact that initially London upheld Brunei against Brooke encroachment, Sultan Abdul Mumin sought a counterweight to British power. In 1865 he granted a ten-year lease on a concession covering present-day Sabah to Charles Lee Moses, the American consul, who had arrived in Brunei the previous year. Moses obtained backing from American and Chinese businessmen in Hong Kong, who formed the American Trading Company and established a farming and trading settlement at Kimanis, about ninety kilometres north of Brunei town. But the venture was dogged by sickness and by bickering among the partners. It was abandoned in 1866 and the American consulate closed two years later.

While this American interlude came to nothing, it showed the sultan's unwillingness to enforce the 1847 treaty, which forbade the cession of territory without British approval, and alerted Britain to the possibility of rival powers intervening in North Borneo.

The British North Borneo Company

In 1875 the American Trading Company was bought by Baron von Overbeck, Austrian consul in Hong Kong, who went into partnership with a British businessman, Alfred Dent. In 1877 Brunei gave them sovereignty over Sabah in exchange for an annual payment, and since the sultan could not in practice exert his sway in the region, which was also claimed by the sultan of Sulu, Overbeck and Dent made a further agreement with Sulu in 1878 to ensure their title. In 1881 Dent bought out Overbeck's share and that same year the British government, alarmed at the possibility of German or French interest in North Borneo, granted Dent a royal charter to form the British North Borneo Company.

This chartered company was the first since the formation of the East India Company at the beginning of the seventeenth century, but its charter was radically different from that of its defunct predecessor. The prototype for several chartered companies formed to develop other parts of the British colonial empire in the final years of the nineteenth century, it was in line with Britain's growing enthusiasm for imperial expansion, when it sought to extend its influence as cheaply as possible but through the medium of its own people rather than through friendly rulers.

The Company was permitted to administer North Borneo, provided it gave facilities to the British navy, and it could not transfer its rights without the British government's approval. It was not given a monopoly of trade, nor was it allowed to interfere with local religion or customs.

Alfred Dent *(By courtesy of the Sabah Information Department)*.

Britain's attitude to Sarawak's relationship with Brunei also began to change. Up to that time London had frowned upon Charles Brooke's attempts to extend his domain at Brunei's expense and in 1874 rejected Charles's proposal that it should either take Brunei under its own wing or, failing that, put the sultanate under Sarawak's protection. In the next few years the climate of opinion in London altered. Labuan was written off as a hopeless disappointment, and Britain became worried about foreign ambitions in the region: Spain's conquest of Sulu in 1882; and the activities in North Borneo of Italians, Germans and the Austrian, von Overbeck. It was concerned too about the Brunei succession, since Sultan Abdul Mumin was approaching his hundredth year but had no designated heir. In 1882 Britain at last gave approval for Charles Brooke to obtain cession of the Baram basin, which became the Fourth Division of Sarawak, and two years later he acquired the Trusan valley.

Now only the heartland of Brunei remained, eyed enviously by both Sarawak and the British North Borneo Company. But Britain did not want to see Brunei disappear and decided to assume paramountcy over the whole of northwestern Borneo. In 1888 Brunei, Sarawak and North

Borneo became British protectorates, the governor of the Straits Settlements was appointed high commissioner for Brunei and agent for Sarawak and North Borneo. The crown colony of Labuan was handed over to the British North Borneo Company.

But the British government did not appoint a resident to the Brunei court, and Sarawak continued to press on the sultanate. In 1890 the local chiefs of the Limbang district of Brunei, which had been in a state of rebellion and virtual independence for the past six years, asked Raja Charles to take them over and rescue them from Brunei's misrule and exactions. The sultan did not acknowledge the cession, but Charles united Limbang with the Trusan valley to form the Fifth Division of Sarawak. London offered to pay compensation to the sultan but the offer was never taken up, so that the British government came to regard this as a cession by default and in 1916 formally acknowledged Limbang as part of Sarawak.

For a time it looked as if Sarawak might swallow up the whole of North Borneo. The Company faced such financial difficulties in its early years that in 1894 it offered to sell part of its territory to Sarawak. Brooke was eager but the terms he proposed were too exacting. The deal was abandoned but in 1905 the Company gave up the Lawas valley to Sarawak, and the following year transferred Labuan to the Straits Settlements.

This completed the territorial arrangements in British Borneo, and the appointment in 1906 of a British resident at the Brunei court, with a brief to advise the sultan and reform the state, brought suspicions and friction between the three protectorates to an end.

Sarawak and North Borneo in the Early-Twentieth Century

By the beginning of the twentieth century Sarawak had achieved peace, stability and a modest prosperity. Oil was found at Miri in 1895 and the Sarawak Oil Company, a subsidiary of the Shell Oil Company, began to exploit this resource in 1910. The introduction of rubber from 1905 provided the first successful plantation crop.

Despite Sarawak's status as a British protectorate, its raja continued to enjoy full internal autonomy with no check on his autocratic powers, and Charles ended his days in an aura of respect amounting to veneration. In 1916 he handed over charge of the government to his eldest son, Vyner, and died in England the following year at the age of eighty-seven. Raja Charles's half century of rule had brought Sarawak to its territorial limit and established efficient administration, a sound financial basis, peace and order.

Against this favourable background the quality of life in Sarawak had improved, though with the minimum of social change or dislocation, and the different communities still lived in isolation having little contact beyond their own river valley. Raja Charles gave some cautious encouragement to education, opening the first government Malay primary school in 1883, and by the early years of the twentieth century there were two government Chinese schools and a multi-racial secondary school.

By the end of Raja Charles's reign, Kuching was an orderly and pleasant small town, boasting mission schools, offices, churches, a hospital, a museum, recreation club, a race track and golf course.

In North Borneo the Company did not enjoy Raja Brooke's freedom of action and was still struggling for survival in the early years of the twentieth century. Its activities were subject not only to the control of the high commissioner in Singapore and the Colonial Office but also of its London directors. The appointment of the Company's governors was subject to the British government's approval, and the first two governors were seconded from the Malayan Civil Service.

The capital of North Borneo, first established at Kudat, was transferred to Sandakan in 1883, and in the same year an advisory council was established on the lines of a colonial legislative council. It appeared as if the territory would conform to a typical crown colony pattern. But the financial tribulations of the infant Company, culminating in the abortive negotiations to transfer North Borneo to Raja Brooke in 1894, led the Company's directors to exert a stronger control and to rush through an ill-conceived and premature programme for economic exploitation. To effect this they removed many experienced colonial officials and appointed a 'new broom' as governor in the person of Leicester Beaufort, a London lawyer, who held office from 1895 to 1900. Beaufort's extravagance, particularly an over-ambitious west coast railway scheme, necessitated new and unpopular taxes, which in turn deterred progress. In 1900 the Company reverted to appointing governors from Malaya but the directors continued to interfere, and in 1904 Governor Sir Ernest Birch, son of Woodford Wheeler Birch and formerly resident of Negri Sembilan, was dismissed at the directors' insistence for suggesting that the Colonial Office should convert North Borneo into a crown colony to save it from their meddling. The position improved in 1910 with the death of William C. Cowie, the most domineering of the board of directors, after which North Borneo reverted to colonial-type administration.

Initially development centred in the northeast, where numbers of tobacco plantations were established in the 1880s and 1890s, but with the introduction of rubber early in the twentieth century the planting industry gravitated to the west coast, where transport facilities were better.

The Company met with comparatively little violent resistance in imposing its rule. The Kadazans, or Dusuns, who were the largest and longest-settled indigenous group, were for the most part leading a

Mat Salleh *(By courtesy of the Sabah Information Department).*

sedentary village life. The semi-nomadic Muruts, swidden farmers and on occasion head-hunters, who had moved north from Kalimantan over the past two or three centuries, showed more resistance and in 1915 staged a local revolt. But they soon came to accept the Company's presence and continued to lead an aloof life in the hilly interior. In many ways the most difficult people to assimilate were the restless and aggressive Muslims of the coast: the Illanuns from the southern Philippines, the Sulus and Bajau. It was Mat Salleh, a part-Sulu, part-Bajau minor chieftain from eastern Sabah who caused the Company most trouble. Mat Salleh's collision with the Company's officials in 1895 began as a misunderstanding but escalated into a widespread rebellion, in which he raised the standard of revolt on the west coast and in the interior. Fighting dragged on until Mat Salleh himself was killed in 1900, and final mopping up operations were completed in 1902.

Despite their differences in experience, there were strong similarities between Sarawak and North Borneo in this period. Both showed economic progress but could not rival the spectacular advances of the western Malay states. Sarawak had few natural resources, North Borneo's were still to be opened up, while their primitive communications and lack of capital held back the economy. Both Sarawak and North Borneo discouraged foreign enterprise and at first provided few attractions to immigrant labour. Whereas Chinese flocked eagerly to the Malay peninsula, special inducements had to be offered to bring immigrants to the Borneo territories. The Company, the north Borneo tobacco companies and Raja Charles Brooke all offered financial assistance to Chinese settlers from the 1880s. With the relaxed attitude towards immigration Sarawak's Chinese population expanded more than tenfold between the 1880s and 1920. North Borneo's attempts to recruit Chinese labour from Hong Kong were at first less successful, since most immigrants wanted to be traders not agricultural labourers, and the majority returned to China. It was only after 1903 that Chinese came to settle in appreciable numbers.

The Company's vicissitudes and the tussle between the London directors and colonial officials also left their mark on North Borneo's economic fortunes. The Company made little profit for its shareholders. For nearly twenty years it paid no dividend at all and it was only in 1909 that it began to produce a steady return of some 5 per cent.

Modest though their progress had been, both territories by the second decade of the century had achieved peace, stability, law and order with their local customs essentially preserved.

CHAPTER 14

Political Consolidation, Economic Expansion and the Plural Society, 1896–1918

The Federated Malay States

The federation of the Protected Malay States in 1896 led quickly to more unified government, increased official activities and economic expansion. As resident-general during the first five years, the vigorous Swettenham succeeded in centralizing administration in Kuala Lumpur and making it more efficient. The civil service, judiciary and police force were streamlined and federal departments created to deal with public works, posts, land, education and other matters. More sophisticated government services brought an influx of British administrators, teachers, engineers, doctors and others.

Swettenham continued to give priority to improving communications. Existing local lines were joined to form a trunk railway, which by 1903 linked Prai in Province Wellesley to Seremban and by 1909 was extended to Johor Bahru. Port Swettenham, the present Port Klang, was opened to traffic in 1901 and a new west-east road constructed from the new port through Kuala Lumpur to Kuantan.

The new system of communications boosted economic enterprise. Tin mining continued to be the major economic activity, particularly in Perak, where the Kinta valley, after its centre at Ipoh was linked with Telok Anson by rail in 1895, overtook Larut as Malaya's main tin-producing district.

Tin

Until well into the twentieth century the Chinese continued to dominate the tin industry. The misfortunes of European attempts to break into the Selangor tin industry in the 1880s deterred further Western investment for a generation. Most Chinese tin mines were small labour-intensive ventures in which owners often worked alongside their employees. With the exception of the Sungei Lembing lode mines near Kuantan, tin came from alluvial sources, which were easy and cheap to

171

exploit by open-cast mining, given an abundant labour force. The first stage of mechanization, involving the introduction of the steam engine and centrifugal pump in the 1880s, led to a rapid expansion of tin mining during the last twenty years of the nineteenth century, and by 1904 the Malay states produced half the world's tin.

After the formation of the Federation, European capital soon began to encroach into the Chinese tin preserve, particularly in the Kinta valley, bringing new mechanized methods such as the gravel pump introduced in 1906, and the tin dredge which was first used in the Kinta valley in 1912. While the Chinese readily adopted the gravel-pump process they left dredge mining, which involved considerable capital outlay and technological expertise, to the big European companies. In 1913 Chinese mines still accounted for 74 per cent of Malayan tin output, but from that time dredging increased in importance until eventually it became the dominant mining method.

Commercial Agriculture

While the tin industry continued to be the major revenue earner until the end of the nineteenth century, commercial agriculture also flourished as peace and stability came to the peninsular states. Gambier, pepper, sugar and coffee cultivation spilled over from the Straits Settlements into the protected states in the late-1870s, but the dramatic expansion of agriculture came in the last years of the century, encouraged by greater security, improved communications and transport facilities, favourable land laws and advances in public health.

With the exception of the Province Wellesley sugar industry, the Chinese dominated most forms of export agriculture throughout the nineteenth century, both in the Straits Settlements and the Malay states: pepper and gambier production, which spread from Singapore to Johor in the 1840s and to Selangor and Negri Sembilan in the 1870s, reaching a peak in the last two decades of the century; tapioca planting, which spread from Melaka to Negri Sembilan in the 1870s. Even in the sugar industry, while European planters were predominant in cultivation and processing from the mid-nineteenth century, Teochew farmers who had first introduced sugar to the district shortly before the British occupation, continued production alongside their bigger European competitors and from the 1870s also moved into the Krian district of Perak.

Gambier, pepper and tapioca cultivation represented slash and burn agriculture on a big scale with an eye to quick profits rather than long-term settlement. European cultivators established the first permanent plantation system, although traditional Western methods of wide planting and regular weeding were unsuited to tropical conditions. Europeans also encountered labor difficulties, which did not trouble the

Chinese who relied on secret societies and clan links for a constant supply of recruits.

It was many years before Western planters found an ideal crop. While sugar continued to be fairly profitable up to the latter years of the century, it was confined to Province Wellesley, and European ventures into spices in Penang, and sugar and spices in Singapore, all ended in failure. For a time prospects for coffee planting looked more hopeful. When blight destroyed Ceylon's coffee plantations in the 1870s, European planters moved to the Protected Malay States, coming first to Perak, then in 1880 to Sungei Ujong and the following year to the Klang valley of Selangor, which became the centre of the Malayan coffee industry. Malayan coffee enjoyed a boom in the 1890s, reaching a peak in 1897, but suddenly collapsed in the face of competition from Brazil. The rather poor-quality Liberian coffee which was the only type suitable for Malayan tropical conditions could not match Brazil's better-quality Arabian coffee.

Rubber

While Brazilian rivalry destroyed the Malayan coffee industry, salvation also came from Brazil in the form of rubber. Brazilian rubber seedlings were sent to the Singapore Botanical Gardens from Kew in 1876, but it was Henry Ridley, appointed director of the gardens in 1888, who first recognized their commercial potential. After many experiments he discovered the most satisfactory method of tapping rubber trees, but planters and officials, notably Frank Swettenham, ridiculed 'Mad' Ridley's campaign to try rubber as a commercial experiment. His first success came in 1895 with a Melaka Chinese planter, Tan Chay Yan, and the following year the Kindersley brothers planted some rubber on their Selangor coffee plantation.

Faced with sudden ruin, in the late-1890s desperate coffee planters turned to rubber just at the time when the need for rubber in the electrical and infant motor car industries produced an upsurge of demand. In 1897 Malaya had only 140 hectares under rubber, but from about 1904 rubber planting became popular. When Ridley retired in 1911 the area under cultivation had increased to 250 000 hectares and by 1920 to one million hectares, by which time Malaya produced 53 per cent of the world's rubber.

Rubber was the perfect crop for Malaya, hardy and disease resistant, capable of growing in a variety of soils and conditions; on undulating land, properly drained alluvial plains or even on abandoned worked-out land. Estates developed along the road and rail communications which had initially been laid down to service the tin industry. Within a few years most prime sites in Melaka, Perak, Selangor and Negri Sembilan had been taken up, and rubber planting spread to Johor, southern

Henry Ridley *(By courtesy of the Arkib Negara Malaysia).*

Kedah and Kelantan as railways or roads were extended into these states, although poor transport facilities at first inhibited the industry's growth in Pahang and east coast states.

During the first two decades of the twentieth century demand for rubber exceeded world supply, and prices soared. European investment, mainly British but also French and others, poured into the Malayan rubber industry, and by the outbreak of the First World War rubber had overtaken tin as the Federation's main revenue earner. Since cultivation required a large capital outlay and afforded no return for a number of years while the young trees grew to maturity, rubber was first grown on large estates. But over the years peasants adopted rubber as a supplementary crop and by 1917 small holdings produced as much as the big plantations.

Rubber supplanted earlier forms of commercial agriculture. Sugar and tapioca, which both went into decline in the 1890s, gambier and pepper, which fell off in the early-twentieth century, had all sunk into insignificance by the time of the First World War. Chinese farmers diverted their attention to rubber and formed a number of companies, notably in Melaka. But, as in the tin industry, it was European enterprise, in the form of Singapore agency houses representing London-based public companies, which soon came to lead in export-oriented agriculture. The new developments in the economy by-passed the Malay ruling class, which had sometimes in the past taken an active part in promoting commercial enterprise, as in the case of the Temenggong Ibrahim of Johor in the mid-nineteenth century gutta-percha, gambier and pepper trade, or the Kedah aristocracy in late-nineteenth century large-scale rice production. In the twentieth century they were left behind by the big European joint stock companies and the tight Chinese family trade networks.

Initially European plantations suffered from labour shortages, since Malays preferred to remain on their own land and take up rubber cultivation as an adjunct to their own traditional farming, while Chinese immigrants chose to work on their own account or for their countrymen on Chinese-owned estates, tin mines or in the towns. European rubber estates came to rely primarily on Tamil immigrants, who had formerly supplied the labour force for the Province Wellesley sugar plantations and later for the Selangor coffee estates.

The southern Indians, who came in their thousands to the Straits Settlements and protected states, were even more transitory than the Chinese, and in order to ensure a steady supply, the colonial authorities negotiated an agreement with the Indian government to import indentured labour. Such labourers were permitted to work on the land or on the construction of roads and railways but not in the mines. They were recruited initially for periods of three to five years to work on particular plantations or projects, after which they could return to India or take up alternative employment. Indentured labourers began to arrive in Perak, Selangor and Sungei Ujong in 1883, but it was the rubber industry which brought them in vast numbers. In the first decade of the twentieth century the Indian population in the Federated Malay States almost doubled, nearly all of the immigrants coming to the three western states.

Since indentured labour was often of poor quality, some estates turned to a *kangany* system, sending a foreman to India to enlist recruits who were given a free passage. But this could not meet large-scale demands for labour, and in 1907 the federal government stepped in to take a more active role. They established a British official as agent in Madras to supervise recruitment, and set up an Indian Immigration Fund to which Malayan estate owners contributed. This financed the recruitment and transport of labourers, who were then allowed to take up employment on any estate. The practice proved more satisfactory for employers and workers alike, so that the indentured system rapidly declined and was finally abolished in 1910. The following year the Federated Malay States set up a Labour Department and in 1912 codified existing labour legislation, covering both Indian and Chinese labour. This code was enforced and was brought up to date from time to time. It laid down minimum standards in housing and medical treatment, and during the 1920s was extended to ban Indian child labour and provide for a certain measure of education. It protected labourers from excessive exploitation or cruel treatment but was weighted in favour of employers, who sought security for their capital investment and a steady labour supply, so that life on the estates was hard, wages were low, and living conditions spartan.

Public Health

The rapid expansion of the rubber industry owed much to a dramatic and timely breakthrough in the battle against malaria, which was the main killer disease in the Straits Settlements and the Malay states. The role of the mosquito in spreading malaria was discovered in 1899, and Dr Malcolm Watson, who arrived in Klang as government medical officer two years later, experimented with draining and spraying swamps, which effectively reduced the disease. Watson's methods were

Sir Malcolm Watson *(By courtesy of the Arkib Negara Malaysia).*

subsequently adopted as regular practice, and, together with the widespread use of quinine, kept the disease within manageable bounds.

At the same time the Institute of Medical Research, which was founded in Kuala Lumpur in 1900, was able to make strides against beriberi, the second most deadly scourge, which had decimated Chinese tin miners living on a basic diet of polished rice. During the early decades of the century some success was achieved in battling against plague, cholera, yaws and smallpox, and in the isolation of lepers.

Opium smoking was gradually brought under control and its worst excesses eliminated. In response to mounting pressure from Baba Chinese reformers and the Chinese Chamber of Commerce in Singapore, an Opium Commission was appointed in 1907 to investigate the problem of addiction. As a result of its report, in 1910 the government abolished the opium tax farm and itself took over responsibility for production and sale of opium, thus ensuring quality control, although opium was still widely used and continued to provide the largest single source of government revenue up to the 1920s.

Peasant Farming

In its eagerness to promote rubber and later oil palm, the colonial government neglected Malay peasant agriculture. During the nineteenth century *padi* or rice planting had expanded appreciably, spreading from the middle reaches of the rivers and from undulating land to the more difficult but fertile coastal plains as in Kedah, Melaka, and Province Wellesley. While rice growing continued to thrive in Negri Sembilan, it advanced more spectacularly in the Siamese-protected states in the north, which produced 83 per cent of the peninsula's rice in the early years of the twentieth century and exported it to other states. Kedah was the major rice-producing region, stimulated by demand from Penang and the west coast states and aided by an enterprising aristocracy which led the way in directing irrigation and drainage works.

In the first decade of the twentieth century the British promoted some works, notably the Krian irrigation scheme in northern Perak, but this was an exception and after 1910, apart from a brief flicker of interest in food production during the First World War and the Great Depression of the early-1930s, official policy neglected peasant subsistence farming in favour of promoting cash crops. Government revenue was employed to improve communications, transport and health facilities in rubber and tin districts, not to further irrigation, drainage or the eradication of disease in rural areas, where the standard of living remained low.

Peasants themselves, in the Malay states and to a lesser extent in the Borneo territories, tended to neglect *padi* growing and divert part of their land to more profitable crops. Immigrant Indonesians at first grew coconuts, as in Lower Perak and west Johor, and later turned to rubber cultivation. The result was that, while rubber brought widespread prosperity, food production was neglected, and with the rapid expansion of population concentrated in the export-oriented sector of the economy, Malaya relied ever more heavily on imported foodstuffs.

Industry

By the late-nineteenth century Malayan trade had switched from the former luxury exotic products, such as spices, gold and pepper, to basic commodities such as gambier, coffee, tin and later on rubber. These led to processing industries, particularly rubber manufacturing and tin smelting.

The Straits Trading Company was founded in 1887 to smelt tin ore. The first modern tin smelter was constructed at Telok Anson and moved to Singapore in 1889, while a new smelter opened at Butterworth in 1902. These not only processed ore from the Malay states but imported ores from the Netherlands Indies and southern Thailand to form the basis for Malaya's first industry.

Oil became the third most important commodity in Singapore's trade. A tank depot was set up on Pulau Bukum at the end of the century. Subsequently Dutch and British oil interests in the region united to form the Shell Company and by 1902 Singapore was the oil supply centre for the Far East.

Economic Progress

The Straits Settlements blossomed in the last quarter of the nineteenth century. After many years in decline Melaka now supported a prosperous agriculture, especially with the advent of rubber. Penang profited from the rich Perak tin trade and from the rapid economic development of the Eastern residency of north Sumatra, particularly when Acheh's long drawn-out war against the Dutch came to an end early in the twentieth century.

But the most spectacular expansion was in Singapore, which became the trade outlet and the financing and servicing centre for operations in the Malay states, and a major port in the chain of British commercial stations extending from the Mediterranean, through Suez and the Red Sea, via India and Penang on to Hong Kong and the Far East. The Suez Canal consolidated Singapore's pre-eminence and the primacy of the Melaka Straits route in east-west international trade. It gave an immediate boost to Singapore's trade, which increased from a little over £stg58 million in 1868 to nearly £stg90 million in 1873.

Despite British suspicions about other Europeans powers' colonial ambitions, the spread of Western imperial control opened up the region to new commercial possibilities. These were encouraged by more liberal trade policies, which Spain introduced in the Philippines in the 1830s and the Dutch in the Indies from the 1860s; by the French colonization of Indochina; by the opening up of Thailand through the Bowring treaty of 1855 and of China through treaties in 1859 and 1860 at the end of the second opium war; by the British annexation of upper Burma in 1886 and the development of Burma's export rice trade; and by the growing primacy of steam over sail, which meant that from the 1880s the bulk of international cargoes were carried in steamers.

The Straits Settlements, and particularly Singapore, became the headquarters of shipping companies, business firms and agency houses which financed and serviced agriculture and mining in the Malay states. From the 1860s Chinese businesses, which were often small concerns based on family or clan associations, formed networks of connections with other ports all over the Nanyang, and with Hong Kong and Shanghai, developing by the twentieth century into big trading empires. Singapore was an excellent centre for such operations, by virtue of its geographical situation and freedom from restrictions.

Western enterprise was virtually confined to Singapore and Penang up to the 1880s, but by the last decade of the century European and Chinese business interests sometimes combined to exploit the opportunities in the Malay states: notably the Straits Steamship Company, which was registered in Singapore in 1890 and came to dominate the regional carrying trade. Singapore's port facilities were modernized in the first two decades of the twentieth century to cope with the growing volume of international trade. Economic expansion following the formation of the Federated Malay States in 1896 and the extension of the trunk railway line through Johor, gave a further boost to Singapore's prosperity, but it also bred a sense of suspicion and jealousy on Kuala Lumpur's part towards Singapore and a reluctance to be drawn into its orbit.

The Northern States

The Federation's progress in its early years was impressive, leading to a concentration of power in Kuala Lumpur and in the hands of the resident-general, as Swettenham had intended. He was promoted to be governor and high commissioner in 1901, at a time when Joseph Chamberlain was at the height of his power as secretary of state for the colonies, and popular enthusiasm for imperial expansion reached its peak in Britain. In tune with the times, Swettenham favoured bringing the remaining Malay states into the Federation, including the northern territories which acknowledged Siamese suzerainty.

In the late-nineteenth century King Chulalongkorn was strengthening his hold over Thailand, modernizing the state, centralizing the administration and trying to bring outlying provinces more firmly under Bangkok's control. This tendency would normally have brought Thailand up against the similar expansionist and centralizing policy of the British in Malaya, but the Thais wished to avoid a clash and the British were anxious to preserve Siam as an independent buffer between British Malaya and French Indochina. The northern Malay states were caught between the Siamese and the British. Siamese rights in the individual states varied and were not strictly defined. Kedah and Perlis were more directly under Siamese control than the east coast states, and Kelantan more firmly under Bangkok's wing than Trengganu.

By the turn of the century Kedah had recovered from its earlier disasters and was exceedingly prosperous. Penang provided a good market for Kedah's agricultural produce and the thirty years leading up to 1910 saw a major expansion in its rice industry, in which the ruling class led the way. Since it was difficult to extract the customary forced labour when Kedah's peasants had been accustomed throughout the nineteenth century to take refuge in Province Wellesley whenever demands on their labour became excessive, it was necessary instead to develop capitalist investment. After land registration was introduced in the 1880s, land ownership came to be regarded not merely as a source of labour but as real property with an intrinsic monetary value of its own, and this encouraged the emergence of a rich peasant class. The royal family and ministers followed up their drainage and irrigation schemes by ploughing back revenue from rice exports into further agricultural development. By 1910 Kedah had a commercialized export economy, based in part on rubber and tin mining in south Kedah, but predominantly on rice cultivation dominated and financed by the traditional indigenous ruling class. At the same time rice milling and marketing were the preserve of a sizeable Teochew Chinese minority.

Kelantan also flourished. By the early-twentieth century, it had recovered from the hurricanes and cattle plague which drove many peasants to migrate to Kedah and other states in the 1870s and 1880s, and abandoned fields were coming back into production. In addition to producing a small surplus of rice for export, it grew maize, sugar-cane, coconuts, and later rubber.

While Trengganu grew rice, pepper and coconuts, it relied less on agriculture and more on industries: silk and cotton sarongs, weapons, brass work and boats. In 1895 Hugh Clifford described Kuala Trengganu as 'the Birmingham of the peninsula' and at that time the town and its environs were the most densely populated region in the peninsula outside of the Straits Settlements. But already cheap imported cloth and metal goods were undercutting Trengganu's products, and by the second decade of the twentieth century its industries were in decline and many of its artisans forced to migrate to other states or to the countryside as farmers and fishermen.

Sultan Zainal Abidin III of Trengganu *(By courtesy of the Arkib Negara Malaysia)*.

During a period of energetic reform in Siam from the mid-1880s Bangkok tightened control over Kelantan and Trengganu. King Chulalongkorn paid two state visits to Trengganu in 1887 and 1889, the first occasions on which a Siamese king had visited the state, and Sultan Zainal Abidin III returned these in 1896. Early in his reign Zainal Abidin, who ruled from 1881 until 1918, revived the practice of sending the *bunga mas* to Bangkok, but he regarded this as a token of friendship rather than vassalage, and Trengganu received favours in return. In 1882, for instance, the Siamese sent relief after most of Kuala Trengganu was destroyed by fire.

Kelantan was compelled reluctantly to accept a Siamese resident commissioner in Kota Bharu in 1894, and in 1900 when the death of the childless Sultan Mansur led to a dispute for the throne, the Siamese installed their nominee, Tengku Long Senik as Sultan Muhammad IV. The new ruler was an unpopular choice, who needed the backing of Siamese troops to maintain his position.

Meanwhile renewed fears about ambitions of other European powers, particularly rumours of alleged German interest in establishing a naval base in the isthmian region, led Britain to make a secret convention with Siam in 1897, by which it promised Siam protection while Bangkok undertook not to grant concessions or cede territory in the peninsula to other powers. While Siam kept this bargain in rejecting German bids in 1899–1900 for the Langkawi islands, Britain became alarmed in 1901 at rumours that dissidents in Patani and Kelantan were looking for German support to throw off Bangkok's yoke.

Accordingly in 1902 Britain and Siam signed a further agreement, in which Bangkok undertook to supervise all dealings between Kelantan and Trengganu and foreign powers, and to exert stricter internal control by appointing Siamese government officials of British nationality to supervise administration in these states. Sultan Zainal Abidin of Trengganu resisted the appointment of such an adviser, despite Swettenham's attempts to get him to accept one in 1902 and again in 1903. But William Armstrong Graham was appointed adviser in Kelantan in 1903, and the British put pressure on Bangkok to appoint a British financial adviser to Kedah in 1905.

Graham remained adviser for Kelantan until 1909, during which time he carried out fundamental reforms in administration, the judiciary, police and prisons, created a public works department and overhauled the revenue system. He encountered much opposition, particularly from R. W. Duff, a British entrepreneur and former police officer from Pahang. After raising financial backing in England, in 1900 Duff obtained from the sultan of Kelantan a concession giving his Duff Development Company exclusive rights to develop an area amounting to one-third of the state of Kelantan. Bangkok ratified this agreement the following year, and the company began planting rubber. But Duff proved to be an embarrassment both to Siam and Britain, quarrelling with Graham and obstructing his work. Eventually the Duff Company gave up its administrative rights but remained on bad terms with Graham and also failed to make a profit.

Despite the 1902 agreement, the British suspected the intentions of German engineers who were making preparatory surveys in the isthmus region for a railway line to link the southern states with Bangkok. At the same time Britain's relationship with France was undergoing fundamental change in the face of the growing German threat in Europe. The Anglo-French *entente* of 1904 drew together the two former rivals, who endeavoured to remove sources of mutual friction overseas. Their agreement to ensure the territorial integrity of Siam's central Menam Chao Phraya basin opened the way to territorial adjustments in the border areas. A Franco-Siamese agreement of 1907, by which Siam transferred its eastern provinces to Cambodia, was followed in 1909 by an Anglo-Siamese treaty, in which Siam surrendered to Britain its suzerainty rights over Kedah, Perlis, Kelantan and Trengganu, in return for a large loan to construct the Bangkok–Alor Star railway line and Britain's promise to give up extra-territorial claims.

Despite their resentment at recent Siamese interference, the northern states were not pleased at the prospect of coming under the British wing. Kedah and Kelantan both petitioned against such a transfer, but none of the four rulers was consulted when the Anglo–Siamese treaty was made. In 1910 the British signed a further treaty with Kelantan, providing for the appointment of a British adviser of similar status to the residents of the Protected Malay States prior to federation. Under the terms of another treaty signed the same year Trengganu undertook to conduct its foreign affairs through the British and to accept a British agent with consular powers, though it resisted the appointment of a British adviser until 1919. No treaty was made with Kedah. The British sent a handful of officials in 1910 but left the general running of the state in charge of the Kedah Malay bureaucracy.

The transition to British rule was not plain sailing. In Kelantan and Trengganu the enforcement of the new land system and imposition of fresh taxes were opposed both by local chiefs who lost their powers to levy taxes and by peasants who did not understand the unfamiliar dues. In Kelantan the appointment in 1912 of a Singapore Malay district officer, who tried to tighten administration, and the substitution three years later of fixed land rents instead of customary levies in kind, sparked off a revolt led by an old man, Hamid Mat Hassan known as To' Janggut on account of his long white beard. To' Janggut, who was a respected local figure, more than sixty years old, a trader and son of a warrior, organized a boycott of the land tax and attracted some 2000 followers. The rebels destroyed the small town of Pasir Puteh, but fighting died out within a few weeks when To' Janggut himself was killed, after which the state settled down to peaceful but slow development.

In all the northern states British protection brought improvement in revenue collection, land administration, police, health and schools. In Kedah British officials supplied backing to an already well-developed civil service, and in Kelantan the British adviser expanded the work begun by Graham in the first decade of the century. The most marked advance was in Trengganu, where Sultan Zainal Abidin III, though a devout and well-meaning ruler, had left executive government to ministers, chiefs and favourites, many of whom were exacting and greedy. In 1911, under British pressure, the sultan drew up a written constitution, which provided for a state council, and in 1913 the British agent was admitted to this body. J. L. Humphreys, who became British agent in 1915 and worked for ten years in Trengganu, first as agent and from 1919 until 1925 as British adviser, made considerable improvements. Until 1920 he was the sole European official in

Trengganu but during the 1920s several others were appointed. Humphreys also worked in co-operation with Haji Ngah, who became *mentri besar* (chief minister) of Trengganu in 1917 and held the office for more than twenty years.

Johor

By 1910 the pattern of British administration was established, boundaries finally drawn both in the peninsula and Borneo, and the process of expansion virtually complete. Only Johor retained internal autonomy, although it had surrendered the right to control its foreign relations under the 1885 treaty. Neither the British government nor the Straits authorities pressed for the acceptance of the British consular officer provided for in that treaty during Abu Bakar's lifetime, nor did they seek to draw Johor into the Federation, which came into being shortly after his death. While Sultan Abu Bakar was extravagant and spent much of his time in foreign travel, living in flamboyant style, Johor was peaceful and stable, giving no excuse for British interference. The British had fewer inhibitions about putting pressure on his successor, Ibrahim, an inexperienced young man aged twenty-two at the time of his accession in 1895, who inherited his father's expensive tastes without his diplomatic ability to court officialdom in Britain or his skill in playing London against Singapore.

For ten years the young sultan pursued an independent line, urged on by his astute, English-educated cousin, Abdul Rahman bin Andak, who became secretary to the Johor government in 1893 and ruled the state during Ibrahim's frequent absences. Abdul Rahman's determination to uphold Johor's independence irritated and alarmed the British authorities. Ibrahim resisted proposals to extend the railway through Johor and he signed away large land concessions to people in England, but the British put pressure on him to sign a Johor Railway Convention in 1904 and to dismiss Abdul Rahman three years later.

The extension of the road system and completion of the railway in 1909, coinciding with the rubber boom, induced British companies to extend their activities to Johor. Numbers of European planters moved into the state, and in 1910, anxious to establish more formal control over development, the British authorities persuaded Ibrahim to accept a British general adviser of rather vague status. In 1914 they used the excuse of a critical report by a prison commission about conditions in Johor Bahru to compel the sultan to give his British adviser powers similar to those of the residents in the Federated Malay States.

Despite this Johor was not drawn into the Federation and continued to enjoy considerable local autonomy. As in the northern states, there were few European officials. It retained its own civil service and government based on the 1895 constitution, in which the sultan governed in conjunction with the traditional ruling class.

Centralization of Government

The vague constitution of the Federated Malay States did not define the powers and functions of the central or state governments. From its inception British policy, as exemplified by Swettenham as

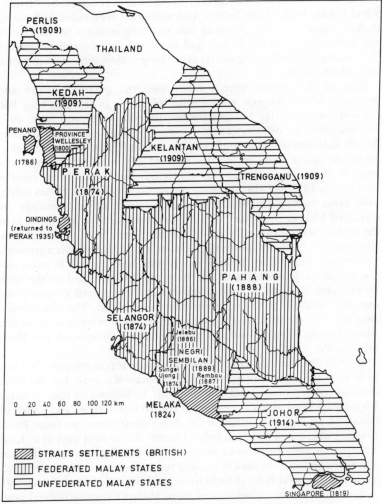

British Rule in the Malay Peninsula in 1914

resident-general and subsequently governor and high commissioner in the period from 1896 to 1903, was to draw the states together under unified administration, with the idea of eventually creating a central legislature and treasury.

Economic progress, the growing sophistication of government and the increase in the number of technical and specialist functions contributed further to the process of centralization, while the new communications systems, cutting across old physical divides, and new towns such as Kuala Lumpur and Ipoh, Seremban and Kuala Lipis by-passing the traditional administrative centres at Klang, Kuala Kangsar, Sri Menan- ti and Pekan, broke down former distinctions between individual states. Within a few years the grouping was an amalgamation rather than a true federation, and the British had in effect taken over direct rule of the country, subordinating nearly everything to the promotion of the tin and rubber industries.

Most of the sultans were content with the greater security and prosperity which the new system afforded them. In the past they had enjoyed great prestige but not necessarily real power and were often overshadowed by officers of state or enterprising lesser chiefs. Under British rule former chieftains became court officials or civil servants, while the rulers were set at the apex of Malay life, honoured and revered, their religious authority respected. But Sultan Idris, ruler of Perak from 1887 to 1916, the most politically vocal of the Malay rulers, soon came to criticize the federation. Swettenham had initially en- couraged Idris to push the case for federation with his fellow rulers on the understanding that they would win back their freedom of action by clipping the residents' powers. A clause in the federation agreement guaranteed that rulers' powers should not be curtailed in their own states, but in practice more and more authority passed to the more remote and inaccessible resident-general, who acquired greater power over the sultans than the residents had ever wielded. The Malay rulers were left with the external trappings and material rewards of authority, while British officials usurped many of the functions of the Malay aristocracy.

In 1897 the four rulers met together with great pomp for the first time in history at a durbar or rulers court in Kuala Kangsar, but the splen- dour of the ceremonial did not cloak the hollowness of their position. Idris complained about the extent of British interference and joined the sultan of Selangor, as rulers of the two richest states, to resist British pressure to create a common federal purse. At the next durbar at Kuala Lumpur in 1903 Idris spoke out more strongly against centralization. He again opposed the idea of pooling resources in a common treasury or creating a central federal legislature, and appealed for a loosening of federal ties and the admission of more Malays to senior official posts. John Anderson, who was appointed from the Colonial Office in Lon-

The first Federated Malay States durbar, held in Kuala Kangsar in July 1897. Seated (left to right): Hugh Clifford, resident of Pahang; J. P. Rodger, resident of Selangor; Sir Frank Swettenham, resident-general; Sultan Ahmad of Pahang; Sultan Abdul Samad of Selangor; Sir Charles Mitchell, governor of the Straits Settlements and high commissioner for the Federated Malay States; Sultan Idris of Perak; Yamtuan Tuanku Muhammad of Negri Sembilan; W. H. Treacher, resident of Perak *(By courtesy of the Arkib Negara Malaysia).*

don to succeed Swettenham, continued his predecessor's energetic policy during his term of office as governor and high commissioner from 1904 to 1911. He wanted to strengthen central federal government, bring the northern states and Johor into the Federation and draw together the Malay states, Straits Settlements and Borneo territories under tighter supervision. The idea of closer association appealed at the time to Singapore which suffered in 1908 from an acute commercial crisis while the Federation was enjoying a boom in rubber and tin.

Anderson was partially successful in his plans. He extended British protection to the Siamese states, put Johor under closer control, appointed a British resident in Brunei in 1906, became high commissioner for Brunei that same year and for Kedah, Perlis, Trengganu and Kelantan in 1909. He created a common federal legislative council in 1909 and replaced the office of resident-general by a chief secretary, who was intended to be a less senior official.

The Malay rulers approved the removal of the resident-general who had curtailed their freedom of action, but again they were disappointed, since in attempting to throw off the resident-general's control, they potentially put themselves at the high commissioner's mercy. It was not the rulers, but the high commissioner who presided over the federal council and nominated its members, so that the sultans found themselves mere advisers in the council.

In practice Anderson's reforms made little difference. His original intention in creating the federal council and demoting the resident-general was to put more power in the high commissioner's hands, to centralize the Federation and integrate the Malay states with the Straits Settlements, but by the last year of his governorship he realized this could not yet be done. The obvious unwillingness of the former Siamese states to join the Federation, the dissatisfaction on the part of Sultan Idris, the objections of Perak and Selangor to the idea of a federal treasury, and the refusal of the Colonial Office, now that Chamberlain was out of politics, to bring force or any undue pressure to bear, brought to an end the expansionist and centralizing policy which had dominated British policy in Malaya and Borneo during the previous thirty years.

From the beginning of the twentieth century until the Second World War, British policy, in principle, was committed to retaining or restoring the authority of the Malay rulers and to decentralizing some of the functions which had accumulated in Kuala Lumpur. But the implementation of this policy came only in fits and starts. After Anderson left in 1911, the constitutional issue faded into the background during the prosperous First World War years. In practice the chief secretary carried out the same functions as the former resident-general, and if anything the federal council only served to give him more authority.

The Plural Society

In the first twenty years of the twentieth century the population of the Malay peninsula including Singapore more than doubled, partly through natural increase and improved medical facilities but mostly through immigration from China, India and Indonesia.

The expansion of agriculture and tin mining in the Malay states and eastern Sumatra in the last quarter of the nineteenth century brought an influx of Chinese immigrants, highlighting abuses in the coolie trade which was run by Chinese secret societies. British and Chinese merchants were opposed to immigration restrictions, but the Straits authorities became increasingly concerned about blatant exploitation and the naked flaunting of secret-society power.

After secret-society riots which paralysed Penang for several days in 1867, the first measure to provide for registration of such organizations was passed in 1869, and in 1877 a Chinese Protectorate was set up in Singapore, with William Pickering as protector of Chinese and registrar of societies. The Protectorate was responsible for boarding incoming ships from China, discharging passengers who had paid their own passages, housing others in government depots until they obtained work, and registering employment contracts. In 1881 its work was extended to cover the supervision of Chinese women and girls, to register prostitutes, and offer a refuge to girls who had been sold or lured into prostitution.

The Protectorate marked a significant change from the previous *laissez-faire* policy. Over the years Pickering worked to undermine the secret societies' power by providing alternative arbitration for disputes, so that the societies lost their legitimate functions. In 1890 they were outlawed in the Straits Settlements and subsequently in the Federated Malay States and survived only as underground criminal 'protection' rackets.

Political upheaval in China and expanding employment opportunities in Malaya increased the volume of immigration in the early years of the twentieth century. Fifty thousand Chinese landed at Singapore in 1880, 200 000 in 1900, 227 000 in 1907 and 270 000 in 1911. Most Chinese immigrants intended to spend only a few years in the Nanyang, but the number of immigrants exceeded returning emigrants throughout the first thirty years of the century. While Chinese women came in increasing numbers, the vast majority of immigrants were still young adult males, and in 1911 the sex ratio among Chinese in Singapore was eight males to one female.

The Chinese were to be found mainly in the towns, the Federated Malay States and Johor. As early as the mid-nineteenth century Singapore and Penang were largely Chinese towns, and by the end of the century the Chinese were the largest community in Perak, Selangor and Johor. The majority of urban settlers were Hokkiens, particularly among the trading and shopkeeping community. Teochews were also primarily urban dwellers and were concentrated in the Straits Settlements and Kedah. Cantonese and Hakkas provided most of the labour force in the tin mines and the Chinese agricultural sector. The smallest and poorest community were the Hainanese, who comprised some 5 per cent of the Chinese in Malaya in the 1920s, most of them unskilled labourers and household servants.

The heaviest influx of Indians came in the first two decades of the twentieth century in response to demands for labourers on the rubber estates and in the construction of roads and railways. Until 1903 Penang was the sole port of entry for assisted Indian immigrants, most of whom settled on estates in Province Wellesley, the Federated Malay States and Johor.

Immigration from the Indies into peninsular Malaya, which had been going on for centuries, speeded up in the last quarter of the nineteenth century when peace came to the west coast states. As in the past, the bulk of the immigrants came from Sumatra; Minangkabaus, Bataks, Achehnese, Mandaling, Rawas, Korinchi, men of Siak and Palembang. But there were also Bugis, Banjermasi from Borneo, and many Javanese, together with Arab sheiks, many of them half-Arab-half-

Achehnese, who came in large numbers in the late-nineteenth century to escape the war in Acheh. A number of Riau Malays moved to the peninsula in the first decade of the twentieth century when the Dutch abolished the sultanate. Most Indonesian immigrants came to the Straits Settlements and the west coast states, while expansion in the Malay population in the northeast states, which were least affected by big migration movements, came about mainly through natural increase.

At the turn of the century about 7000 Indonesians came each year to Singapore, as the centre for embarking on the pilgrimage to Mecca. Some stayed for a lifetime, accumulating funds for the journey or working off debts on the return voyage. Most Minangkabau and Javanese came as rice farmers, and the majority of Bataks and Mandaling also settled on the land, but the Bugis and Rawas were mainly adventurers and traders.

Within the peninsula new opportunities encouraged interstate migration, which had always been a feature of Malay society; particularly among members of the large raja class, who inherited titles and aristocratic rank but not necessarily wealth, and among *hajis*, those who had acquired social and religious prestige by performing the pilgrimage to Mecca and often gathered together bands of followers to set up pioneer settlements and carve out a new role for themselves.

Indonesian immigrants usually came to settle and were less transitory than any of the other communities. While they came from mixed backgrounds, most shared a common Muslim culture and were close in customs, dress, food and lifestyles. The Sumatrans, who sprang from the same stock as peninsular Malays, assimilated most easily. Javanese and Banjermasi did so with more difficulty, but they also were Muslims and readily adopted the Malay language, which had been the lingua franca of the archipelago for centuries and used by the Dutch as the local language of administration in the Indies. Old hostilities between Bugis and peninsular Malays softened in face of the influx of the more alien Europeans, Chinese and Indians with their disruptive influences.

Indian Muslims sometimes married local Indonesian–Malay girls and were half assimilated into the indigenous population. But on the whole Indian, Chinese and European immigrants did not merge with the local population or with each other. In earlier times Asian intermarriage had been common and produced the Baba Chinese of Melaka and the Tamil/Arab/Malay communities of Kedah and Melaka. Of the Europeans, only the Portuguese actively encouraged their countrymen to settle down permanently and marry local wives, but many Dutchmen and early British settlers also took Asian brides. From the latter years of the nineteenth century, with the arrival of large numbers of Chinese, Indians and Europeans, intermarriage was frowned upon by all communities, each ethnic group seeking to preserve its own identity.

The different racial communities were divided in geographical distribution and in employment. Malay preference for remaining in their villages, following their traditional way of life as rice-growing peasants or fishermen, was consolidated by land reservation schemes introduced in 1913 to protect Malays from losing their plots to the land-hungry rubber industry. The Chinese concentrated in tin mining or Chinese-type agriculture or as shopkeepers in the new commercial towns, such as Taiping or Ipoh, rather than in older Malay administrative centres. Indians, mainly recruited under official schemes which forbade their employment in mines, were mostly to be found on rubber plantations or in transport, or, in the case of the better educated, as government clerks.

Education

Divided in language, custom, religion, dietary laws, marriage and funeral ceremonies and in employment, the communities were forced further apart by education. British policy, adopted first in the Straits Settlements in the early-1860s and extended later to the Protected Malay States, aimed to provide mass primary vernacular education for the indigenous population, with some provision for English-medium education among the elite, but the colonial power took no responsibility for educating immigrants in their native languages. Government-financed primary schools aimed to achieve literacy in Malay in a four-year course, and this system persisted up to the Second World War. After the Federation was formed the authorities tried to enforce primary schooling among the Malays, but such legislation remained a dead letter in the face of opposition from parents, who objected to the secular nature of the schooling, suspecting that pressure might be put on their children to adopt Christianity, and who also resented the loss of their children's earning power. Many Malay boys and most girls did not attend school at all and few stayed the full four years. In Selangor, where the authorities made special efforts to enforce attendance, in 1901 probably one-third of eligible Malay boys attended the government primary schools.

While a number of British officials worried about the poor quality of vernacular Malay education in the early years of the century, little was done to change it until the appointment in 1916 of Richard Winstedt as assistant director of education for the Federated Malay States with special responsibility for Malay schooling. As assistant director until 1921, director from 1924 to 1931, and president of Raffles College from 1921 to 1931, Winstedt devoted a large part of his long career in Malaya to education, specifically among the Malays. He improved teacher training, introduced special textbooks and incorporated practical training in basket-making, weaving and gardening. This system of education served its purpose in keeping the mass of Malays undisturbed in their

Sir Richard Winstedt *(By courtesy of the Arkib Negara Malaysia).*

traditional way of life, but was too rudimentary to enrich their appreciation of their own culture and did not qualify them to enter the mainstream of economic and social life.

The Colonial Office and most early-twentieth century British officials in Malaya discouraged the provision of wide-scale, English-medium schooling as being irrelevant, inappropriate and unsettling, but they wanted to educate upper-class Malays in the English tradition in order to absorb them into the administration. In 1890 William Maxwell, resident of Selangor, opened a 'raja school', which admitted twelve boys from the Selangor royal family.

To meet the criticisms levelled by Sultan Idris at the 1903 durbar and to train more Malays for government service, a Malay residential school was established in Kuala Kangsar in 1905, and in 1909 became the Malay College. Modelled on Britain's exclusive independent boarding schools, it restricted entry to upper-class Malays, including the sons of royalty and aristocracy from the unfederated Malay states, and was designed in particular to train an elite for the Malay Administrative Service, which was established in 1910. From 1921 onwards Malay administrative officials could obtain promotion to the more senior Malayan Civil Service, but only ten such appointments were made in the first ten years.

Some English-medium schools were established in the Straits Settlements and larger Malayan towns, usually run by Roman Catholic, Anglican and Methodist Christian missions. For many years even leading schools, notably Singapore's Raffles Institution and the Penang Free School, provided only primary education and did not expand into the secondary stage until the later years of the nineteenth century. English-medium schooling failed to meet the growing demand for clerks and junior officials, and a critical report by a commission of inquiry into English education in the Straits Settlements in 1901 sparked off moves to improve English education in the colony.

In the Federated Malay States English-medium schools developed slowly. Apart from a Central School set up in Taiping in 1883 and the raja school in Selangor, the first government English school was Kuala Lumpur's Victoria Institution founded in 1893. Unlike the privileged Malay College at Kuala Kangsar, government English schools in this period were mediocre institutions, educating middle-class children of all communities to be clerks and teachers. The majority of pupils were urban Chinese and Indians.

While in principle the colonial authorities did not undertake to provide immigrants with education in their own language, they subsidized Christian Anglo-Tamil mission schools and from 1905 set up a number of government Tamil schools in the Federated Malay States. They also encouraged employers to provide Tamil estate schools but did not force them to do so until 1923. Tamil education in government, mission, and estate schools was of rudimentary standard, only fitting pupils for unskilled labour.

Apart from one Chinese school established in Selangor in 1885, up to 1920 the British colonial authorities took no responsibility for providing Chinese schooling and the Chinese were left to organize their own schools. Chinese philanthropists provided a few dialect schools, which taught the classics by rote according to the traditional system, while some Chinese children attended English-medium schools, but during the nineteenth century there were few Chinese children in Malaya and little demand for Chinese-medium education. In the early-twentieth century Nanyang Chinese became interested in the movement to reform education in China. Under the influence of the exiled reformer K'ang Yu-wei, who spent a number of years in Singapore and Penang in the first decade of the century, 'modern' Chinese schools, including the first schools for Chinese girls, sprang up in the Straits Settlements and the major towns in the Federation. These were primary schools but offered an up-to-date curriculum, teaching in mandarin rather than local dialects. The first secondary or middle school was opened in Singapore in 1919, and numbers of others were established in other large towns during the 1920s, so that Chinese education was unique in providing the only opportunity in the vernacular schools to advance to the secondary level.

Education policy linked the English-educated upper classes of all races but for the masses it divided one ethnic group from another and created a rift between the elite and lower classes within each community: between the aristocratic Malay, schooled in the British tradition, and the English-educated Chinese or Indian professional man and white-collar clerk on the one hand, and the vernacular-educated Malay peasant, Tamil rubber tapper or Chinese tin miner on the other.

This was particularly marked in the Chinese community, where the new modern schools blurred former dialect differences but created sharper divisions between the Chinese-educated and the English-educated, Baba Chinese had assimilated fairly well into Straits society, marrying local wives, adopting Malay dress, evolving their own Malay patois, often attending English-medium schools and sometimes adopting Christianity. Upper-class Babas' familiarity with European ways and the English language gave them business contacts with the Western commercial sector and an entry to public life as legislative or municipal councillors. With the expansion of English-medium schooling more Straits Chinese entered English schools, and the most talented profited from the Queen's scholarships established in 1889 to send outstanding local students to universities in Britain. While there was no opening for English-educated Chinese in government administration, except at the clerical level, they entered the professions as lawyers, doctors and teachers, and Straits Chinese leaders drew closer to the colonial regime, founding the Straits Chinese British Association in 1900.

The Chinese Community and Chinese Nationalism

But in 1901 only 10 per cent of Singapore Chinese were Straits born, and immigrants, arriving in increasing numbers in the early-twentieth century, kept aloof and separate from other communities, clinging to their own customs and language, marrying only pure-blooded Chinese. Having no entree either to government or the Western professions, they concentrated in the business sector, where they had the reputation of being more aggressive and enterprising than their Straits-born counterparts.

Despite the growing divergence between the Straits-born and the China-born, and between the English-educated and Chinese-educated, the interest of Straits Chinese in their motherland was stimulated by improvements in steamship connections, by Chinese vernacular newspapers, of which the first was published in Singapore in 1881, and by Peking's newly-awakened interest in its countrymen overseas. After centuries of prohibition on emigration when the Chinese government had no contacts with overseas Chinese, the Manchus relaxed emigration restrictions in the 1860s and formally repealed the ban in 1893. Peking set up the first of a number of Nanyang consulates in Singapore in 1877 and from the 1890s used the Singapore consulate as the centre for harnessing the loyalty, money and technical skills of the Nanyang Chinese, in order to help bolster up China's economy against Western pressure and encroachment. The Singapore consulate collected funds for China throughout the Nanyang, sold Chinese honours and titles, and promoted cultural activities. In 1906 Peking set up a Chinese chamber of commerce in Singapore and in 1909 asserted the principle of *jus sanguinis,* which claimed all persons of Chinese descent through the male line as Chinese nationals, regardless of where they were born or how long their family had lived abroad. These demands on the loyalty of the overseas Chinese started a process which was continued after the fall of the Manchu empire and strengthened throughout the period of Kuomintang rule in China.

Straits Chinese leaders were excited by the Hundred Days' Reform which swept China in 1898, and the Straits Settlements provided a haven for exiled reformers, notably K'ang Yu-wei, who fled from China when the short-lived movement failed. Sun Yat-sen's revolutionary followers also came to the Straits Settlements and in 1906 set up a Singapore branch of the T'ung-ming Hui, or Chinese Revolutionary League. Singapore and Penang became the centre for Chinese revolutionary sympathies in the Nanyang, and Straits-born and China-born alike were exhilarated by the successful revolution which overthrew the Manchu empire in 1911. When the T'ung-ming Hui re-organized itself as the Kuomintang, took control in China and set up branches in the Nanyang, the Singapore committee included several eminent Straits Chinese, such as Dr Lim Boon Keng, the first Chinese Queen's scholar and a legislative councillor.

The Muslims and Reform Islam

While the Chinese in Malaya were engrossed in events in their homeland, many Malayan Muslims were caught up by the Reform Islam movement, which originated in the Middle East in the latter half of the nineteenth century and was brought to Malaya by a small Cairo-educated minority and by more numerous pilgrims returning from Mecca. The reformers, or *Kaum Muda,* sought to strengthen and purify Islam to enable Muslims to cope with the modern world in which they were being left behind. Most of the early leaders of the *Kaum Muda* movement were either Arabs or *Jawi-peranakan,* who were local-born

Dr Lim Boon Keng.

Muslims of mixed Malay-Indian descent. They set up schools and produced reformist vernacular Malay newspapers, notably *Al-Imam*, or *Leader*, which first appeared in 1906. With its stress on self reliance, the movement appealed primarily to Muslims in the Straits Settlements ports, particularly in Singapore, the centre of the Mecca pilgrim trade, focal point for Indonesian immigration and the economic and cultural centre for the Malayo-Muslim world in Southeast Asia at the turn of the century. The Malay vernacular press took root in Singapore but after the First World War the focus of the Reform Islam movement swung to Penang. It was less popular among rural Malays, since it challenged the sufist, syncretist form of religion, which had absorbed pre-Muslim *adat*, ritual, magical practice and the propitiating of spirits that was so strong a feature of Islam in rural Malaya. But in the towns the Reform Islam movement created greater differences between Malays and Chinese.

In 1921 the population of the Malay peninsula, including Singapore, numbered almost 3 300 000, of which approximately 49 per cent were Malays, 36 per cent were Chinese, and 14 per cent were Indian, with Europeans, Eurasians and other communities accounting for less than 1 per cent. In Singapore a little over three-quarters of the inhabitants were Chinese, a proportion which has remained almost constant from that time. Unrestricted immigration and expanding employment opportunities created a plural society in which ethnic communities lived separate, but not at that stage conflicting, lives although different education systems and diverging national interests were widening the rift. In the Borneo territories immigration increased in the early-twentieth century but had not changed the character of the population to the same degree, since employment opportunities were fewer and living conditions less healthy. In Sabah attempts to recruit Indians in the period 1887-1926 were unsuccessful, passages for Hong Kong Chinese had to be subsidized up to 1927, and to a large extent labour requirements were met by Javanese, recruited from 1907 as contract labourers, who made up one-third of Sabah's work force in 1921.

By the end of the First World War the economic pattern was established, with development concentrated in the Straits Settlements, the western Federated Malay States and Johor. The eastern and northern states, which had been the richest and most heavily populated region of the peninsula before the nineteenth century, had become sleepy backwaters, and the Borneo territories, where communications and facilities were less advanced, fell further behind the peninsular states in the race for economic progress.

CHAPTER 15

The Inter-War Years, 1918-41

Up to the end of the second decade of the twentieth century the history of the Malay peninsula under British tutelage seemed to be one of sustained economic progress, increasing administrative efficiency, and political calm, with little evidence of social dislocation or racial friction. Even the Malay ruling class's qualms about its waning political control were soothed by the compensations of wealth and security. While the indigenous population was protected in its possession of land and traditional way of life, immigrants provided plentiful and willing labour for developing the export economy. Mining and plantation agriculture supplied the bulk of the revenue, from which further improvements in administration and economic infrastructure could be financed, without imposing extra burdens of taxation on the peasantry.

But in the period between the two world wars many assumptions of official policy came to be questioned. These years were marked by economic uncertainty with periodic booms and slumps, since Malaya, as a primary producer, was heavily dependent on a fluctuating United States economy. Alien immigrants came to outnumber the Malay population, and more of these settled permanently in Malaya, raising the question of the government's obligations to provide education, social welfare and eventually to grant immigrants political rights. The assimilation of such large bodies of immigrants was more difficult since in this period they were often involved in and absorbed by political events in their mother country: in China, India and, to a lesser extent, the Netherlands Indies.

In view of these developments the *laissez-faire* economic policy and complete freedom of immigration were challenged in the inter-war years and the British authorities, the Malay ruling class and non-Malay Asians began to question the political structure.

The 1921 census revealed a spectacular increase in the immigrant population of Malaya during the preceding decade, and immigration continued to grow during the 1920s, reaching an all-time peak in 1927 when 360,000 Chinese came to Singapore. The Malay population's initial feeling of indifference to immigration turned to concern in face of the huge numbers who poured into the Malay states in the boom years of the mid-1920s. This developed into alarm when the 1931 census revealed that for the first time non-Malays outnumbered the indigenous population by 2 230 000 to 1 930 000.

China and the Malayan Chinese

At the same time the colonial authorities became increasingly concerned about the disruptive effects of Chinese nationalism upon the Straits Settlements and the Malay states. Prior to the First World War, the British deplored the remittance to China of funds which could have been employed in developing Malaya but were otherwise not concerned about the interests of the overseas Chinese in politics in China. Between the wars the British became increasingly worried at Chinese patriotism which was aimed against Japan, with whom the British wished to keep on friendly terms; and also at the potentially subversive influence in the Chinese schools.

In 1919 mass demonstrations among the Chinese protesting against Japan's acquisition of Chinese territory under the terms of the Versailles peace treaty spilled into violence in Singapore, Kuala Lumpur and Penang. Alarmed at the prominent part played by school students in these riots, in 1920 the authorities passed a Registration of Schools Enactment which, for the first time, gave them a measure of supervision over the Chinese schools. The law roused opposition from Chinese teachers and community leaders but was followed in 1923 by further attempts to bring Chinese schools under control when grants were offered, subject to supervision. In 1925 a second school registration Act empowered the government to refuse registration for teachers guilty of subversion.

The colonial authorities were also worried about the spread of communism among the Chinese community. In 1923 the Comintern, formed by Lenin to promote and control the international communist movement, set up a Far Eastern Bureau in Shanghai and worked to infiltrate the Kuomintang in China and the Nanyang. Communist agents came from Shanghai to Singapore in 1924 and established a base among the left-wing Kuomintang supporters in the Straits Settlements and the Federated Malay States. They concentrated in particular on Singapore night schools which attracted young Hainanese, the poorest of the Chinese communities. In 1926 a Communist Youth League was formed in Singapore, but when the Kuomintang broke with the communists in China the following year, only left-wing extremists remained loyal to the communist cause in Malaya. They formed a Nanyang Communist Party in 1927 but could attract little support. For a time the majority of Chinese in Malaya were content with their renewed prosperity and approved the Kuomintang's efforts in reuniting China.

For its part, the Kuomintang set out with renewed vigour and considerable success to woo the Nanyang Chinese. In 1927 it set up an education bureau to supervise Chinese education overseas. It supplied teachers and textbooks, and encouraged the use of standard Chinese rather than local dialects as the medium of instruction, thus helping to renew loyalties to China while breaking down provincial cultural barriers. The Kuomintang government also encouraged Malayan Chinese to send their children to China for education. In 1929 China passed a Nationality Law renewing the late Manchu claim that all Chinese descended through the male line remained Chinese nationals and could not throw off their citizenship. These moves met with an enthusiastic response, particularly among the China-born and Chinese-educated in Malaya. Teachers brought in from China had no experience of Malaya so that, at best, Chinese schooling did not fit children to adapt to their new country and was racially divisive, while much of the teaching was actively hostile to colonial rule.

Political Reform Proposals

The high prices commanded by tin, rubber, and other primary products produced a buoyant Malayan economy during the First World War but encouraged over production, particularly in the rubber industry, where ambitious planting schemes came into full bearing about the time the boom broke in 1920. Tin prices held fairly firm, but rubber, which had fetched a price of Straits $5 per pound in 1912, fell to 20 cents in 1922.

Since it was so heavily dependent on rubber and tin export taxes, official revenue slumped too, and in 1923 the government appointed a committee to consider cuts in official expenditure. On economy grounds the committee recommended a measure of decentralization in the Federated Malay States, and these proposals struck a chord of sympathy among the Malay rulers in the Federation. They had suppressed their objections to the loss of their political power during times of prosperity but now came to envy the comparative freedom of action enjoyed by their counterparts in the unfederated Malay states.

Decentralization proposals were put forward in 1925 by the high commissioner, Sir Laurence Guillemard, who suggested abolishing the post of chief secretary and handing over his functions to the residents and state councils. While the rulers welcomed these proposals, European and Chinese businessmen, miners and planters objected strongly, fearing decentralization would bring inefficiency and make the Federated States more dependent on Singapore. The press and the unofficial members of the legislative council voiced alarm, so that Guillemard felt obliged to compromise. The state councils were given wider financial powers, but the chief secretary remained and the federal council retained its legislative power, although it was enlarged in 1927 to include more non-officials and Malays. In addition to the one Malay member drawn from Perak as the premier state, three further non-official Malay councillors were brought in to represent the other three states. The council now comprised thirteen officials and eleven non-officials, all nominated by the high commissioner. At the same time the Malay rulers withdrew from the council. In future they were to sign laws passed by the council and to meet at an annual rulers' durbar.

Guillemard's successor, Sir Hugh Clifford, who had served in Pahang in the 1880s and returned to be governor of the Straits Settlements and high commissioner of Malaya in 1927 began his period of office by reaffirming the policy of keeping faith with the Malays.

The adoption of any kind of government by majority would forthwith entail the complete submersion of the indigenous population, who would find themselves hopelessly outnumbered by folk of other races, and this would produce a situation which would amount to the betrayal of the trust which the Malays of these states, from the highest to the lowest, have been taught to repose in His Majesty's government.

At the same time W. G. A. Ormsby-Gore, parliamentary undersecretary for the colonies who visited Malaya in 1928, noted in his report that 'Our position in every state rests upon solemn treaty obligations . . . they were, they are and they must remain Malay states'.

But Clifford was already ill when he came to office, and his three years as governor were a time of aimless drift. These years were crucial, since they coincided with the peak of prosperity, followed by the dramatic break in the American boom which plunged the world into the 'Great Depression.'

The Great Depression

In 1923 trade had begun to revive and by the mid-1920s Malaya was enjoying unprecedented prosperity. Tin prices reached a peak in 1926, and the price of rubber recovered to some extent as a result of a production restriction scheme adopted by Malaya and Ceylon in 1922, on the recommendations of the Stevenson Committee, set up to devise solutions to the industry's problems. The full benefits of restriction were limited by the refusal of the Netherlands Indies to join the scheme, but voluntary restriction brought some improvement in prices since Malaya and Ceylon between them had supplied 70 per cent of the world's rubber in 1922. In 1928 the price rose to 30 Straits cents a pound and the Stevenson scheme was dropped.

When the boom broke once again in 1929, Malaya was hard hit since the United States was its chief customer. Tin prices fell from £ stg284 in

1926 to £ stg120 in 1931, while rubber sank to an all-time low of less than five Straits cents a pound in 1932. Government revenue dropped dramatically. Thousands of planters, rubber tappers, miners and labourers were thrown out of work, many officials were retrenched and the remainder suffered severe wage cuts. The Depression caused widespread hardship at all levels of society and in all communities, even among subsistence peasant farmers who had grown a few rubber trees as a supplementary cash crop.

The Great Depression brought into the open long-standing fears about anomalies and problems in the economy, the plural society, the constitutional structure, and the impact of colonial rule on the nature of society.

The first priority was to put the economy back on its feet, to restore tin and rubber prices as quickly as possible, and to try, as a long-term measure, to diversify the economy in order to make Malaya less dependent on its two major products.

Restriction schemes, applied to both tin and rubber production, produced a short-term amelioration. In 1931 Malaya agreed to restrict tin production, along with the other main world producers, Bolivia, the Netherlands Indies and Nigeria. The agreement was renewed in 1934 and again in 1937, and tin prices recovered to hold fairly steady throughout the 1930s. After considerable wrangling, in 1934 all the major rubber producers, including the Netherlands Indies, Vietnam and Thailand, agreed to restrict production, and this pact was renewed in 1938. Rubber prices recovered to some degree but remained low up to the outbreak of the Second World War.

As a result of the Depression and the continuing need to compete in a buyers' market, the tin and rubber industries were forced to modernize and become more efficient. This speeded up mechanization in the tin industry and the dominance of dredge mining. Rubber estates merged into larger and more economic units, and the Rubber Research Institute, which had been founded in 1926, stepped up its work to improve the quality of rubber.

These developments strengthened the Malayan economy but had some painful social consequences. Rubber restriction schemes hit small holdings harder than the big, often foreign-owned, plantations. Similarly the large tin producers had a better chance of survival and by 1939 two-thirds of Malaya's tin mines were European owned and highly mechanized, consolidating a trend which had been going on for a quarter of a century. On the eve of the First World War Chinese producers still accounted for 74 per cent of Malayan tin exports, but in the next twenty years the Western public companies with large capital resources were in a better position to open up new tin-bearing lands. While Chinese producers remained active in the tin industry, by 1930 they were responsible for only 40 per cent of Malaya's tin exports and by 1939 for only one-third. Thus in a quarter of a century the tin industry changed from a predominantly Chinese enterprise comprising hundreds of small concerns to a predominantly European industry dominated by a few large companies.

Attempts to diversify agriculture made only modest progress, notably in palm oil and pineapples. Oil palms, which were first planted commercially in 1917, proved particularly suited to good well-drained soils in Perak and Selangor. The palm-oil industry was a Western enterprise, requiring considerable capital and a large estate, since palm oil needed to be processed in the immediate vicinity. Pineapples, which were the only crop suited to soggy soils, were grown in Johor, and supported a remunerative Chinese-owned pineapple canning industry. But it was difficult to find a crop as ideally suited as rubber to the Malayan soil and climate. Rice and other food crops were neglected, so that Malaya continued to import much of its basic food requirements. Nor were any steps taken to improve the fishing industry.

The Great Depression coming after a time of great prosperity created economic competition for the first time between the different racial communities, whose activities up till then had been complementary. In the towns Indians and Chinese competed with growing numbers of English-educated Malays for clerical jobs, while many unemployed immigrants moved to the country to try to wrest a living from subsistence farming.

Constitutional Change

In 1930 Clifford was succeeded by Sir Cecil Clementi, formerly governor of Hong Kong, a vigorous and determined leader, who tried to come to grips with the economic crisis and with long-standing constitutional and racial problems in Malaya and the Straits Settlements. His tenure of office was one of the most dramatic, controversial and unsettling in Malayan Communist Party, withdrew government grants from Chinese faced with problems of Chinese nationalism, Clementi intended to curb Chinese troubles in Malaya. He banned the Kuomintang, broke up the Malayan Communist Party withdrew government grants from Chinese schools, censored the vernacular press and imposed the first restrictions on immigration.

The Kuomintang had flourished under Clifford's lax rule, and Clementi's ban roused strong objections both from the China-born and Straits Chinese. So did his censorship of the vernacular press, which was predominantly Chinese, and the withdrawal of subsidies from vernacular schools, which were also mostly Chinese.

But the greatest objections came to the new immigration laws which were deliberately aimed at the Chinese. In 1930 Immigration Restriction

Ordinances imposed the first quotas on immigration into the Straits Settlements and Federated Malay States in an attempt to cope with the problems of unemployment brought on by the slump. Many unemployed immigrants returned voluntarily to their homeland, and the government repatriated many Indian labourers at government expense. During the early 1930s for the first time emigration exceeded immigration figures, and the numbers of new Chinese immigrants coming to Singapore fell from 242 000 in 1930 to less than 28 000 in 1933, of whom only 14 000 were young male adults.

The restrictions, though a startling departure from the Straits Settlements' traditional free immigration policy, were accepted as an economic necessity during the slump, but in 1933 the law was replaced by an Aliens Ordinance, which imposed permanent quota restrictions on non-British male immigrants. This law was aimed primarily at the Chinese, since Indians could enter freely as British subjects, and it roused the united objections of the China-born and Straits-born Chinese. The Chinese chamber of commerce protested, as did legislative councillor Tan Cheng Lock, descendant of a Baba Chinese family which had settled in Melaka three centuries before.

The government has no fixed and constructive policy to win over the Straits and other Malayan-born Chinese, who are subjects of the country, and foster and strengthen their spirit of patriotism and natural love for the country of their birth and adoption . . . One is driven to the conclusion that the Bill is part and parcel of an anti-Chinese policy, probably with a political objective, based on distrust and fear.

Clementi's immigration policy was in fact part of his plan to pull Malaya together into one efficiently administered country, to consolidate the general British policy of recognizing it as a Malay country and to revive Guillemard's attempts to give force to this principle.

The initial stage involved restoring to the Federated States the same control over domestic policy enjoyed by the unfederated states, after which Clementi hoped to draw together the Straits Settlements, the Federated and unfederated Malay states, and possibly the three British-protected Borneo territories, into a league.

With Colonial Office approval, at the ruler's durbar in 1931 Clementi announced plans to transfer responsibility for most departments from the federal to state governments, subject to the overall supervision of departmental directors in Singapore. The high commissioner proposed also to abolish the post of chief secretary and to incorporate the colony and all the peninsular states into one customs union.

These plans were warmly welcomed by the Malay rulers whose withdrawal from the federal council after 1927 led to further erosion of their powers, and the proposals also fell in with Colonial Office policy.

But they provoked an outcry; from Chinese in the Federated Malay States who did not want to be subject to Malay-dominated state governments; from Chinese, Indian and European business interests in the Federation who alleged the state councils would be inefficient, slow and corrupt, and who feared to be drawn into Singapore's orbit; and from Straits Settlements businessmen who did not want to sacrifice the free-port status of Singapore and Penang to a Malayan customs union.

The idea of a customs union was jettisoned on the recommendation of a committee comprising Straits Settlements businessmen and officials. But in view of the uproar in Malaya and queries in the British parliament concerning the rest of the proposals, in 1932 Sir Samuel Wilson, permanent under-secretary for the colonies, came to investigate the position. Despite widespread opposition, he upheld Clementi's view and reported that while a centralized federal government would make for economic efficiency, decentralization was 'probably the greatest safeguard against the political submersion of the Malays' and 'the maintenance of the position, authority and prestige of the Malay rulers must always be a cardinal point in British policy'. The decision was therefore made to decentralize in stages but to retain financial control at the federal centre.

Despite widespread protests the first stage of decentralization was put into effect. The post of chief secretary was abolished in 1935 in favour of a more junior federal secretary. The rulers came to play a more active role and the residents once more assumed effective executive leadership in each state. The powers of state councils were extended, including the right to legislate on some matters, and their membership was enlarged to bring in European, Chinese and Indian non-officials. By 1939 six departments had been largely transferred to state control: education, medical services, public works, agriculture, forestry and mining.

But there was no enthusiasm for proceeding to the second stage of constitutional reform envisaged by Clementi: to draw the different units together. The unfederated states, which enjoyed financial autonomy and considerable administrative independence, had no wish for closer integration. Nor was there any proposal to force them into any such union. As Sir Samuel Wilson had insisted, 'His Majesty's Government has no intention of requiring the ruler of any unfederated state to enter, against his will, into any kind of Malayan league or union'.

In the Straits Settlements colony the form of government remained essentially unchanged from 1867 up to the Second World War. Penang grumbled at Singapore's dominance but prospered quietly. The Straits Settlements Association, founded in 1868 to protect Straits commerical interests, had in its early years been a source of lively opposition, a thorn in the flesh of the Colonial Office and the colonial governor. After

calming down in the mid-1870s, it sprang to life in the early-1890s to
uphold Straits merchants' objections to allegedly excessive demands
made on the colony for defence expenditure, but from the late-1890s
the Association's interests became almost exclusively commercial. In
1920, in order to bring the Federated States within the scope of its activities, the Association was wound up and a British Malaya Association
formed in its place. But the Singapore branch of the Straits Settlements
Association refused to disband itself and in the 1920s became a lobby
for constitutional reform.

After the early years of friction during Ord's regime, colonial rule settled down in the mid-1870s to a placid routine. While preserving control by means of an official majority, the governors consulted non-
officials, particularly on matters of taxation, and a governor had to
report and justify any case where he overruled their unanimous opinion.
In practice the only real friction arose over the size of the military con-
tribution, and up to the 1920s there was no public demand for constitutional change.

In 1920 Sir Laurence Guillemard appointed a committee, which
recommended creating an unofficial, predominantly Asian, majority on
the legislative council, leaving the governor with the power to suspend
proceedings. The Straits Settlements (Singapore) Association, comprising mainly European members, welcomed this suggestion but it was rejected by the Colonial Office. As a compromise Guillemard introduced
changes in 1924, by which the legislative council was enlarged to
twenty-six members, with equal numbers of officials and non-officials,
leaving the governor with the casting vote. The Singapore and Penang
chambers of commerce were each allowed to nominate one non-official,
the rest being nominated by the governor on a racial basis: five Europeans, three Chinese, one Malay, one Indian and one Eurasian. The
governor then nominated two non-official legislative councillors to sit
on the executive council.

In 1930 the Straits Settlements (Singapore) Association called for an
executive council comprising equal numbers of officials and non-
officials, and suggested that non-officials should be elected by a panel of
British subjects. There was no popular support for these proposals,
which were 'a ludicrous scheme' and 'crass folly', according to the *Straits
Times,* giving too much power to European commercial interests.

By that time the major initiative in demanding constitutional reform
had passed to the Straits Chinese British Association, and notably to
Tan Cheng Lock, born in Melaka in 1883, a Melaka municipal councillor from 1912 to 1922, legislative councillor from 1923 to 1934, and
executive councillor from 1933 to 1935. In 1928 Tan Cheng Lock called
for an unofficial majority and direct election of representatives to the
legislative and executive councils by locally domiciled residents of all
races. Subsequently the Straits Chinese British Association of

Tun Tan Cheng Lock *(By courtesy of the Arkib Negara Malaysia).*

Singapore, Penang and Melaka petitioned Governor Clementi for the appointment of an additional Chinese legislative councillor to represent each of the three settlements and for a Chinese member on the executive council. The governor refused. Incensed by the discriminatory legislation on immigration and education during the Great Depression, Tan Cheng Lock and the Straits Chinese British Association continued to press for reform in the 1930s and tried to rouse support in the British parliament, but without success. Throughout the inter-war period constitutional reform remained the interest of only a small majority of Europeans and Straits Chinese without any public clamour to back them.

While all senior Malayan Civil Service appointments in the colony were restricted to Britons with European ancestry on both sides, some provision was made in the 1930s to associate Asians more closely in the middle range of administration. The Straits Medical Service was opened to Asians in 1932, the Straits Settlements Civil Service was created in 1934 and the Straits Legal Service in 1937. But they only provided a few appointments on the bottom rung of the ladder to the minority who could acquire the requisite qualifications, which normally meant university and professional training in Britain. In the Federation more Malays were appointed to government service in the 1930s and larger numbers were promoted from the Malay Administrative Service to the Malayan Civil Service. But the rulers of the Federated States stood firm against admitting non-Malay Asians into the administration, except to certain technical posts. On this the rulers supported the sultan of Selangor, who insisted at the 1939 durbar that immigrants had no rights but were 'privileged to live in peace and prosperity by the courtesy of the people of the country'.

The Straits Chinese leaders realized that the way to professional and ultimately to political success lay in providing better opportunities for higher education. They had been the force behind the opening of a medical school in Singapore in 1905, which became the King Edward VII College of Medicine, and in 1919 they persuaded the government to celebrate Singapore's centenary by founding Raffles College. The Straits Chinese and other local communities gave generously to the setting up of Raffles College as the nucleus of a university, which was designed to promote Malay and Chinese as well as English studies. But the government, and particularly Winstedt as director of education and principal of the college, was averse to creating a frustrated Western-educated Asian elite for whom there was little place in pre-war colonial society. After many delays the college finally opened in 1928, with a small annual intake of students, the vast majority of whom were destined for a teaching career in the English-medium schools. The colonial authorities had no enthusiasm for creating a university. In 1938 a commission headed by Sir William McLean recommended uniting Raffles College with the Medical College to form a university college but decision on this was deferred.

Most politically-active Chinese in Malaya were not concerned with local constitutional reform but with events in their own country, and after the Japanese invaded China in 1937 Singapore became the centre of the Nanyang Chinese National Salvation Movement. It was led by Tan Kah Kee, a Hokkien immigrant who came to Singapore in 1890 at the age of seventeen and made a fortune in business, which he devoted to educational and philanthropic works in China and Malaya, and to the support of Chinese patriotism.

The Sino–Japanese war rallied the sympathies of the China-born and Chinese-educated in Malaya and restored the fortunes of the Kuomintang and the communists which had been at a low ebb in the early-1930s. Both were illegal but the Kuomintang had formed underground branches after Clementi's ban, and in 1930 the Comintern set up a Malayan Communist Party in Singapore, whose objective was to set up a republic of Malaya. The organization was uncovered and broken up in 1932 but began to recover with the arrival of an Annamese Comintern agent, Lai Teck, who became secretary-general in 1934. The party infiltrated youth organizations and trade unions with some success and exploited labour grievances to promote a large number of strikes in 1936 and 1937, particularly among Hakka and Hainanese labourers and tin miners. Its most notable success was at the Batu Arang coal mine in Selangor, where the communists set up a soviet commune which had to be broken up by force. After the Chinese Communist Party joined forces with the Kuomintang in 1937 to form a united front against Japanese aggression, the Malayan Communist Party was able to exploit patriotism among the Chinese in Malaya and to infiltrate the national liberation movement. Anti-Japanese feeling mounted to fever pitch as the Japanese invaded southeast China, taking Amoy and Canton in 1938, and the following year the Nanyang Chinese National Salvation Movement reached the height of its power, organizing financial relief and marshalling recruits for the China campaign, leading boycotts of Japanese shops and goods. By the time the Second World War broke out in 1939, the Malayan Communist Party, although still illegal, could probably command an allegiance of some 37,000 members in Singapore and peninsular Malaya.

For the moment the party's growing strength was not reflected in active opposition to the colonial power, which took a more conciliatory attitude to the Chinese community after Clementi's departure. Immigration restrictions remained but in 1935 Clementi's successor, Shenton Thomas, allotted more financial backing to Chinese schools, including those which used mandarin as the medium of instruction.

Malay Nationalism

The growth of Malay nationalism was impeded in the inter-war period by the division of the peninsula into different states, the variety of Malay–Indonesian communities and the rift between the Malay elite and the masses. But an incipient sense of nationalism took root in the form of opposition to the threat of being swamped by alien elements, particularly the Chinese. The 1931 census revealed that in the Federated Malay States the Chinese were now the largest single community, comprising nearly 42 per cent of the population, with the Indians more than 22 per cent and Malays less than 35 per cent.

While British administration was benign and well meaning, its impact on the Malays was not entirely beneficial. The peasants were better off than their fathers or grandfathers but still remained at the bottom of the social and economic scale. They were freed from slavery and debt bondage, which was eliminated in Selangor and Perak in the early-1880s, in Pahang in the early years of the twentieth century and in the northern states in the following decade, finally disappearing in Trengganu in 1919. They enjoyed settled rents, low taxes, security in possession of their land and incentives to improve their property, but in general their incomes were low and they received no government help in

improving rice agriculture or in marketing facilities. Competition from
the more highly commercialized Burmese and Thai rice industries
depressed the price of rice. They resented exploitation by immigrant
middlemen in milling their rice and marketing their crops, fish and
other produce.

Only in Trengganu did discontent break out into violence in this
period when in 1928 an inland chief, Haji Drahman, an ardent Muslim,
incited peasants to refuse payment of land rent and briefly seized Kuala
Brang. But the rising subsided with the arrest and exile of its leader. It
was not a nationalist movement but rather a conservative backlash
against modernization, along the lines of To' Janggut's rebellion (see p.
183), thirteen years earlier. The *Kaum Muda* reform movement made
no headway in the ultra-conservative states of Kelantan and
Trengganu, where orthodox religious leaders held sway among the
peasants. Throughout the peninsula the Malay peasantry were docile
and not yet politically awakened.

While the English-educated Malay elite ruled in co-operation with
the British, they insisted on a 'Malaya for the Malays', and the liberal
Western education at the Malay College, followed by experience gained
in the state councils, bred a new generation of young independent-
minded Malay leaders. But the greatest change was among urban
middle-class Malays. Originally influenced by the Reform Islam
movement, which had been dominated by Arabs and Indian Muslims,
by the 1920s modern-minded Malays wanted to throw off external
Muslim influence. In 1926 the first Malay political association, the
Kesatuan Melayu Singapura, or Singapore Malay Union, was founded
by Mohammed Eunos bin Abdullah, 'the father of Malay journalism'.
Born in Sumatra in 1876, Eunos Abdullah, was educated at Raffles
Institution and began his career as a journalist in 1907. Appointed first
as a justice of the peace, in 1922 he became the first Malay municipal
commissioner in Singapore and two years later the first Malay legislative
councillor. Membership of the Singapore Malay Union was confined to
Malays from the peninsula and archipelago, excluding Arabs and
Indian Muslims. Most of the leaders were English-educated, middle-
class traders, junior officials and journalists, who wanted to improve the
Malays' lot, to win better opportunities for Malays in education and
employment. The Singapore Malay Union set up branches in Penang
and Melaka in 1937 and inspired the founding of Malay associations in
the peninsular states. In 1939 the first annual conference of Pan-
Malayan Malay Associations was held in Kuala Lumpur, forerunner of
the influential post-war United Malays National Organization.

The Singapore Malay Union leaders were conservative in outlook, not
seeking to produce a social revolution or to overthrow the colonial
regime, but to obtain more say and status within the existing system for
indigenous Malays, as distinct from alien Chinese, Indians or Arabs.

At the same time a more radical Malay left wing emerged among the vernacular-educated, many of them from humble backgrounds. Ironically many Malay radicals were graduates of the Sultan Idris Training College, established by Winstedt in Tanjong Malim in Perak in 1922 to train Malay teachers for the vernacular primary schools, which were designed to keep the Malays content with their traditional lot. To this end the college concentrated on practical manual subjects, excluded study of the English language and confined Malay studies to the primary level. Despite this, the college awakened students to Malay social problems, stimulated their interest in the more radical Indonesian nationalism, and revived sentiments of a common Malay–Indonesian tradition, which had been torn apart when the Anglo–Dutch treaties of 1824 and 1871 split the region into artificial units under British or Dutch control.

Pahang-born Ibrahim bin Haji Yaakob, who entered the college in 1929 at the age of eighteen, came into contact with Indonesian and Comintern leaders, such as Tan Malaka, who fled to Malaya after the abortive communist revolution in Indonesia in 1927. In 1937 Ibrahim bin Yaakob, together with Ishak bin Haji Mohammed, formed the *Kesatuan Melayu Muda* or Union of Malay Youth, which sought to achieve speedy independence for Malaya and to produce a more equal society. It opposed not only the British but also the Malay upper class in the peninsular states and the Singapore Malay Union in the colony for co-operating with the colonial regime and accepting social inequality. The *Kesatuan Melayu Muda* appealed to the vernacular-educated, many of them schoolteachers and journalists; to Malay graduates from the Technical School started in 1925, the Federal Trade School founded in 1926, and the Serdang College of Agriculture created in 1931, and in general to Malays who were frustrated by official education policy. By the 1920s many Malays, particularly in the towns, were losing their distrust of secular government schools and sought English-medium education for their children as the gateway to white-collar jobs, but only a minority of Malays could gain scholarships to English-medium schools, and only a handful of gifted Malay commoners gained entry to the Malay College in the inter-war period. Others wanted to improve the quality of Malay vernacular education and resented the government's refusal to open Malay secondary schools.

The Borneo Territories

Between the two world wars the Borneo territories drew no closer to peninsular Malaya, despite British protection and common control from Singapore. While the peninsula forged ahead in economic development and more sophisticated administration, the Borneo territories lacked the base for such development. Economic growth was deterred by poor communications, labour shortages and by the policy of the Brooke regime and the British North Borneo Company, both of which were reluctant to open up the territories to outside capitalist exploitation but lacked the capital to develop the region themselves.

In Sarawak government became more professional, less personal and less autocratic. This largely reflected the personality of Raja Vyner Brooke, the last white raja who ruled Sarawak from 1917 until 1946. Born in 1874, he had served in Sarawak since he was twenty-three years old and from 1904 had on occasion taken charge of the government in his father's absence. But Raja Charles had little confidence in his heir, thinking him an idle, extravagant playboy who spent too much time abroad. He preferred his more dependable younger son, Bertram, whom he insisted on associating closely with the government as *tuan muda*. In his political will, drawn up in 1913, Raja Charles urged his successors to spend most of their time in Sarawak, to devote their energies and resources to caring for their people, to keep free of debt, and he stressed that 'the state of Sarawak is not private property'.

Despite some resentment on Raja Vyner's part, the arrangement worked smoothly for many years. Bertram had no ambition to dominate Sarawak and worked amicably alongside his brother. Vyner Brooke lacked his father's strength of character. He was content to delegate responsibility and in some ways this eased the way to more modern and less personal administration. A chief secretary was appointed in 1923, a secretary for Chinese Affairs in 1929 and a chief justice in 1930. The governor of the Straits Settlements as chief agent for Sarawak interfered little, and administration proceeded peacefully at a simple level by consulting the indigenous people although making no formal provision for representation.

To mark the centenary of Brooke rule, in September 1941 Raja Vyner Brooke promulgated a constitution, under which he renounced his autocratic powers and would in future rule with the consent of the Supreme Council. The Council Negri was to become the legislature, meeting twice a year and having control over finance. The new constitution was intended to be the first step in moving to responsible representative government, but initially the councils were to comprise officials and non-officials nominated by the raja. Vyner Brooke created the new constitution on his own initiative, not in response to any public pressure, and the proclamation was received with general apathy. But the proposal was opposed by his brother, and by Bertram's son, Anthony Brooke, who saw it as a move to exclude himself from the succession. According to Sarawak law, leadership had to pass through the male line, but Vyner Brooke had no sons, Bertram was ill and living in London, and the raja was on bad terms with his nephew, Anthony, who joined the Sarawak service in 1936 at the age of twenty-four and was proclaimed *raja muda* three years later. For a few months he took charge of the government in his uncle's absence but his high handedness alienated older officials, four of whom resigned, and Raja Vyner withdrew his title.

At the same time Vyner Brooke came under the strong influence of Gerald MacBryan, an erratic and enigmatic character, who had started his career as a cadet in Sarawak in 1920, had resigned on several occasions but been re-appointed. In 1935 he became a Muslim, married a Sarawak girl and made the pilgrimage to Mecca. An expert on Malay and Dyak custom and steeped in their ways, MacBryan was disliked and distrusted by the European community and was deported in 1936. Four years later he was given permission to return briefly to Sarawak to deal with family matters, but in 1941 he suggested making a settlement of the Limbang problem by offering some amends to the sultan of Brunei, who had never formally acknowledged Sarawak's rights over the territory. Vyner was so pleased with MacBryan's handling of these negotiations that he appointed him his private secretary and subsequently chief secretary of Sarawak. This roused considerable opposition, particularly from Anthony Brooke, who suspected MacBryan was aiming to control the state himself by letting the succession pass to Vyner's daughters or grandson. Castigating the new constitution as an 'impersonal and revolutionary monstrosity', Anthony Brooke went to Singapore to protest in September 1941 and was dismissed from the service by Raja Vyner for abandoning his post.

The Colonial Office gave a cautious welcome to the constitutional change, which did not need their approval since it was an internal matter. London tried to persuade the raja to accept a British resident but he would agree to receive only a defence and foreign affairs adviser. An agreement between Britain and Sarawak to this effect was signed in Kuala Lumpur in November 1941 but the Pacific war broke out before it was published.

In North Borneo after 1910 the Company's London directors left administration largely under Colonial Office supervision and many North Borneo officials continued to be recruited from the Malayan Civil Service. Some attempt was made to increase local participation in administration, notably by Douglas Jardine, who was governor from 1934 to 1937. Jardine created a Native Chiefs' Advisory Council, reviving the custom of calling an annual conference of chiefs which had prevailed in the period from 1897 to 1917. Some advance was made in the provision of vernacular education for the indigenous Malays, Dyaks and Kadazans in schemes laid down in 1921, but there was even less opportunity for English-medium education than in peninsular Malaya.

On the eve of the Second World War the Borneo territories were peaceful, comparatively prosperous and healthier than in the past, since the first vigorous steps had been taken to combat malaria. The wealthiest region was the tiny state of Brunei, where rich new oilfields were discovered at Seria in the 1930s. It was ironic that the small area left unswallowed by Sarawak and North Borneo should prove to be the most richly endowed part of the old sultanate.

In both North Borneo and Sarawak rubber was the most important export product. In North Borneo the North Borneo Company was concerned with administration rather than commercial profit and never paid high dividends. In the period from 1925 to 1928 it paid out 1.5 per cent, with the onset of the slump it offered no dividend at all from 1928 to 1937, but revived a payment of 2 per cent between 1937 and 1941, which was a time of rising prosperity. The centre of economic development and population growth shifted from the east to the west coast, where the expensive white-elephant railway scheme now came into its own, as rubber estates grew up along the line.

Labour problems were partially solved during this period, with a fairly steady flow of Chinese, mainly Hakka, immigrants, so that by the mid-1930s about 8000 were arriving each year. North Borneo abandoned its assisted passage scheme for Chinese in 1927, ended Javanese contract labour arrangements in 1933, and in 1937 put the first restrictions on Chinese immigration.

Sarawak's economy was based on agriculture. Its oil production, which reached a peak in 1926, declined in the 1930s and the Miri field was almost worked out by the time the Pacific war broke out. The government tried to induce Ibans to lessen their dependence on hill rice by settling down to permanent wet-rice farming and by diversifying into rubber. But the Ibans were reluctant to abandon their traditions, and in general rubber planting appealed more to immigrant Chinese. In 1941 Sarawak laid down plans for agricultural expansion, to work through co-operatives of local small-holders under state encouragement, in keeping with the Brooke policy to retain Sarawak for the benefit of the indigenous population. Kuching intended to devote surplus revenue to agricultural development, but both Sarawak and North Borneo were hampered by shortage of revenue, particularly with the low level of rubber prices in the 1930s, and since they were not crown colonies they did not qualify for colonial development funds.

Eve of Second World War

On the eve of the Second World War the British territories in Southeast Asia could look back on decades of peaceful progress since the Straits Settlements became a colony in 1867 and the other states were successively brought into the British orbit. The population had been drawn within the pale of the administrative and judicial systems, British rule bringing security and peace everywhere, some measure of education and improvements in public health and medical facilities, particularly in the towns. In line with international agreements to supervise the distribution and eventually eliminate the use of opium, in the late-1920s, Britain pledged to suppress opium smoking in its Far Eastern territories within fifteen years. Restrictions on opium smoking were tightened up during the 1930s, civic improvements led to better health, and in Singapore the Singapore Improvement Trust, created in 1927, began slum clearance.

But progress was uneven. Malaya had the highest living standards in Southeast Asia and was more advanced than the Borneo territories. Within the peninsula the traditional role of the states was reversed in that Kelantan, Trengganu and to some extent Pahang were isolated and neglected, while the west-coast tin and rubber-producing states prospered. The railway system was extended to Kelantan in 1931 but did little to develop the northeast, and the road along the east coast was poor. Food crops were ignored in favour of mining and export agriculture, producing raw materials which did not encourage industrialization, except small-scale processing of rubber, tin, palm oil or pineapples for canning. Low-grade iron ore deposits, notably at Bukit Besi near Dungun in Trengganu which were worked from 1928, were exploited by the Japanese and shipped to Japan. Apart from small deposits of inferior coal at Batu Arang in Selangor, the peninsula also lacked energy resources to develop industry.

While the pattern of British administration and territorial boundaries was established by the first decade of the twentieth century with the governor of the Straits Settlements acting also as high commissioner for the Federated and unfederated states and Brunei and as British agent for Sarawak and North Borneo, the thirty years which followed produced little sign of unity. Despite the growth of new towns and communications systems, which challenged the identity of traditional societies, the Malay peninsula was still a collection of states without any sense of nationhood. Apart from Negri Sembilan, all the peninsular states as in traditional times were named after and centred on major river basins, retaining their individuality, so that state loyalty remained strong. In the Federated Malay States the decentralization policy of the late-1930s enhanced the sense of separateness, while the unfederated states had no official relationship with the Federation or with each other. Everywhere the isolation of Malay rural life encouraged parochial attitudes. Only English education cut across racial barriers in linking the elite, but this did not create a united nationalist force. For the masses a plural education system rose out of the plural society and in turn helped to consolidate it. And these divisions were accentuated by differences in culture, language, religion, employment, and political loyalties outside of British Malaya and Borneo.

CHAPTER 16

War and Occupation, 1941–5

From 1902 when Britain signed the Anglo–Japanese alliance and decided to concentrate its fleet to protect its home waters, it in effect handed over to Japan the major responsibility for defending Britain's Eastern empire. The First World War had little direct impact on Malaya. The German cruiser *Emden* raided Penang harbour in October 1914 but was destroyed a few weeks later. A mutiny among the Indian garrison in Singapore in February 1915 caused a momentary scare but was soon put down. Britain emerged on the winning side, but the First World War marked the end of its imperial expansion and, although it still seemed to be in complete command of its empire in Southeast Asia, it was in a sense on the defensive. Relatively its naval power was in decline, but in the inter-war years it attempted to add a significant strategic capacity to Singapore's role as a commercial centre.

Britain let the Japanese alliance lapse when it came up for renewal in 1921, and in its place the United States, Britain and Japan signed a Naval Limitation Treaty in Washington in 1922, by which the three powers agreed to limit the size of their navies and not to construct naval bases within an agreed zone. Britain's intention was to continue to keep its naval forces in home waters and if necessary to dispatch ships to the East to meet any threat to India, Australia or the Far East. It needed an Eastern base for docking and repair work and for this purpose in 1923 began construction of a naval base at Singapore, which was outside the restricted area laid down by the Washington Agreement. Singapore was too far away to be a threat to Japan, and the base was designed with a purely defensive intent, strategically placed to protect not only British territories in Southeast Asia but also the gateway to the Indian Ocean and to Australasia.

Work on the base proceeded slowly and was suspended in 1929 during the international slump but later resumed in face of Japan's increasingly belligerent policy in the Far East. In 1931 Japan occupied Manchuria, in 1936 it terminated the Washington Agreement and the following year it invaded China. From that time the construction of the Singapore base speeded up and was completed in 1941. Sited on the northern coast of Singapore island, it was ringed with fortifications and protected by a seaplane base and airfields.

Malayan defence plans rested on the premise that Japan was too far distant to launch any surprise attack, and that only sufficient military and air cover was needed to protect the naval base until reinforcements from the home-based fleet could arrive. As early as 1937 senior British commanders in Malaya warned the British government of the potential danger of an invading force attacking from the north down the Malay peninsula and striking Singapore before Royal Navy contingents could reach the Far East. They argued the need for defence works in Kedah and Johor, but these were not constructed. Airfields were built at Kota Bharu and Kuantan to counter any enemy landing on the northeast coast of the peninsula but were allotted inadequate military protection. With the Japanese navy based 2700 kilometres away and no Japanese airfields within striking distance of Malaya, the danger seemed remote.

War in Europe 1939

The outbreak of war in Europe in 1939 changed the position dramatically. After the Germans overran France the following year, the Vichy-controlled administration in French Indochina gave Japan bases in south Vietnam, which brought their fleet to within 1200 kilometres of Singapore and their planes within 500 kilometres of north Malaya. The German invasion of the Soviet Union in June 1941 freed Japan from any Russian threat and allowed it to concentrate on Southeast Asia, whence it drew oil from Indonesia, and rubber, tin, bauxite and iron from Malaya to wage war in China.

Britain had to weigh the possibility of war in the East against dangers on its home front and heavy commitments in fighting in North Africa. It built up its army in Malaya but most of the troops were ill-trained and inexperienced, many of them newly recruited in Australia and India. Their equipment was inferior and they had no tanks or anti-tank guns. In December 1941 Britain dispatched two warships to Singapore, *Prince of Wales,* which was the pride of the Royal Navy, and *Repulse,* but no aircraft carrier or other supporting ships to form an effective Far East naval force. There were few aircraft and these were obsolete. Britain planned to build up its force in Malaya by the spring of 1942 but in the meantime it hoped for peace.

There was little sense of danger in Malaya and morale was high. After the slow economic recovery during the 1930s, the war in Europe meant all-out production and prosperity. As producer of nearly 40 per cent of the world's rubber and nearly 60 per cent of its tin, mainly for the United States market, Malaya was a 'dollar fortress', Britain's most important hard-currency earner. After a brief flurry of communist labour trouble launched in sympathy with the Russo–German non-aggression pact of August 1939, the Chinese Communist Party ordered the Malayan Communist Party to consolidate the anti-Japanese front and to call off anti-British activities. The German invasion of Russia in June 1941 brought the communists and Kuomintang together in Malaya in opposition to Japan and its German allies, and Chinese of every political persuasion supported the British war effort. But the British were anxious not to provoke Japan into war and found the anti-Japanese activities of the Chinese an embarrassment.

The Pacific War

In July 1941 the United States, Britain and Holland froze Japanese assets and put a complete embargo on trade with Japan, forcing it to choose between abandoning its invasion of China or seizing by armed force the essential war materials it needed from Southeast Asia. Having failed to get the embargo lifted by diplomacy, the Japanese government determined to go to war, and on the night of 7–8 December 1941 (Malayan time) launched simultaneous and surprise attacks on the American naval base at Pearl Harbour, on the Philippines, Hong Kong and Malaya. A subsidiary force landing at Kota Bharu put the airfield out of action, while the main Japanese army landed at Singora in southern Thailand, whence they moved swiftly to invade Kedah.

The Japanese pre-emptive strike took the defenders by surprise, and the British had no opportunity to put into force a proposed 'Matador' plan to enter south Thailand and ward off a Japanese landing. Within twenty-four hours the Japanese air force had destroyed most of the Commonwealth planes and seized the north Malayan airfields. Within three days they had sunk *Prince of Wales* and *Repulse,* which had sped north without air cover in a desperate attempt to prevent further Japanese landings in north Malaya. The naval base was empty, and the Commonwealth army, which had been designed as an ancillary force to protect the naval base and airfields, now had to take the brunt of the Japanese attack.

In command of the air and sea, the invaders pushed forward, enveloping the Commonwealth forces and compelling them to withdraw rapidly down the one main trunk road in order to avoid being cut off from the rear. On 7 January the Japanese won the day at Slim river, forcing the defenders to abandon central Malaya. Four days later the Japanese took Kuala Lumpur, and on 16 January they broke through the Australian lines at the Muar river in north Johor, which was the last defensive position on the peninsula. On the final day of January the last Commonwealth soldiers withdrew across the causeway to Singapore and the island was under siege.

Belated attempts were made to rally the local population for defence.

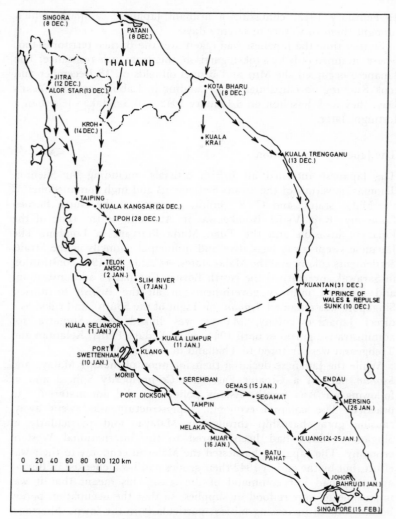

The Japanese Invasion 1941–2

Communists were released from prison and Chinese leaders combined to form a Chinese Mobilization Committee. Chinese of all ages and different walks of life rushed to join a militia, Dalforce, which was hastily formed and given rudimentary training.

On 8 February the Japanese invaded, and the defending troops fell back on the crowded town, which had doubled its population to about one million people with the influx of refugees from the mainland. After a week of heavy fighting final unconditional surrender came on

15 February 1942, climaxing a brilliant Japanese campaign which brought them to victory in seventy days.

By that time the Japanese had taken over the Borneo territories too, where, manned only by a token garrison, there was little resistance. The Japanese occupied the Miri and Brunei oilfields on 18 December and took Kuching on Christmas Day. Landing in Labuan on New Year's Day, they took Jesselton on 8 January 1942 and Sandakan less than a fortnight later.

The Japanese Occupation

The Japanese interned all British officials, including Sir Shenton Thomas, governor of the Straits Settlements and high commissioner of the Malay states, and C. R. Smith, governor of the North Borneo Company. Raja Vyner Brooke was in Australia at the time of the Japanese invasion and the Tuan Muda Bertram in London. The Japanese swept away legislative and municipal councils in the Straits Settlements colony and the Malay states, set aside the 1941 constitution in Sarawak, overturned the North Borneo Company's administration, and installed military governments in all the British territories. Singapore was renamed *Syonan*, or 'Light of the South', and ruled as a direct Japanese colony, Malaya was linked with Sumatra for administrative purposes until 1944, while Kedah, Perlis, Kelantan and Trengganu were restored to Thailand in August 1943.

While the Japanese declared their intention of making Malaya and *Syonan* part of a Greater East Asia Co-prosperity Sphere and of following an 'Asia for the Asians' policy, this did not materialize in practice. The colonial economic superstructure was swept away, causing great hardship throughout Malaya, and particularly in Singapore which had been geared to the international Western economy. The Japanese harnessed the Malayan economy to their war effort, but by the end of 1942 their armies had been checked in Burma and they had lost command of the seas. This meant that it was impossible to import food or supplies, so that the occupation period became one of increasing misery, particularly in the towns. Shortages led to a 'black market' and runaway inflation when the currency, which the Japanese issued with reckless abandon, became worthless. It was a time of starvation, ill-health and massive unemployment.

While the Japanese preached a doctrine of Asian equality and brotherhood, the treatment which they meted out to the various communities was markedly different. The Japanese were harsh on Eurasians, bullying them into forgoing their semi-privileged position in the colonial hierarchy. Their attitude to the Chinese varied, treating some with great brutality but recognizing others as indispensable business partners. Indians were courted as desirable friends in fighting the British colonial regime in India, while the Malays as the indigenous people were potential allies in creating a government in league with the Japanese.

The Japanese planned to retain Singapore as a permanent direct colony and strategic base, but to convert peninsular Malaya ultimately into a protectorate. Unlike other countries in Southeast Asia which they overran, the Japanese found no strong Malay nationalist movement which they could build up as a puppet government. They released Ibrahim Yaakob, Ishak Haji Mohammad, Ahmad Boestamam and other *Kesatuan Melayu Muda* leaders, whom the British had imprisoned in 1940, and they promoted Malay Administrative Service officials to senior bureaucratic posts under Japanese state governors. At first the Japanese intended to replace loyalty to the Malay rulers by homage to the Japanese emperor. To this end they cut royal pensions, trimmed the rulers' powers and suspended the state councils. But within a few months the Japanese, like their British predecessors, came to recognize the sultanates and the aristocracy as the soundest props for their own political power and a better vehicle than the radicals for channelling the support of the Malay population. In January 1943 the sultans' titles were recognized, promises were given to restore their pensions, their property was guaranteed, their supreme authority in matters of Malay custom and the Muslim religion once more acknowledged, and every honour and courtesy shown to them. In December 1944 a nation-wide Malayan Conference of Religious Councils was convened in Kuala Kangsar to add prestige to the sultans' religious authority, although their political power was restricted.

The Japanese also came round to recognizing the necessity for Chinese co-operation in running the economy. In the early days of the occupation many Chinese were treated with cruelty. In an attempt to root out anti-Japanese, Kuomintang and communist sympathizers, who had used Singapore as their centre before the Pacific war, the Japanese rounded up the entire Chinese adult male population of Singapore for screening in the first week of the occupation and massacred countless thousands. At a conservative estimate 5000 perished but the actual figure may have been five times as high. After that the Japanese organized an Overseas Chinese Association, under the leadership of the ageing Dr Lim Boon Keng, and through this organization forced the Chinese community to raise a crippling 'donation' of Straits $50 million, which was collected by a levy organized by the prominent Chinese on their community throughout Malaya. But the Japanese, like the British, depended on Chinese support to oil the wheels of the economy. Many large firms, such as Mitsui and Mitsubishi, set up concerns in Malaya and large numbers of Japanese businessmen came to run them, but the Chinese were essential middlemen and in some cases became the real power behind the Japanese front men in business associations.

Despite the fact that they consigned Tamil rubber tappers as forced labour on the Siam–Burma railway project, where they died in their thousands, in general Japanese policy was gentle towards the Indians. Before the invasion they sent Indian Independence League agents to stir up trouble among Indian troops in Malaya and induced Captain Mohan Singh, a regular army officer, to set up an Indian National Army to fight alongside the Japanese for Indian liberation. Following the surrender in Singapore nearly half the Indian Commonwealth troops were enrolled in the Indian National Army and those who refused, including all the Gurkhas and most Muslims, were imprisoned, sent to work camps in the Netherlands Indies, or executed. In May 1942 Rash Behari Bose, the founder of the Indian Independence League, who had lived in exile in Japan for more than twenty years, came to Singapore and set up branches of the League throughout Malaya, attracting thousands of Indian civilian members. But the movement flagged as Indians became convinced that Rash Behari Bose was a Japanese puppet and that the Japanese intended the Indian National Army to be an instrument of propaganda, not an effective fighting force. Mohan Singh was arrested in December 1942, but the movement sprang to life again in July 1943, with the arrival of Subhas Chandra Bose, former president of the Congress in India, who had escaped to Germany and was then smuggled to Singapore by submarine. A dynamic and militant leader, Subhas Chandra Bose proclaimed the *Azad Hind* or provisional government of Free India in October 1943 and attracted Indians from all over Southeast Asia, but mostly from Malaya, to join the Indian National Army. Early in 1944 Bose moved his headquarters to Rangoon and the Indian National Army joined Japanese forces on the Burma front, but the campaign was a disaster. The Indian National Army disintegrated in the retreat and Bose himself died in an air crash in August 1945.

In accordance with their policy of orienting the occupied countries towards Tokyo, the Japanese tried to introduce a uniform education system, using Japanese and the Malay vernacular as the media of instruction, and sent carefully selected youths to Japan for training. But language difficulties and ethnic plurality defeated their attempts to unify education, and of the 400 to 500 young Southeast Asian students sent to Japan only a dozen came from Malaya and Singapore.

The Japanese did not visualize setting up an independent government in Malaya in the foreseeable future and their policy vacillated according to the fortunes of war. As the tide turned against their armies, their administration became nervous and erratic but they made more attempt to win the co-operation of the local population, in order to give them a vested interest in resisting the return to colonial rule. In late-1943 and early-1944 the Japanese set up advisory councils in each state and city, comprising the Japanese resident as chairman, the sultan, and Malay, Chinese, Indian, Eurasian and Arab representatives nominated by the Japanese. Unlike the pre-war state legislative councils, the Japanese advisory councils were purely consultative bodies, meeting merely to receive instructions, usually about the war effort. The Japanese also created communal bodies to represent the interests of the various ethnic groups, in the form of Malay, Eurasian, Indian and Arab Welfare Associations, along the lines of the Overseas Chinese Association.

In the summer of 1944, when the war was going badly for the Japanese, they set up *epposho* or clubs for the Chinese in Penang, Kuala Lumpur and Singapore to discuss problems concerning the economy, and in June 1945 at a time of mounting crisis they extended this idea by creating *hodosho*, or 'help and guide the people offices' in each state. Presided over by Japanese civil officials, these were designed to bring together young representatives of all communities.

The Japanese made no promises of independence for Malaya and looked on *Syonan* as Japan's key point in the Nanyang, but politically-aware Malays saw an opportunity to gain their own freedom in conjunction with Indonesia, where the nationalist movement was more advanced. In September 1944 the Japanese agreed in principle to grant independence to Indonesia and encouraged Malay interest in order to defuse discontent over the cession of the northern states to Thailand the previous year. In May 1945 the secretaries-general of the military administrations of Malaya, Java, Sumatra and Celebes met in Singapore to discuss the question of Indonesian independence, and at a second conference late in July 1945 they formed a KRIS *(Kesatuan Ra'ayat Indonesia Semenanjong* or Union of Peninsular Indonesians) organization under the leadership of Dr Burhanuddin Al-Hemy and Ibrahim bin Haji Yaakob. Ibrahim met Sukarno and Hatta briefly at Taiping, when the Indonesian leaders were *en route* from Saigon to Jakarta on 12 August 1945, but by the time the first KRIS meeting of representatives from all the states and the Straits Settlements met in Kuala Lumpur five days later, the war had suddenly come to an end, and Ibrahim Yaakob escaped to Java.

While a number of Indians and Malays actively opposed the Japanese regime and Malay dissidents formed an underground movement, the major resistance came from the Chinese. The survivors of Dalforce, the Chinese militia, and numbers of communists fled to the jungles and formed a Malayan People's Anti-Japanese Army. While it carried a three-star flag, representing the Chinese, Indian and Malay communities, it was essentially a Chinese force and was dominated by the Malayan Communist Party. The Japanese were ruthless in their attempts to wipe out communism, and in the first year of the occupation arrested the entire Singapore city committee and eliminated nearly forty communist guerrilla leaders who assembled from all over Malaya at Batu Caves in Selangor in September 1942. The survivors regrouped and by 1944 attracted many non-communist, anti-Japanese Chinese recruits. From 1943 British officers were parachuted into Malaya or landed by submarine to join the Chinese guerrillas, and large quantities of arms and ammunition were dropped to the Malayan People's Anti-Japanese Army in preparation for the coming Allied invasion.

The Malayan guerrillas carried out scattered raids, and in Sarawak renewed head-hunting among the Iban made the countryside unsafe for the Japanese, but the only open rebellion came in North Borneo. A force of Chinese and Bajaus, led by Albert Kwok, seized Jesselton briefly in October 1943 but were quickly overpowered, and a further plot in North Borneo was unmasked at the planning stage the following year, leading to mass executions.

The Malayan People's Anti-Japanese Army bided its time, the communist leadership planning to use the coming showdown between the Japanese and British to establish a communist republic in Malaya. It anticipated that the battle for the re-occupation of Malaya would be long and fierce. The Japanese were prepared for a determined resistance and conscripted the local population to build and man defences.

British War-time Planning for Post-war Reconstruction

Throughout the period of the occupation the link between Britain and the territories in Malaya and Borneo was broken and little was known of what was going on in the occupied countries, so that the British government operated in the dark in formulating its post-war reconstruction plans. Colonial Office officials had long wanted to see constitutional reform in Malaya and were thwarted by the slow pace of change in pre-war years. In the words of Edward Gent, head of the Eastern department of the Colonial Office in September 1941, 'a merely static policy of ignoring undoubted interests . . . is a barren policy'.[1] The dramatic collapse of the colonial administration provided the opportunity for Gent, who became assistant permanent under-secretary for the colonies in 1942, to draw up plans with a small group of Colonial Office colleagues for a radical restructuring of the country, with the object of achieving administrative efficiency and ultimately a sense of national cohesion in which settled immigrant communities would have an assured and equal place. The Colonial Office also felt it was time to put North Borneo and Sarawak on a more modern footing by replacing the anachronism of personal white raja rule, however paternal, and of chartered company government, however enlightened and willing it might be to subordinate profit to good administration.

An initial proposal to group the Federated and unfederated Malay states, Straits Settlements and three Borneo territories into one confederation was set aside as premature, and in 1944 the British government accepted in principle Gent's alternative plan to incorporate the Federated and unfederated Malay states, Penang and Melaka into a Malayan Union, leaving Singapore, together with the Cocos Keeling and Christmas Islands, as a separate crown colony. At the same time the war cabinet authorized negotiations with the directors to buy out the British North Borneo Company. Each territory would have its own governor, while a governor-general, stationed in Singapore, would superintend all British possessions in Southeast Asia. Detailed execution of the schemes was worked out by Malayan and Borneo planning units, comprising the handful of former officials available.

The Malayan Union meant uniting the states into a centralized union, in which the sultans would relinquish nearly all their powers, and laws would be made by a central legislative council. All persons born in the Malayan Union or Singapore and those who had lived there for ten out of the previous fifteen years would automatically become citizens, while naturalization would be granted on application to people with five years' residence in the country.

Singapore was excluded from the proposals at that stage largely because London did not want to jeopardise the delicate negotiations for peninsular re-organization. This involved persuading each individual ruler to abrogate his rights and to accept the principle of liberal citizenship provisions for non-Malays. The inclusion of Singapore would only add to complications, since a major stumbling block in achieving constitutional change before the Second World War had been the resistance of both the traditional Malay leadership and foreign business circles in the Federation to being subordinated to Singapore's commercial interests. There were also problems about the island's status as a free port and strategic base, and it was anticipated that it would be a long time before Singapore reverted to civil rule, since it would remain the centre for Allied operations in Southeast Asia in what was expected to be a long drawn out campaign to win the war in the East, long after the rest of Malaya had reverted to civil rule.

All the normal channels of communication with local opinion were closed and, apart from a token consultation with the London-based British Malaya Association, which represented British commercial interests, Gent sought no outside advice. He took little account of representations which were sent to him from individuals and associations with experience of Malaya. These included detailed proposals from Malayan refugees who escaped to India where they formed a Malayan Association of India, largely comprising Europeans, Eurasians and Jews, and an Overseas Chinese Association, headed by Tan Cheng Lock. Most of these recommendations indicated a preference for a federation and the inclusion of Singapore in any post-war settlement, which ran counter to the British government's thinking, but London expected that a long period of military administration after the reconquest of Malaya would give plenty of time for consultation and negotiation 'to test the temper of the people'. Meanwhile it went ahead in secrecy, fearing to reveal its plans lest the Japanese exploit these for propaganda purposes.

The Malayan Union meant a drastic departure from the policy adopted towards Malaya up to the Second World War, which explicitly re-iterated that Malaya was a Malay country in which the British ruled in alliance with the Malay sultans and in trust for the Malay people. But in the light of pre-war agitation among Indians and Chinese, the indications of strong feelings shown by the Indian National Army and the Malayan People's Anti-Japanese Army, and the expected emergence of China as a great power and India as an independent Dominion, the British expected renewed agitation for more political powers on the part of the immigrant communities. They did not anticipate unfavourable Malay reaction, and believed that the new arrangement would satisfy the aspirations of Chinese and Indians who had made Malaya their home and would induce a sense of nationhood, in which it would be possible to work towards self government.

Both the British North Borneo Company and Raja Vyner Brooke were content to see their territories pass to the Colonial Office, which was in a better position to inject the large doses of capital needed for rehabilitation and development. Raja Vyner, Bertram and Anthony Brooke were all out of Sarawak during the Japanese occupation. For a time Vyner Brooke held his supreme council in Sydney but disbanded it in April 1942 and created a commission in London under Tuan Muda Bertram. The raja returned to England himself in June 1943, with Gerald MacBryan as his secretary, and the Brookes continued their family arguments, much to the British government's embarrassment. The Borneo planning unit moved to Australia in 1945, but nothing was known in England of conditions in Japanese-occupied Sarawak or possible public reaction to the Brookes' return. While Vyner himself felt too old to resume the government, Anthony Brooke, who was very conscious of the 'Brooke mantle', bombarded the Colonial Office with suggestions and was anxious to rehabilitate the old regime if the population would take the Brooke family back. He was released from military service at the end of 1944 to become officer administering the government of Sarawak and wanted to return immediately the Japanese were expelled. But the Colonial Office wanted to wait until the position cleared, preferring to see Sarawak become a crown colony or revert to Malay rule, possibly under Datu Patinggi, the senior Malay chief and direct descendant of the sultan who had ceded Sarawak to James Brooke.

The Australians re-occupied Labuan in June 1945 and by early July were in control of Brunei and parts of the coastal areas of Sarawak and North Borneo. But the British were still preparing for their invasion of Malaya when the war came to an end with unexpected suddenness after the destruction of Japanese cities by atomic bombs early in August 1945 induced the emperor to surrender.

1. Edward Gent in Colonial Office minute, 23 September 1941, Public Record Office, London, CO 273/667, 50429.

CHAPTER 17

Nationalism and Independence, 1945–63

Return of Colonial Power

Most Western colonial regimes met with violent resistance in trying to re-impose their rule in their Southeast Asian colonies, ignoring the development of nationalism during the years of war and occupation. Malaya was unique in that here the British were initially welcomed back with enthusiasm but were themselves unwilling to put the clock back and were soon overwhelmed by the reaction against their schemes for streamlining the administration and assimilating the different immigrant communities.

The Colonial Office foresaw little difficulty in implementing what it considered to be a just, rational and realistic policy whereby 'each of the races forming the population of Malaya must have full opportunity of helping to build the country's future and reaping the benefits of their efforts, provided they in fact regard Malaya as an object of loyalty'.[1] The British government recognized that, despite assurances repeatedly given to the Malays, colonial rule had permanently changed the character of Malaya by bringing in alien settlers in such numbers that provision had to be made to grant them political rights and a place in the administrative structure. The pressure for this had been growing over the past ten to fifteen years. The curb put on immigration during the Great Depression, which was designed to keep the foreign element in check, in practice encouraged more permanent settlement by reducing mobility and discouraging immigrant Chinese from returning home lest they would be barred from coming back to Malaya. The Pacific war and the Japanese Occupation kept people rooted in Malaya, so that by 1945 the immigrant population was more settled than ever before.

The colonial power was prepared to admit that the change from a country of transients to permanently domiciled communities dictated the need to weld a plural society into a multi-racial one, to expand the functions of government in the fields of education and social welfare, and to set the country on the path to ultimate self government.

Malayan Chinese and Indians were expected to welcome the proposals for a Malayan Union citizenship. This would allay the pained concern voiced in the 1930s by Tan Cheng Lock and other Straits

Chinese who, feeling themselves to be part of Malaya, resented the discriminatory immigration and education policy against the Chinese and feared for the future position of their community. It would satisfy the aspirations of Indians, who on the eve of the Pacific war had been clamouring for greater opportunities.

Little opposition was expected from the Malays. While Malay Associations were formed in the various states in the late-1930s in view of increasing worry over immigration figures, competition for employment and demands from immigrants for a share in administration, there was no unity in Malay nationalism before the Second World War. The eleven states represented at the conference of Malay Associations held in Singapore in 1940, which included representatives from Brunei and Sarawak as well as peninsular Malaya, rejected proposals to form a joint association, preferring to work individually for Malay interests in their separate states.

Chinese and Indians who had contributed to Malaya's prosperity and were domiciled in the country, sometimes for several generations, wanted permanent and equal political status. The British wished to foster this sense of cohesion and belonging as a prelude to modernization and self government by encouraging immigrants to look on Malaya as 'home'. But what immigrants regarded as equality, meant to the Malays a foreign intrusion which threatened to destroy the character of their country. Before the Second World War the Malays had been content to leave the economy to foreigners, provided they retained political supremacy. Now they awoke to the fact that they were not only outnumbered in their own country and had lost the lion's share of its wealth to outsiders, but those outsiders now wanted equal political status too, and the colonial government backed these claims.

To Malays this was a gross betrayal of all the premises upon which British–Malay rule was based and a violation of their rights. But non-Malays came increasingly to regard those rights as outdated privileges.

To reconcile these conflicting interests would have been a formidable undertaking at any time, but the difficulties were compounded by the abrupt end of the war in mid-August 1945 which threw the various communist, Malay nationalist and British political schemes out of gear. This precipitated the British into implementing their new schemes without the anticipated extended period of consultation and persuasion. The premature launching of these proposals, which had been drawn up in an artificial, bureaucratic situation in London without consulting either Malayans or British officials who had worked in Malaya, released powerful forces latent in Malayan society. The Malayan Union proposal was the catalyst which for the first time brought the Malays together, to sink their parochial loyalties into a common Malay nationalism. The constitutional innovations brought into the open lurking fears and unspoken worries, provoking intense reaction and counter reaction. It exposed the issue of communalism, the ethnic and religious divisions and antipathies which up to that time had been delicately veiled, shattered the complacent calm of pre-war Malaya and brought out the full force of racialism on political, economic and social grounds, which was to be the dominating problem in post-war Malaya.

None of this was obvious in the euphoric days which immediately followed the British return. For a few weeks after the Japanese collapse the 7000-strong Malayan People's Anti-Japanese Army had carried out a reign of terror against alleged collaborators, many of whom were Malays. This in turn sparked off racial violence among Chinese and Malays in many parts of the country, notably in Johor, Negri Sembilan and Perak. But the return of the British put an end to the terror.

The Malayan People's Anti-Japanese Army did not contest the restoration of British rule. While the guerrilla leaders were dedicated communists, pledged to work for an independent Malayan republic, many of the army's rank and file at that time were merely anti-Japanese. Nor could the Malayan People's Anti-Japanese Army hope to be a match for the powerful Allied force which had been poised to drive the Japanese out of the Malay peninsula. The Malayan Communist Party was forced to adopt a soft line, so that Commonwealth forces landed unopposed at Penang, Singapore and Morib in Selangor early in September 1945, and by the end of the month the British military administration was in effective occupation of the whole peninsula, Sarawak and North Borneo.

The Malayan Communist Party's co-operation came as a relief to the British government, who had feared the communist-dominated guerrilla army as potentially the most dangerous force in post-war Malayan politics. At the same time a party manifesto issued on 25 August 1945 calling for 'a democratic government in Malaya with an electorate drawn from all races of each state and the anti-Japanese army' embarrassed London, since they felt that the communists had 'rather stolen their thunder' and that they had 'lost that element of surprise for their progressive policy which would politically have been so valuable'.[2] On paper the declaration came so close to the Colonial Office's own plan that London feared its long-deliberated schemes might instead appear to have been hastily forced upon it by the Malayan Communist Party.

London was anxious to replace military administration by civil government as quickly as possible and to settle the constitutional future of the various territories. Civil administration was resumed in Malaya, Singapore and Sarawak in April 1946, when the peninsular states and settlements were amalgamated under the Malayan Union. Singapore became a separate crown colony and Sarawak was temporarily restored to the Brookes. Military government persisted a little longer in North

Borneo while London completed the negotiations for buying out the British North Borneo Company, but in July both Sarawak and North Borneo became crown colonies, the last colonies which Britain acquired and at a time when colonialism was in retreat. Labuan was included in the North Borneo colony and the capital transferred from Sandakan to Jesselton.*

North Borneo accepted the change readily, since colonial status opened the way to British government funds for economic reconstruction and development. The British North Borneo Company was an outmoded instrument of government, the longest surviving of its generation of chartered companies. For many years it had conformed to the normal colonial pattern, and many of its officials transferred to the new service.

In Sarawak constitutional change did not run so smoothly. Despite doubts at the Colonial Office and among the Brookes themselves, Sarawak welcomed the white rajas back.[3] While Raja Vyner Brooke, who was seventy-two years old in 1946, felt he had neither the energy nor resources to develop the country and was content to hand Sarawak over to Britain, Anthony and Bertram Brooke and senior Malay officials in the Sarawak administration put up strong opposition to the change. Sarawak's future was debated heatedly in the British parliament, but a parliamentary commission which was sent to investigate the situation in Sarawak reported a majority in favour of the transfer.

In May 1946 the Council Negri agreed to the raja's proposals by a narrow majority, and the new crown colony came into being in July 1946, based upon the 1941 constitution. Many still refused to accept the change and some Malay officials resigned. But demonstrations which culminated in violence and the assassination of the governor, Duncan Stewart, in 1949 shocked the opponents of colonial rule. In 1951 Anthony Brooke formally relinquished his claims and colonial government came to be accepted peacefully.

Malayan Union

In the peninsula, in October 1945 London hurriedly dispatched an emissary, Sir Harold MacMichael, to renegotiate the treaties with the Malay rulers in order to pave the way for the new constitution. MacMichael, who had seen distinguished service in Palestine and East Africa but had no previous experience of Malaya, conducted his mission with a speed reminiscent of the way in which Swettenham had foisted the idea of federation on the Malay rulers in 1895. At the time it seemed easy. MacMichael informed the Colonial Office ten days after he reached Malaya, 'the impression I receive is that the new policy was

* Renamed Kota Kinabalu after independence.

almost taken for granted and is regarded as eminently reasonable'. Dazed and concerned lest they might be charged with collaboration with the Japanese, all the rulers signed the treaties making over their jurisdiction to the British. The ageing and respected Sultan Ibrahim of Johor led the way and the rulers of the Federated Malay States and Perlis readily followed suit, although the new treaties were only accepted after some discussion in Kelantan and Trengganu and with heated argument in Kedah. Within a few weeks MacMichael returned to London with his mission completed.[4]

He succeeded initially largely because the new constitutional scheme had been launched into a political vacuum and came as a surprise in Malaya, which had no well-developed nationalist movement to cope with such a situation. The Japanese, despite their professed intention to work for Asian unity, had left the different ethnic communities more deeply divided than ever and created new divisions within the communities, such as the split between the upper class and radical Malays. The Malayan Communist Party, the only political party in existence at the end of the war, was still almost entirely Chinese in composition, while the sudden end to the war stifled the KRIS organization at birth.

The first protests against the formation of the Malayan Union and the separation of Singapore came from former governors and European Malayan Civil Service officials. Shenton Thomas claimed that Singapore was 'the only natural capital in Malaya' while Clementi objected that to exclude Singapore from the Malayan Union was 'to cut the heart out of Malaya'.[5]

Former Malayan Civil Service officials protested forcibly at what they regarded as a gross betrayal of trust in the reneging on all pledges given repeatedly to the Malay leaders over the years. Since the beginning of the century Malay paramountcy had been acknowledged. While British officials dominated the executive government, the Malayan Civil Service up to the Second World War was conscious of administering the Malay states by right of treaties made with the rulers. In 1945 they still adhered to the principle expressed by Sir Hugh Clifford in 1927: 'The States were, when the British government was invited by their rulers and chiefs to set their troubled houses in order, Muhammadan monarchies; such they are today, and such they must continue to be.' And in December 1941, as the Japanese invaders swept through Malaya, Prime Minister Churchill had told the governor, Sir Shenton Thomas, to assure the sultans that, in gratitude for their large contributions to the British war effort, 'we shall see them righted in final victory'.

Recovering from their initial shock and taking heart from former officials' protests, the rulers protested at the way in which the MacMichael mission had browbeaten them into submission. Some blamed Sultan Ibrahim for so readily leading the way, and there was a move in Johor to depose him. The rulers objected that the union implied colonial annexation. They were even more incensed against the liberal citizenship provisions, which would have given immigrant communities equal political status to the indigenous Malays, denying the premise that Malaya was and always would be a Malay country. Meeting at Kuala Kangsar, the rulers proposed to go to London to protest, but the initiative was taken out of their hands by a new political force: the United Malays National Organization (UMNO).

Formed in March 1946, on the eve of the inauguration of the Malayan Union, by Dato Onn bin Ja'afar, *mentri besar* of Johor and a founder member of the former KRIS, UMNO grew out of the pre-war Malay Associations, which had been formed to protect Malay interests but had hitherto been unable to sink individual state jealousies to make a common cause.

The Colonial Office anticipated a backlash conservative movement of Malay rulers resenting the loss of privileges, but they were astonished to find mass support rallying behind the sultans, who during the years of

Dato Onn bin Ja'afar *(By courtesy of the Arkib Negara Malaysia).*

British protection and the Japanese Occupation had increasingly become the symbol of Malay identity. In pre-war days the British had nurtured the rulers' role as spiritual leaders of their people. They were brought together at regular durbars, which for the first time welded them into a cohesive group. During the Occupation, Japanese concern to boost the rulers' religious authority at the expense of their political powers gave them prestige within their own community without associating them too closely with the hated Japanese administration.

Now they became the focus of Malay nationalism. This was a slow development because before the Second World War the Malays felt more loyalty to individual states than to Malaya as a country. They were not bound together by a centralized government nor by a religious organization, since Islam had no hierarchy. Yet loyalty to the sultanate and the Muslim religion were the distinguishing features of Malay character and thus became a symbol of nationalism.

Before the war this had drawn Malays together in face of immigrants but not against the colonial power. Now it served to unite them in emotional opposition to the Malayan Union scheme, drawn up by London civil servants with no feel for the country.

Malay nationalism matured almost overnight. UMNO quickly formed branches in the major towns and organized protest meetings throughout the country, claiming transfer of sovereignty from the rulers to Britain was invalid because the sultans had been pressed into signing away their rights, and the proposed citizenship was unfair to the indigenous people. By the time the Malayan Union came into being in April 1946, with Gent as governor, Malay opposition had crystallized. The rulers refused to attend Gent's installation, and Malays boycotted the advisory councils.

UMNO was a new departure in Malay nationalism, because it was dominated by the traditional ruling class, who had formerly worked in partnership with the British. Startled by the passionate and concerted intensity of Malay feeling and responsive to parliamentary and press criticism in Britain, London agreed to withhold the citizenship proposals and modify the Malayan Union. In mid-1946 a working party was set up under the chairmanship of Malcolm MacDonald, the newly appointed governor-general of the Malayan Union and Singapore, to consider UMNO's proposal for a federation with stricter citizenship requirements and more safeguards for Malays and their rulers. The only feature of the original Malayan Union scheme which UMNO wished to retain was the separation of Singapore, in order to avoid putting the Chinese in a majority.

Meanwhile the intensity of conservative Malay nationalism in turn roused other disparate groups into political action, including many who had shown little interest in the original constitutional proposals or the opportunities which the liberal Malayan Union citizenship laws offered them.

In October 1945 some former KRIS leaders, notably Mokhtarruddin, Dr Burhanuddin Al-Hemy and Ishak Haji Mohammed, formed a Malay Nationalist Party, dedicated to working for a radical Malaya within an independent Indonesia. The Malay Nationalist Party attacked UMNO as an aristocratic party and saw both the Malayan Union and the proposed federation as threats to its ideal of Indonesia Raya, a Greater Indonesia into which the Malay peninsula would be merged.

A Malayan Democratic Union, formed in Singapore in December 1945 under the leadership of mildly left-wing, English-educated, middle class professional men wanted to see Singapore part of the Malayan Union and objected to UMNO's insistence on the exclusion of Singapore.

Opposition groups formed a Pan-Malayan Council of Joint Action under the chairmanship of Tan Cheng Lock, incorporating the Malayan Democratic Union, the Straits Chinese British Association, the Pan-Malayan Federation of Trade Unions and various communal, commercial, women's and youth organizations. The Malayan Communist Party, who saw the separation of Singapore as a threat to its goal of a united communist Malaya, was not itself a formal member but lent its support. The Council allied with the *Pusat Tengga Ra'ayat* (People's United Front or PUTERA), dominated by the Malay Nationalist Party. Renamed the All-Malaya Council of Joint Action (AMCJA) in August 1947, for a time it attracted the support of Chinese chambers of commerce in Singapore and the peninsula, and organized trade shut downs and mass rallies in the major towns in protest against the exclusion of Singapore. The Council drew up *People's Constitutional Proposals,* which demanded a Malayan federation including Singapore, with an executive council responsible to a legislative assembly to be elected by all adults domiciled in Malaya regardless of race. But the British refused to accept the All-Malaya Council of Joint Action as general spokesman for non-Malay opinion. Ignoring the *People's Constitutional Proposals,* the British went ahead in agreement with UMNO and the rulers to form the Federation of Malaya in February 1948.

The Malayan Union and a separate Singapore were conceived as a civil servant's dream and subsequently became a politician's nightmare. The fate of the scheme closely paralleled Gent's own career. As first governor of the Malayan Union he had to face the opposition which smothered his brainchild, and he was killed in an air crash soon after the formation of the Federation of Malaya in 1948.

The Federation of Malaya, 1948

The new Federation had a strong central government, comprising a high commissioner, a federal executive council of seven officials and seven non-officials, and a federal legislative council, but the rulers were to be sovereign in the Malay states and the various states and settlements kept their own individuality and considerable local powers. While the Federation of Malaya Agreement was committed to provide for 'the means and prospects of development in the direction of ultimate self government', initially all seventy-five legislative councillors were nominated, although two-thirds of them were non-official. A common Malayan citizenship was offered on stricter terms, demanding from immigrants a residence of fifteen out of the previous twenty-five years, a declaration of permanent settlement and the ability to speak Malay or English. About three million of Malaya's five million population qualified for citizenship in 1948, of whom 78 per cent were Malay, 12 per cent Chinese and 7 per cent Indian.

The constitution and citizenship arrangements under the new Federation calmed Malay fears, but the British refusal even to entertain discussion of the *People's Constitutional Proposals* swept under the carpet real issues which needed to be faced: the question of Singapore and its relationship with the rest of Malaya; the problem of achieving a political independence in which minorities would be adequately protected; the need to break down divisive barriers of education, occupation and wealth which often ran along communal lines.

Though hastily abandoned, the idea of Malayan Union had some merit. It was in some ways a well-conceived scheme, cutting through the limitations which frustrated pre-war developments, and attempting to create a multi-racial Malaya, based on equality of citizenship. If the proposals had been introduced tactfully and slowly, the Malayan Union might have been instrumental in creating a firmer foundation for the development of Malaya than the federation which replaced it in 1948. As it was, the Malayan Union was implemented clumsily and then abandoned in favour of a Federation of Malaya, again with undue haste and insufficient consultation. When the Malayan Union was jettisoned, Britain accepted UMNO's concept of a Malay nation into which immigrant groups would have to fit, and from this premise difficulties were to develop.

Post-war Economic and Social Policy

Constitutional debate was waged against a background of struggle to repair the ravages of war and restore the economy. Tin dredges had been destroyed in the British retreat and rubber estates neglected during the Japanese occupation, but the world-wide, post-war hunger for primary products supported a vigorous recovery of the tin and rubber industries, which received a further boost with the Korean War boom in the early-1950s.

The post-war colonial regime also determined to play a more active role in providing a better standard of life. The Labour government in Britain favoured more liberal and positive colonial administration in the fields of education and social welfare, which also fitted the changed character of the population in Malaya and Singapore. A more settled community with a more even numerical distribution between the sexes and between age groups demanded education, housing and better living conditions as well as political rights.

Before the war the Chinese Protectorate and Labour Departments protected immigrant Chinese and Tamil labourers and immigrant women and girls from exploitation but the care of the old, poor, destitute, orphans, and handicapped — indigenous and immigrant — was left almost entirely to private charity. The Occupation compounded problems of poverty and in April 1946 a Social Welfare Department was created, although the major role in social work remained in the hands of charitable bodies.

In the inter-war years the control of opium smoking and other improvements raised health standards, particularly in the towns. In 1943 Britain decided to suppress opium smoking throughout its colonies and the prohibition was put into effect on the re-occupation of Malaya. Dramatic advances in medical knowledge led, in the immediate post-war years, to the elimination or containment of malaria, leprosy and polio, and speeded up the cure for tuberculosis which was the most serious killer disease. But tuberculosis was fostered by chronic over-crowding and bad housing conditions, and its prevention depended on a vigorous housing programme which did not come for many years.

Official expenditure on education increased nearly ten-fold in Singapore and Malaya in the first post-war decade, but could not cope with the increasing demand of a rapidly expanding population. In 1949, to meet the need for large numbers of teachers and administrators, Raffles College merged with the King Edward VII Medical College to form the University of Malaya, which was located in Singapore but also served the Federation of Malaya and the Borneo territories. Despite increased government expenditure, the objectives of introducing free, compulsory primary education and unifying the education system in Malaya could not be attained in the early post-war period, while in Singapore disproportionate spending on English-medium schools led to mounting discontent and frustration among the vernacular educated, particularly the Chinese.

The Communist Emergency

After the failure of the constitutional campaign, the unnatural AMCJA–PUTERA alliance fell apart, the Chinese chambers of commerce and the Malayan Communist Party withdrew their support, leaving UMNO to dominate the political scene. But the new Federation had scarcely come into being before Malaya was plunged into a state of Emergency when a communist revolt broke out in June 1948.

The insurgency arose only indirectly from the communist failure to abort the Malayan Federation and was caused in the main by setbacks in the communist campaign to control the labour movement, changes in international communist policy and upheaval within the Malayan Communist Party itself.

The communists had emerged from the Second World War with new-found strength in Malaya and Singapore. While the party had been harried by the Japanese and many of its leaders arrested, it had built up prestige as a patriotic resistance movement during the Occupation and exploited this advantage during the outwardly co-operative phase immediately after the war. Legalized for the first time in its history, the Malayan Communist Party was admitted in 1945 to a share in policy making through membership of the governor's Advisory Council in Singapore. It also used the misery, shortages and hardships of the immediate post-war years to enlist support.

The Malayan Communist Party's first steps towards securing a Malayan republic were to master the labour movement and to influence constitutional development through such organizations as the Malayan Democratic Union and the All-Malaya Council of Joint Action.

In October 1945 it created a General Labour Union in Singapore and similar organizations followed in the Malay states. With its headquarters in Singapore and branches in other Malayan towns, the party operated through the General Labour Union to build up support among workers and gear the infant trade union movement to its political ends. In January 1946 the General Labour Union organized a general strike in Singapore and the following month all the unions incorporated in the General Labour Unions of Singapore and Malaya formed a communist-dominated Pan-Malayan Federation of Trade Unions.

At first the party had considerable success. The British wished to encourage a democratic labour movement and took a tolerant view. The party played on genuine grievances and hardships, and 1946 and 1947 saw widespread strikes throughout Malaya, particularly on rubber estates.

But the economic tide had begun to turn. As conditions improved, food supplies increased, wartime shortages disappeared and disillusioned workers realized they were being manipulated for political ends without achieving significant material benefits.

The party was rent by internal discord with the defection in March 1947 of its secretary general, Lai Teck, who absconded with the party's funds following accusations of treachery. A Vietnamese, who had studied communism in Russia and France before coming to Singapore in the early-1930s, Lai Teck became secretary-general of the Malayan Communist Party about 1934 after the whole central committee was arrested. He may have been an agent for the British special branch even at that early stage and later became a Japanese agent during the

Occupation. Lai Teck's loyalty to the Malayan Communist Party does not seem to have been questioned, despite the fact that he was probably responsible for betraying other communist leaders into the hands of the Japanese in the Batu Caves incident in 1942, and after the war he resumed his contacts with the colonial special branch. His ultimate exposure came as a great shock to the communist rank and file, and under its new secretary-general, a former occupation guerrilla leader, Chin Peng, the party turned away from the soft line which its fallen idol had promoted.

By then the Malayan Communist Party was also reviewing its policies against the changing background of international communism. A Southeast Asian Youth conference, sponsored by the Soviet-controlled World Federation of Democratic Youth met in Calcutta in February 1948, with representatives from throughout Southeast Asia, including two from the Malayan Communist Party. While local communist parties may not have been given specific instructions, the climate of opinion at Calcutta favoured militant action. Coming out of its immediate post-war pre-occupation with internal reconstruction, Russia gave a new impetus to international communism, and the conference was to be followed by risings in Burma, Indonesia and Indochina as well as in Malaya.

The Malayan Communist Party failed in one trial of strength in February 1948 when a Singapore Harbour Board strike petered out, and this coincided with the collapse of the campaign which the party had supported against creation of the Federation of Malaya. An attempt to organize a mass May Day rally in Singapore also failed, following which most communist leaders retreated into the jungle.

While the Malayan People's Anti-Japanese Army had disbanded itself peacefully at the end of the war, it had stowed away arms caches, and its organization had remained intact through an Old Comrades' Association, so that the force could be quickly re-assembled.

The murder of three European planters in Perak in June 1948 sparked off the communist revolt. The colonial authorities, having lost their contact with the communist movement after the unmasking of Lai Teck, were unprepared, with only a small number of troops. At first the initiative lay with the guerrillas, who embarked on indiscriminate attacks against both European managers and local employees on rubber estates and tin mines, with the object of disrupting the economy. By a mixture of persuasion and intimidation they extracted money, food, medical supplies and information, particularly from Chinese rural squatters, who probably numbered half a million.

Despite large-scale troop reinforcements which were rushed to Malaya, the British seemed bogged down in an insoluble guerrilla war. In 1950 the director of operations, Lt General Sir Harold Briggs, inaugurated a plan to resettle the isolated Chinese squatters in about

500 fenced 'new villages', where they would be cut off from contact with terrorists, allowed out to work but forbidden to take food and supplies, and placed under night curfew. In the same year war executive committees were created at district, state and federal levels to co-ordinate military, police and civil administration. But these arrangements took time to produce any effect, and in 1951 morale plunged to its lowest point when the liberal high commissioner, Sir Henry Gurney, was ambushed and killed by communist terrorists.

Gurney's successor, General Sir Gerald Templer, a tough and forceful soldier, was appointed joint high commissioner and director of operations in February 1952. He vigorously promoted the Briggs resettlement plan and anti-guerrilla operations generally. At the same time, realizing that military suppression on its own was self defeating, he initiated a campaign to 'win the hearts and minds of the people'. The guerrillas were already slackening their indiscriminate terrorism, since violence and the destruction of their livelihood were alienating the local population. By the end of 1953 the communists were on the defensive, although a further seven years elapsed before the Emergency officially came to an end.

The communist insurrection failed partly because, by 1948, the worst post-war hardships were over and the opportunity to exploit genuine misery had faded, but also because the Malayan Communist Party appeared to be exclusively Chinese, and this, coupled with Muslim revulsion for Marxism, created almost universal Malay opposition to communism at that stage. The party found some supporters among poor Indians in the towns but hardly any among Indian rubber tappers. Even among the Chinese, it was almost entirely the urban poor and rural squatters who backed the party, which was shunned by well-to-do Chinese, including many former members of the Malayan People's Anti-Japanese Army.

The colonial regime countered the communist guerrillas' claim to be a Malayan people's liberation army fighting for independence for all races, by hastening the process towards self government, so that the communist Emergency accelerated political independence. At the same time it meant that independence was granted to conservative forces, since the first impact of the Emergency was to destroy all left-wing political organizations, which had become tainted by association with the communists during the constitutional debate about the Malayan Union and the Federation. Emergency regulations promulgated in the Federation and Singapore in 1948 permitted arrest and detention without trial and proscription of political parties. The Malayan Communist Party and Malay Nationalist Party were immediately banned with all their associate organizations, and Malay Nationalist Party leaders were jailed. In Singapore the Malayan Democratic Union, which by 1948 was heavily infiltrated by communists, disbanded itself to avoid proscription. This left only the conservative parties: the United Malays National Organization in the Federation and the Progressive Party, founded in Singapore in 1947.

Constitutional Progress in Malaya and Singapore

For several years the Emergency inhibited the growth of radical politics, the development of trade union activity or liberal political ideas. While the British government wished to encourage democratic trade union-ism, the climate of fear and repression frustrated the formation of unions.

On the other hand independence was negotiated in a fairly amicable spirit, since both UMNO and the Singapore Progressives wished to gain political independence by constitutional means, sharing the British concern to preserve the economic and social *status quo.*

As a prelude to self government in Malaya and Singapore, the British set out to develop and work through existing institutions by Malay-anizing the civil service, expanding popular participation in local government, and enlarging representation and responsibility in legislative and executive councils. The first municipal elections were held in Singapore in 1949 and in Kuala Lumpur in 1952, while provision was made for elected councils in the new villages.

Singapore's initial constitutional progress was more rapid than Malaya's, although for some years the same atmosphere of political repression precluded the development of radical political parties. While fighting did not spread to Singapore, the Emergency regulations were enforced, and between 1948 and 1953 hundreds of left-wing radicals were arrested.

The first elections for a small number of seats in the Singapore legislative council were held in 1948 and further elections for a larger number in 1951. The electorate was virtually confined to English-speaking British subjects, which excluded the majority of Singaporeans, particularly the China-born. There was thus little mass enthusiasm for politics, but the British were happy to work through a conservative group of English-educated professional men. The Singapore Progressive Party, formed to contest the first 1948 election, was an upper-middle-class party, but was multi-racial, as nearly all Singapore political parties were to be, in contrast to those in Malaya.

Meanwhile in the Federation the legislative and executive councils continued to be wholly nominated bodies, but from 1951 the high commissioner nominated non-official councillors as 'members' or ministers in charge of specific departments. The Singapore Progressives were anxious to see Singapore follow suit.

In Malaya the British insisted on ensuring the well-being and protection of racial minorities before agreeing to political independence.

Tunku Abdul Rahman Putra *(By courtesy of the Arkib Negara Malaysia).*

They attempted to spread responsibility by appointing Chinese and Indian as well as Malay members, but the Federation of Malaya Agreement, in effect, meant working in collaboration with the traditional Malay ruling class in any attempt to assimilate immigrant communities into an independent Malayan society and secure a peaceful transition to independence.

At the first federal legislative council meeting Dato Onn bin Ja'afar called for 'a consciousness of membership in a united Malaya ever moving towards a final conception and acceptance of a nationality of the peninsula and a self-governing entity'. As member for home affairs, Dato Onn wanted to achieve racial harmony by opening membership of UMNO to non-Malays. When he failed to get support from the rest of his party, he resigned from UMNO in 1951 to create a non-communal Independence of Malaya Party, aiming to secure independence within seven years. The leadership of UMNO passed to Tunku Abdul Rahman, a Cambridge-educated lawyer and brother of the sultan of Kedah.

The Kuala Lumpur municipal elections of 1952 posed a trial of strength between UMNO and the Independence of Malaya Party. In order to combat Dato Onn's multi-racial party, UMNO formed an electoral pact with the Malayan Chinese Association, which had been formed by Dato Tan Cheng Lock in 1949 as an anti-communist party for Malayan-domiciled Chinese. The success of this alliance in the election induced UMNO and the Malayan Chinese Association to form an Alliance party, which the Malayan Indian Congress subsequently joined in 1954. Thus the temporary alliance became a permanent nation-wide party, embracing the major races, but all three organizations were largely English-educated and middle or upper class in their leadership.

Tunku Abdul Rahman and the other Alliance leaders favoured communal alliances and associations with other ethnic parties as a first stage in winning independence, in the belief that once the colonial yoke was thrown off, Malayans of all races would settle down to create one united nation, so that, within a generation, common citizenship and a common education system would make ethnic differences irrelevant.

After his rout at the Kuala Lumpur municipal elections, Dato Onn went on to found a new Party Negara. But the future belonged to the Alliance. The chief impact of the Independence of Malaya Party had been to drive UMNO and the Malayan Chinese Association together. It meant that Malaya was committed to winning independence on the basis of an alliance of communal organizations.

Political tension relaxed as the colonial government gained the upper hand over the communist guerrillas. The influx of large Commonwealth forces, Templer's firm handling of the situation, and a surging economy boosted morale. UMNO leaders in Malaya and Progressives in Singapore pressed for a greater share in government. In 1954 Britain promised independence for Malaya once the communist Emergency was over, and in 1955 granted new constitutions in the Federation and Singapore, which vested responsibility for many functions in largely elected governments, with elected majorities in the legislative councils.

The 1955 elections produced contrasting results in the Federation and Singapore. In Malaya the Alliance, calling for *merdeka* or independence, was swept to power, gaining all but one of the elective seats. In face of this popular support, Britain agreed to grant full independence within two years, after assurances from the Alliance government about the form of constitution in a plural society, citizenship, and safeguards for the position of the rulers.

The Rendel Constitution

In the 1955 elections in Singapore the Progressives and other moderates were soundly and unexpectedly beaten by radicals, who had taken advantage of the thaw in political repression to form new parties to fight the election: the Labour Front, created in 1954 under the leadership of a lawyer, David Marshall, and supported largely by white-collar trade unionists; and the more extreme People's Action Party (PAP), also formed in 1954. Led by English-educated radicals, under the effective leadership of Lee Kuan Yew, in alliance with pro-communists and militant trade-union leaders, the PAP brought Chinese-educated and English-educated radicals together for the first time in a militant anti-colonial movement.

David Marshall's Labour Front won through to be the largest single party and formed a coalition government with Alliance members, in co-operation with the colonial ex-officio members. It was a difficult period of minority government, very different from the Federation, where the colonial authorities bowed to the Alliance victory, recognizing that it had an overwhelming mandate to work towards full authority and independence. In Singapore the colonial government was shocked, expecting a Progressive victory with a slow orderly route to self government, so that at first the governor attempted to browbeat the new government.

Lee Kuan Yew.

Marshall was impatient by nature and competition with extremist left-wing opposition from the People's Action Party goaded him on. The Labour Front regime was a stormy period, troubled by strikes, violent labour disputes and riots over education. The Malayan Communist Party, though still operating illegally, was able to infiltrate schools and trade unions to exploit genuine frustrations among students and workers over poverty and appalling housing conditions. The encouragement of English-medium education caused rising discontent among the Chinese-educated, and trouble in Chinese schools led to the dismissal of teachers and expulsion of students. Wages were held artificially low by a clamp down on trade union activity. This created resentment since the country was experiencing a boom as a result of the Korean War. Playing on this bitterness, communist leaders organized labour unions, notably the Singapore Factory and Shop Workers' Union, formed in 1954 and built up rapidly by its militant secretary-general, Lim Chin Siong. By 1955 the union had organized crippling strikes, securing better wages and conditions and attracting a large following, while communist cells in the Chinese schools had brought student support to labour disputes.

Marshall himself resigned as chief minister in 1956 after an unsuccessful bid to persuade London to grant Singapore immediate internal self government. The Labour Front, despite strikes, riots and demonstrations went on to defuse the most explosive issues: notably education, by laying down a policy to give equal opportunities for all four language streams and train all children to be bilingual; citizenship; and localization of the civil service. This culminated in securing agreement from London for full internal self government in Singapore by 1959.

Independence for the Federation of Malaya

The newly elected Alliance government which came to office in the Federation of Malaya in 1955 declared the communists could no longer claim to be fighting for independence, since this had now been obtained by constitutional means. They offered an amnesty to terrorists in order to end the Emergency, and in 1956 Tunku Abdul Rahman and Tan Cheng Lock, together with David Marshall, chief minister of Singapore, met Chin Peng at Baling. But no agreement was reached and the Emergency dragged on for another four years. The terrorists steadily lost ground and cleared districts were declared 'white areas' where the night curfew and other restrictions on everyday life were raised, until by 1960 the Emergency was declared to be over and the remnants of Chin Peng's forces retreated into hiding in southern Thailand.

Malaya attained independence in 1957 a prosperous country with stable political institutions, a sound administrative system, a good infrastructure of education and communications, a country with excellent resources and a thriving economy based on export agriculture and mining.

The 1957 constitution, derived from the Federation Agreement of 1948, remains fundamentally in force to this day. It created a federation with a strong central government, headed by a constitutional monarchy of king and parliament. The nine rulers were to choose one of their number in order of precedence to be *yang di-pertuan agong*, or supreme head of state for five years. Parliament consisted of two houses; a *Dewan Rakyat* or House of Representatives directly elected by universal suffrage, and the Senate or *Dewan Negara* representing state assemblies and special interests. In addition each state and settlement retained certain powers with its own elected government and ruler or governor. All born in Malaya after independence were to be Malayan citizens, but Malays were guaranteed special rights for ten years.

The Alliance leadership was essentially a conservative, English-educated, upper-middle-class, propertied group, who did not want to see radical social or economic change. They continued to welcome foreign investment and capitalist enterprise and did not plan any nationalization or socialist measures. Malaya continued to rely on Britain for defence and took an anti-communist stand.

The English-educated elite, having more in common with each other than with the mass of their own ethnic communities, genuinely believed in the possibilities of moulding a multi-racial society. They aimed to create national unity by a common education policy and by helping Malays become as prosperous as immigrants by giving them a head start in education and employment. Consequently the emphasis in the early years of independence lay in rural development and education for nation building, which was the particular concern of Tun Abdul Razak, the deputy prime minister.

The government aimed to expand education, to offer six years of free primary education for all children, at first retaining Malay, Chinese, English and Tamil primary schools but laying down a common syllabus with compulsory instruction in Malay and English. Malay secondary education was to be developed with the ultimate object of using Malay as the major language of instruction in all schools, and a *Dewan Bahasa dan Pustaka* or Language and Literary Agency was created in 1959 to promote *Bahasa Melayu* as the national language.

Health facilities were extended among the rural population, particularly under the Second Malayan Five Year Development Plan of 1961-5, since in 1957 the bulk of health facilities had been concentrated in the towns, whereas 60 per cent of the population had lived in the country.

The Alliance government saw free capitalist enterprise, with some government supervision and guidance as the most efficient instrument

Tun Tan Siew Sin *(By courtesy of the Arkib Negara Malaysia).*

for eradicating poverty and transforming an underdeveloped society into a modern prosperous one. Domestic and foreign investment was encouraged by the finance minister, Tan Siew Sin.* A First Malayan Five Year Development Plan (1956-60) aimed to expand agriculture, particularly rice cultivation; to diversify into alternative cash crops in order to lessen the dependence on natural rubber, which was depressed because of competition from synthetic rubber; and to develop secondary industries. But diversification proved difficult, and rubber and tin remained the mainstays of the economy.

While the Alliance continued to dominate politics in the Federation, new opposition parties appeared in the *Dewan Rakyat* after the first elections in 1959; a religious-based Pan-Malayan Islamic Party, which attracted a strong following in the Malay majority northern states; and two left-wing parties, the Socialist Front and the People's Progressive Party, which aimed to cut through ethnic barriers but in practice attracted only non-Malays. In state elections in 1959 the Alliance

* Tan Siew Sin, a son of Tun Tan Cheng Lock; minister for commerce and industry 1957-9; finance minister 1959; became president of the Malayan Chinese Association in 1961 after his father's death.

retained control of all states except Kelantan and Trengganu, which fell to the Pan-Malayan Islamic Party.

Singapore and the PAP Government

Malaya's success in achieving *merdeka* drove Singapore to seek a similar independence but, since the state seemed too small to be viable, all responsible Singapore parties aimed to achieve independence through merger with the Federation. This policy was consistently pursued by the Progressives, the Labour Front and the People's Action Party.

When the secretary of state outlined the policy for the Malayan Union in 1945, he stressed that Singapore had ties with the mainland but should not be forced prematurely into a union. But from the decision taken in 1945 to make Singapore a separate colony its eventual emergence as an independent unit was virtually settled, despite the preoccupation of Singapore politicians over the next twenty years with achieving union with peninsular Malaya.

When the Singapore crown colony was formed in 1946, it preserved many links with the Malayan Union and subsequently with the Federation of Malaya: immigration, currency, university education, income tax and many other aspects. The British government declared in 1946 that 'It is no part of the policy of His Majesty's government to preclude or prejudice in any way the fusion of Singapore and the Malayan Union in a wider union at a later date should it be considered that such a course was desirable'. But in practice the two territories took diverging paths.

By the time the Federation of Malaya was formed in 1948, the Malay leaders opposed including Singapore, which would have meant a Chinese majority. The course of events in Singapore in the decade which followed confirmed this antipathy and strengthened the resolve of Alliance leaders not to seek closer association. In contrast to the Federation's gentlemanly upper-class politics, the nationalist movement in Singapore became increasingly radical and militant, harnessing mass support through trade unions and students, which was distasteful and alarming to Malayan leaders.

At the same time Singapore's need to join the Federation intensified. In face of widespread unemployment, a soaring birthrate and with newly independent nations in the region, notably Indonesia and Malaya itself, attempting to cut out Singapore's traditional middleman role to build up their own independent economies, Singapore politicians sought a Malayan common market which would provide additional employment opportunities.

In 1959, when Singapore was granted full internal self government, the electorate, expanded by the new citizenship qualifications to give dominance to the Chinese-educated, swept the People's Action Party to power. Under Lee Kuan Yew's premiership, the new government was pledged to introduce a programme of active social reform and to secure full independence within four years through a merger with the Federation.

The early years of the new government were troubled. The electoral victory was followed quickly by rifts within the party's ranks between moderates and left-wing extremists. Lee Kuan Yew's moderates wanted to build up the economy by encouraging private local and foreign investment to reduce unemployment, to finance an ambitious programme of social reform and produce stability to impress the Federation. Lim Chin Siong's radical wing aimed at a socialist, and eventually communist, society with the extinction of capitalism.

This led to conflict with trade unions and dissensions within the party, and the loss of a crucial by-election in the spring of 1961 threatened to topple the PAP moderates. Now Tunku Abdul Rahman and the Federation leaders began to dread the prospect of an independent communist Singapore, which would be a permanent communist threat to Malaya. This fear, outweighing concern over the disruptive potential of a Singapore within Malaya, led Tunku Abdul Rahman to reverse his policy, and in May 1961 he mooted the possibility of a closer association. This was eagerly welcomed by the PAP ruling group but precipitated a break with the left wing. While the Malayan Communist Party was dedicated ultimately to creating a communist pan-Malayan republic, the radicals had no wish in the short term to see Singapore absorbed into a conservative, anti-communist, Malay-dominated regime. In a bid to take over power, Lim Chin Siong's radicals challenged the government in the assembly, failed by a narrow margin to overthrow it and then broke away to form an opposition party, the *Barisan Sosialis,* in July 1961, which continued to oppose the merger.

Negotiations between Singapore and Malaya continued for the next two years. As in 1948 the UMNO-dominated federal government feared a simple merger in which Chinese would comprise 43 per cent of the total population outnumbering the 41 per cent Malays, and to redress this imbalance Kuala Lumpur sought to create a larger Malaysian federation including the Borneo territories: Sarawak, British North Borneo and Brunei. The British welcomed this move to settle the problem of the future of its smaller dependencies which had hitherto defied solution.

Post-war Development in Borneo

After the Second World War Britain had tried to encourage uniformity wherever possible between Malaya, Singapore and the Borneo territories. Joint departments had been established where applicable between Singapore and the Malayan Union (later the Federation of Malaya). While it was considered premature to create a unified civil service for Malaya, Singapore and Borneo, the Borneo services were upgraded and adopted Malayan practices. The aim was to create a common feeling of citizenship in the three Borneo states, with a view to their eventual amalgamation, and there was talk on a number of occasions of a confederation of all five territories, although in practice they developed along different lines.

The establishment of crown colony rule brought steady if unspectacular economic and social progress in Borneo, which escaped the peninsula's political troubles and was unaffected by communist insurgency. Commercial agriculture was developed, particularly in North Borneo, with schemes to promote rubber, palm oil and copra production and above all exploitation of timber resources, which became North Borneo's main export and chief revenue earner from 1959. There was some improvement in *padi* cultivation, but both states remained rice importers. Communications were improved, with road building schemes to connect the main settlements in North Borneo being launched in 1954, and new roads built to link the river valleys of Sarawak. The expansion of the economy and increased revenue provided funds for improved social services, education and health measures, although on a lesser scale than in Malaya.

Constitutional change came slowly in the wake of the reforms introduced in the Federation and Singapore in the mid-1950s. In Sarawak a new constitution in 1956 provided for an elected unofficial majority in the Council Negri, chosen by indirect election from municipal and divisional councils. A further constitutional amendment in 1963 reduced the numbers of ex-officio and nominated members in the Council Negri to a handful and provided for the Supreme Council to comprise a chief minister and a majority of members from the Council Negri. Constitutional progress was even slower in North Borneo, where the legislative council did not attain a non-official majority until 1962.

The oil-rich state of Brunei was able to offer generous social benefits and free education to all its people but remained a constitutional anachronism. In 1959 the British resident was withdrawn and Sultan Sir Omar Ali Saifuddin assumed executive authority. The sultan granted a constitution but in practice remained an absolute monarch, nominating his privy council, council of ministers and legislative council.

After granting independence to the Federation of Malaya in 1957 and setting Singapore on the path to self government, Britain hoped to see its other territories in Southeast Asia come together in a viable association. In 1958 it pushed the idea of a North Borneo Federation, to comprise Sarawak, North Borneo and Brunei, but this was rejected by the Sultan Omar, who felt that Brunei's interests were closer to peninsular Malaya than to its neighbours. Without Brunei a Borneo federation was doomed, since its oil revenues were essential to the success of such a state.

The Malaysia Proposal

Bringing the Borneo territories into the proposed Malaysia federation had attractions for all the parties concerned.

Britain welcomed the guarantee of a settled future for the Borneo dependencies. The labour-hungry Borneo states offered the prospect of jobs for Singapore's unemployed, while the merger opened up opportunities for North Borneo and Sarawak to attract capital and labour, modernize the economy and achieve political independence.

At first Sultan Omar was enthusiastic about joining Malaysia. He had long favoured such a link in view of strong ethnic affinity, and Kuala Lumpur looked forward to the addition of the Brunei Malays. The Federation of Malaya saw the incorporation of Borneo as a means to counterbalance the Singapore Chinese, although in fact nearly one-quarter of Sabah's population were Chinese and in Sarawak they made up nearly one-third of the population and were the largest single community. Of the indigenous people, most of those who called themselves Malays were not ethnically Malay but were local people of the coastal regions who had been converted to Islam. The peoples of the interior, Dyaks, Kadazans, Muruts and others, were rarely Muslim but adhered to a much older animism, although numbers had been converted to Christianity in the immediate post-war years.

Initial negotiations proceeded fairly rapidly. Britain dispatched the Cobbold Commission to Borneo in 1962, which after a rushed inquiry reported a unanimous desire for the transfer, although the majority of the population was probably unaware of the implications of the change and accustomed to accept the authorities' recommendations. A referendum in Singapore in September 1962 confirmed popular support for joining, and Sultan Omar's enthusiasm for bringing Brunei into Malaysia grew warmer after a rebellion sparked off by the radical Brunei Party Rakyat in December 1962. The party, led by Azahari, opposed the idea of Malaysia, demanded a share in the administration and challenged the sultan's autocratic rule. The rebellion was quickly suppressed, the party was banned and its leaders were arrested or fled into exile.

But the final months of the Malaysia negotiations were soured by internal disputes and external threats. Haggling over financial arrangements led to bad blood between Singapore and the Federation, while Sultan Omar of Brunei, a man of independent spirit, objected to Kuala Lumpur's claims upon Brunei's oil wealth. Unhappy about the Federation's tax proposals and objecting to the position allocated to him among the other rulers, Sultan Omar preferred to retain freedom of action, even if this meant remaining dependent to some extent on Britain, and at the last minute he refused to join Malaysia.

Brunei's decision was a blow, but the new federation also faced active opposition from outside: notably from the Philippines, which claimed North Borneo as a former dependency of Sulu, and from President Sukarno of Indonesia, who denounced the creation of Malaysia as a neo-colonialist plot and declared a policy of confrontation.

After months of hard bargaining, the Malaysia Agreement was finally signed in July 1963. To satisfy the United Nations that Filipino and Indonesian objections were unfounded, a commission was sent to confirm that the people of Sarawak and North Borneo were willing to join the new arrangement, and in September 1963 the Federation of Malaysia came into being, comprising the former Federation of Malaya, Singapore, Sarawak and North Borneo, which was renamed Sabah.

Malaysia's constitution derived basically from the former Federation of Malaya, comprising a constitutional monarchy and two-chamber central parliament. Each state had its own ruler,* constitution and elected legislative assembly.† Singapore had a special status with more autonomy than the others, its own executive government and control over a large proportion of its revenue. But it had less representation in proportion to its population in the central government.

At the time of the formation of Malaysia in 1963, the Malays comprised 40 per cent of the population, Chinese 43 per cent, Indians and Pakistanis 9 per cent and indigenous people of Borneo and other races 8 per cent. In peninsular Malaysia the Malays were the largest single community, comprising nearly 50 per cent of the population of 7.2 millions, the Chinese 37 per cent, Indians and Pakistanis 11 per cent. In Borneo the indigenous peoples were in the majority but were made up of a number of different tribes.

1. Colonial Office minute, 6 September 1945, Public Record Office, London CO 273/675, 50823/46.

2. Supreme Allied Command South East Asia to Foreign Office, 1 September 1945, Public Record Office, London, CO273/675, 50823.

3. Telegram from Limbang to Raja Vyner Brooke, July 1945, Public Record Office, London, CO 531/238/31, 53115/12.

4. Sir H. MacMichael, *Report on a Mission to Malaya, October 1945-January 1946*, Colonial Office No. 194, His Majesty's Stationery Office, London, 1946.

5. Sir Shenton Thomas to Colonial Office, October 1945, Public Record Office, London, CO 273/675, 50823/17; Sir Cecil Clementi to Colonial Office, February 1946, Public Record Office, London, CO 273/676, 50823/35.

* Governors in Melaka, Penang and Sarawak; *yang di-pertuan negara* in Singapore and Sabah; rulers in the remaining states.

† Sarawak's assembly was still known as the Council Negri.

CHAPTER 18

Malaysia, Brunei and the Republic of Singapore

The new Federation of Malaysia was scheduled to come into being on 31 August 1963 but, in deference to Indonesia's objections, arrangements were postponed until mid-September, in order to allow the United Nations survey team to confirm that the majority of the population in Sabah and Sarawak favoured incorporation in Malaysia.

Meanwhile in Singapore the ruling People's Action Party declared Singapore's independence on the originally stipulated date and exploited the popularity it had gained as a result of the successful negotiations to enter Malaysia to call a snap election. It secured a comfortable majority over the *Barisan* opposition, which had lost most of its leaders when Lim Chin Siong and half of the party's central committee were arrested earlier in the year on charges of complicity in the Brunei revolt. Thus the political situation in Singapore at the inception of the new federation was more stable than at any time since 1955.

But Malaysia had a troubled start. Manila and Jakarta refused recognition and Indonesia, rejecting the findings of the United Nations mission to Borneo, adopted a militant 'Crush Malaysia' stand. While the brunt of this confrontation fell on Sabah and Sarawak, where the Indonesians made military incursions along the borders, Jakarta also landed commandos in peninsular Malaysia in August and September 1964 and sent saboteurs to Singapore.

Indonesian confrontation won little support from the local population, but the threat failed to draw the component parts of the federation closer together. All parties to the Malaysia Agreement stood to gain in the long run, but from the outset there was friction and resentment, which in the case of Singapore and Kuala Lumpur soured relations to breaking point.

The difficulties were partly economic, partly political and racial. While a Malaysian common market seemed essential for Singapore's growing industrial production thereby solving its unemployment problems, the island was badly hit in the short term by confrontation and the sharp decline of trade with Indonesia. There was also resentment of the central Alliance government's allocation of quotas and its taxation policy, which operated unfairly against Singapore industry.

But the major sources of friction were political and communal. Singapore and Kuala Lumpur resented each other's attempts to intervene in what they considered to be their internal affairs. The Singapore government, intent on building up a multi-racial society of equal opportunity, refused to extend to Singapore Malays the same privileges which applied in peninsular Malaysia and accused Malay extremists and Indonesian agents of stirring up racial disharmony in Singapore which erupted in bitter and unprecedented communal riots in July and September 1964.

At the same time the central Alliance government deplored Singapore's attempt to break into federal politics in the 1964 elections, when the People's Action Party unsuccessfully challenged the conservative Malaysian Chinese Association's claim to represent the Chinese community. The People's Action Party campaigned for a re-alignment of federal politics along socio-economic instead of communal lines, but the Singapore leaders were out of touch with the depth of feeling in the peninsular states. While they claimed to represent non-communalism, to the Malay electorate they embodied Singapore Chinese aggression. The election unleashed passionate racial emotion, in which the People's Action Party was soundly trounced.

The Alliance was even more incensed when the ruling Singapore party then went on to form a Malaysian Solidarity Convention in May 1965 in conjunction with other radical opposition parties in the peninsula and Borneo, calling for 'a democratic Malaysian Malaysia' with political alignments based not on ethnic considerations but on 'common political ideologies and common social and economic aspirations'. The call for racial equality was premature, in practice appealing almost exclusively to non-Malays since equality implied the withdrawal of Malay privileges and exacerbated racial tensions.

Escalating friction, exasperation with the People's Action Party leaders, and fear that he was losing control over right-wing Malay extremists, who alleged that Singapore's leaders were plotting to seize control in Malaysia and called for their arrest, drove Tunku Abdul Rahman to decide that Singapore must be expelled. The separation was ordered in August 1965, almost without warning, and in face of Lee Kuan Yew's protests Singapore was forced to become a separate independent republic despite its leaders' previous predictions that it could not survive on its own.

If the break had to come, the actual timing was fortunate. The communists were in no position to exploit the rift, the British continued to underwrite the defence of Singapore and Malaysia, and both countries were profiting from the general buoyancy of the international economy, and in particular the boom in tin prices. Despite these mitigating factors, since the Federation of Malaysia had been formed primarily to absorb Singapore, the island's expulsion caused immediate problems for all the constituents; peninsular Malaysia, Sarawak, Sabah, and most of all Singapore.

Singapore

Separation destroyed the premises upon which Singapore politicians had based their policy since the end of the Second World War. Up to that time the island had not been considered a viable state since it seemed too small to defend itself, too poor in natural resources and overburdened with population to devise a sound economy. Now, suddenly, it was on its own, cut off from its economic hinterland from which it had derived a large measure of its past prosperity and upon which its plans for developing industry and employment opportunities depended. It had to build up an adequate defence capability, devise economic policies to sustain its industrialization programme, and create a sense of nationhood where none existed.

Grave though these problems might be, Singapore's position was not entirely bleak. The merger with Malaysia, painful though it was at the time, averted chaos which seemed inevitable in 1963, saved the ruling regime and weakened the communist movement in Singapore. By 1965 local, regional and international conditions helped Singapore cope with the crisis of separation. At home, while *Barisan Sosialis* leaders condemned Singapore's independence as spurious and boycotted its parliament, the party was in no position to take direct militant action. Lim Chin Siong and other leaders had been in gaol for two years, and the party suffered a further blow when the Indonesian Communist Party was destroyed following an abortive communist coup in Indonesia in September 1965, barely a month after Singapore's break with Malaysia.

The next year the new Indonesian regime called off confrontation against Malaysia and Singapore and this, set against world economic growth, gave Singapore the chance to prosper. Profiting from its own excellent commercial infrastructure, Singapore took advantage of the situation in the late-1960s and early-1970s to build up its economy. Its problems were stark and demanded an all-out drive for maximum efficiency and growth. Abandoning those aspects of socialist policies which no longer fitted an isolated society living on its wits, it adopted a mixed economy, combining private enterprise with state participation and offering incentives to private capital.

Britain's decision in 1968 to close its military bases within three years posed an immediate threat not only to Singapore's security but to its economy, since the bases were the biggest single employer of labour and accounted for 20 per cent of the economy. But the government used the

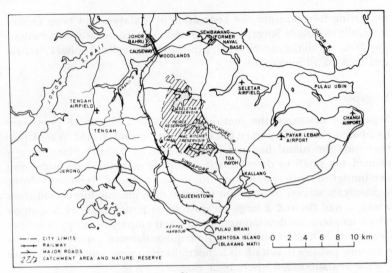

Singapore

crisis to rally the population with a renewed sense of urgency. In the 1968 elections the ruling party gained every seat, giving it a new mandate to push through tough labour legislation, enforcing discipline, restricting trade union activity and providing arbitration to avoid strikes. Singapore encouraged foreign and local capital with considerable success, attracting substantial investment from the developed countries, notably from the United States but also from Western Europe and Japan. By 1969 Singapore claimed to be the busiest port in the Commonwealth and by 1975 the third largest port in the world. In the early-1970s foreign capital poured into Singapore, mostly into the newly developed regional oil industry but also into precision engineering, electrical and other industries. Despite a setback during the oil crisis in the mid-70s, Singapore's per capita income rose from US$700-800 per annum in 1965 to more than US$2500 in 1977, by which time foreign investment accounted for the bulk of employment and more than 90 per cent of direct exports.[1]

Profits from its dynamic economy were taxed to provide benefits in education, housing, public health and urban renewal, while a vigorous and successful family-planning programme helped improve standards of living. The government aimed to persuade, and if need be, force people out of poverty by their own efforts but to discourage a welfare state, so that the amount paid out in public assistance dropped dramatically in the decade after independence.* What was given came in small amounts with the application of a stringent means test.

* 22,241 cases in 1966 to 6640 in 1976.

To create a sense of national identity Singapore's leadership stressed its separateness and sense of achievement and superiority, breeding an abrasive, arrogant attitude which alienated its neighbours, particularly Malaysia. Singapore had committed itself to the path of competitive, dynamic growth, posing strains within its own society and friction with its neighbours.

In building a sense of nationhood Singapore differed markedly from Malaysia. Despite its cosmopolitan population, communalism had never been a serious issue in Singapore. On the other hand it needed to play down its image as a Chinese city state in an alien region and could not use a Chinese identity to build up a cultural nationalism. Its only salvation lay in creating a secular, multi-racial state, encouraging communities to take pride in their cultural roots and language but conforming to a common national character. Despite its association with colonial rule, English became increasingly Singapore's lingua franca, a unifying force within the state and an effective link with the world of international commerce.

Singapore's nationalism had been largely based on the labour movement by creating militant anti-colonial unions. After independence, Singapore's leadership had to tame these unions and left-wing extremists in order to mollify investors and stabilize the economy. The crisis posed by the announced British pull-out in 1968 presented the opportunity to jolt the unions into accepting a changed role.

Economic success and positive energetic government leadership found the answers to separation but at a cost of growing author-itarianism. While democratic forms were maintained and regular elections held, from 1968 the People's Action Party monopolized all seats in the parliament, with the ruling group strengthening its hold on the party, parliament and the state.

Initially Singapore leaders spoke in terms of eventual re-unification with Malaysia. The separation agreement provided for co-operation in defence, foreign policy and economic affairs, but almost immediately Singapore and Malaysia imposed immigration restrictions and set out to produce competitive economies and independent defence systems. The reduction of political tensions and economic success resulted, within a few years, in Singapore's acceptance of separation as inevitable and even beneficial.

Malaysia: Sabah and Sarawak

The separation of Singapore came as a shock to Sabah and Sarawak, particularly the latter which had traditionally been more closely linked with Singapore than with the peninsula. It came at a time when the two states had scarcely begun the process of assimilation into Malaysia.

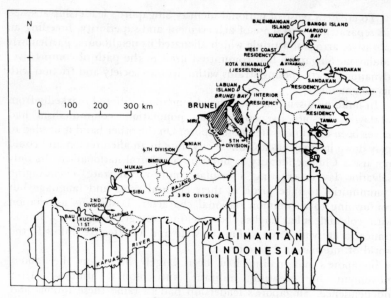

Sarawak and Sabah

Since Kuala Lumpur had been so anxious to attract them into the federation largely as a counterweight to Singapore, the Malaysia Agreement guaranteed a considerable amount of local autonomy, which the central authorities soon came to regret. In attempting to bring Sarawak and Sabah into line with federal policies, Kuala Lumpur failed to appreciate the different character of the Borneo people, particularly the Sarawak Malays, who, as descendants of indigenous converts to Islam, shared the attitudes of other non-Muslim Borneo people rather than peninsular Malays. An initial much resented influx of Malay officials from the peninsula was soon abandoned in favour of appointing locally-recruited officials. While this inhibited the growth of an integrated civil service and common federal policy, it helped the two states to accept the link with the peninsula, especially as the economic and social benefits of federal development planning began to take effect.

The incorporation of Sabah and Sarawak into Malaysia encouraged the rapid development of political parties. Hitherto the Borneo states had virtually no political experience and passed from fully fledged colonial rule to complete independence without the opportunity for gradually acquiring political experience.

Both were controlled by governments which ostensibly supported the central government in Kuala Lumpur. Sabah was dominated by the United Sabah National Organization led by Tun Datu Mustapha bin

Datu Harun which, together with the Sabah Chinese Association, was a member of the Malaysian Alliance. Tun Mustapha, who rose from obscurity to power and riches, was a dynamic personality, an orator of charisma, and was intensely ambitious. A devout Muslim, Mustapha encouraged the mass conversion of the animist peoples of the interior. Controlling patronage and actively promoting Sabah's interests, Mustapha's position for many years seemed all powerful and he effectively ruled the country for thirteen years from the formation of Malaysia in 1963.

In Sarawak, the Sarawak United People's Party and the Sarawak Chinese Association, which supported the Malaysian Alliance, won an overwhelming majority in the 1963 state elections, but there were a number of opposition parties, notably the Sarawak National Party.

Tun Datu Haji Mustapha *(By courtesy of the Sabah In-formation Department).*

Peninsular Malaysia

In comparison with Singapore, Sabah and Sarawak, peninsular Malaysia, in 1965, outwardly enjoyed a more stable situation. The separation of Singapore meant that the peninsula needed to develop its commercial services to replace traditional dependence on Singapore. But it was rich in natural resources, with an excellent communications system, a well-established economy based on agriculture and mining, a sufficiently large domestic market and labour force to support new industry, and was not burdened with over population.

Unlike Singapore, peninsular Malaysian independence owed nothing to trade-union politics and it had no need subsequently to placate the labour movement. But it was built on Malay nationalism which, in its turn, unleashed dangerous communal emotions.

Malayan society was distorted by the uneven distribution of wealth and economic activity, with socio-economic divisions falling largely along ethnic lines, with a predominantly rural Malay peasantry and largely urbanized Chinese and Indian communities. It needed to redress the balance between urban and rural communities, between the developed west coast states and the backward east, which meant that, unlike Singapore, it could not go for all-out economic advancement, but had to sacrifice a measure of efficiency in the interests of building a more just society. The preponderance of Malays in secure, highly paid government positions was to the minorities an irritant that could not be eradicated without further reducing the economic power of the Malays.

The First Malaysia Development Plan 1966–70

The first five-year Malaysia Development Plan, launched in 1966, gave priority to the expansion of agriculture, as the country's main economic activity, employing more than half the population and contributing 50 per cent of foreign exchange earnings. The plan aimed to work towards producing self sufficiency in rice, expanding rubber and oil palm production, exploiting forestry and fisheries and encouraging diversification into new crops.

Large-scale rubber replanting schemes were launched, oil palm under cultivation more than doubled in these years, and emphasis was placed on rice cultivation, traditionally neglected by the colonial regime. A Padi Cultivators Act, passed in 1967, provided security of tenure, an Agricultural Bank was set up in 1969, many schemes were promoted to supply fertilizers, encourage mechanization and double cropping, while irrigation schemes in Kelantan and the Muda basin in Kedah extended production. Communications were improved in Sabah to provide all-weather roads linking Kota Kinabalu with Sandakan and Kudat.

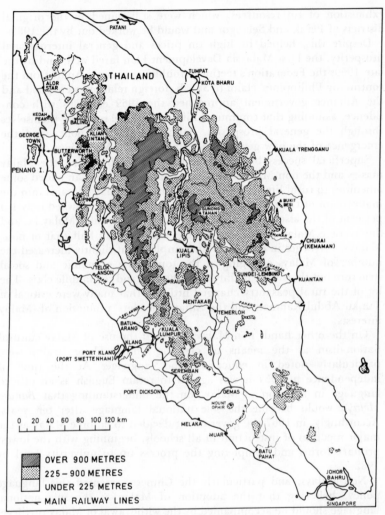

Peninsular Malaysia

There were shadows over economic development: the declining price of rubber, the failure to find a crop which would replace rubber as the major product, the difficulty in industraliziation in view of the traditional reliance on export agriculture and mining,* and the approaching

* In 1963 only 6 per cent of the work force was in industry. D. W. Fryer, *Emerging South East Asia: a Study in Growth and Stagnation*, (McGraw Hill, New York, 1970). p.269.

exhaustion of tin resources, which were still mined in the original districts of Perak and Selangor and would be worked out by the 1980s.

Despite this, helped by high tin prices and general international prosperity, the First Malaysia Development Plan fared well, and by the late-1960s the Federation's teething troubles were over. Apart from the continuing Philippines' claim to Sabah, foreign relations were good and the Alliance government approached the 1969 elections with confidence, assuming that communal differences were resolving themselves through the general prosperity, national education policy and the emergence of the new generation of independent Malaysians.

Superficial success belied social tensions, both among the Malay masses and the non-Malays. While the First Malaysia Plan added some amenities to rural life, it did little to bring the Malay peasants into the mainstream of the country's economy. In 1969 Malays owned only 1.5 per cent of the assets of limited companies in peninsular Malaysia, and the average Malay per capita income was less than half that of non-Malays. Privileges in education and employment slightly increased the number of Malays emerging at the top of the economic and social structure but these were mainly from the rich and the middle class. The lot of the rural peasantry changed little, so that many were critical of Tunku Abdul Rahman and the Alliance leaders' promotion of Malay interests.

On the other hand, non-Malays resented the use of Malay cultural nationalism as the means of creating unity. These strains were particularly noted in education and language. At the time of independence in 1957 it was agreed to retain English as an official language in addition to Malay, on the understanding that *Bahasa Melayu* would become the sole national language after ten years. Accordingly, in 1967 the government decided to enforce Malay as the major medium of instruction in all schools, beginning with the lowest primary forms and completing the process up to university level by 1982.

Non-Malays, and particularly the Chinese, resented this language policy, believing that the adoption of Malay as the sole national language should be accompanied by the withdrawal of Malay privileges in land ownership, civil service recruitment, university and higher education opportunities and business licences.

Disappointed Malays turned to the right-wing Pan-Malayan Islamic Party, while non-Malays, disillusioned with the ability of the Malaysian Chinese Association and Malaysian Indian Congress to protect their interests, turned to more radical parties: the Democratic Action Party, reformed from the remnants of the People's Action Party after the disastrous 1964 election and calling for equality and justice for 'have-nots' of all races; the People's Progressive Party, based upon Chinese and Indian support mainly from Ipoh; or the *Gerakan Rakyat*

Malaysia, the Malaysian People's Movement, a new multi-racial party formed in 1968 to replace the Socialist Front, which had fallen apart two years earlier.

Crisis of 13 May 1969

At the general election held in May 1969, the Alliance based its campaign on its past record and achievements as the only party capable of maintaining secular multi-racial government. To the right the Pan-Malayan Islamic Party stood for strengthening Islam and promoting Malay interests and culture. To the left the *Gerakan* adopted a platform of social reform, economic progress and the submerging of communal issues. The People's Progressive Party and the Democratic Action Party called for racial equality, for English, Chinese and and Tamil to be recognized as official languages alongside the national *Bahasa Malaysia* and for equal treatment for all four education streams.

The election was charged with emotion, since it hinged upon the political position of the non-Malays and the fate of their languages and culture, and the results came as a shock. The Alliance won but their vote fell by 10 per cent, depriving them of their two-thirds majority. UMNO lost some ground to the Pan-Malayan Islamic Party in north Malaysia, but the Malaysian Chinese Association lost half its parliamentary seats to radical rivals and withdrew from the Cabinet and from state executive councils. Victory opposition rallies by *Gerakan* and Democratic Action Party supporters in Kuala Lumpur provoked Malay counter demonstrations which led to violence in the capital. In two days of rioting hundreds of people, mainly non-Malays, were killed, with widespread destruction of property. The army was called in and the government declared a state of national emergency, suspended the constitution, disbanded parliament and called off elections in Sabah and Sarawak, which had been scheduled later in May.

While rioting and bloodshed were confined mainly to the capital, the violence exposed deep-seated tensions. It came as a personal blow to Tunku Abdul Rahman, father figure and architect of Malayan independence. And it challenged the basic principles upon which the Alliance leaders had consistently based their policy: namely Tun Abdul Razak's stress on rural development and education for nation building, and Tan Siew Sin's confidence in uplifting general economic prosperity by a liberal capitalist free-enterprise policy. Hitherto the Alliance leaders had been confident that they were succeeding in slowly creating a united Malaysia. Now it became obvious how little had been done to satisy the aspirations and still the fears of the Malay masses.

This led to a dramatic change in the direction of state policy, based upon fresh ideology and a new economic policy, in which the government took a more positive role in restructuring society, aiming to improve the condition of the Malays rapidly and at the same time to maintain national unity and tolerance, in an attempt to eliminate racial differences within the next generation.

A National Operations Council under Tun Abdul Razak took over the government. Most members were Malay, but in January 1970 an advisory National Consultative Council was set up with representatives from various communities and groups.

Tunku Abdul Rahman retired in September 1970, to be succeeded by his deputy, Tun Abdul Razak. The new prime minister lacked the charisma of his predecessor but used his gifts as an efficient administrator and patient negotiator to steer the country into peaceful development.

The *Rukunegara,* a declaration on national ideology issued in August 1970, laid down five principles of national harmony for all Malaysians: loyalty to the *yang di-pertuan agong* and Malaysia; loyalty to the constitution; respect for Islam and indigenous custom; belief in the rule of law; and moral behaviour. It was forbidden to discuss sensitive issues, such as the special position of indigenous peoples, the national language, citizenship rights, and the sovereignty of the rulers.

New Economic Policy

At the same time the government launched a New Economic Policy designed to combat poverty and raise standards of living in general, but in particular to give the Malays an equitable place in the economy. The goal was not to take from non-Malays but to create fresh sources of wealth for those hitherto left out. Communalism was dangerous when communal issues coincided with socio-economic ones. In the early-1970s Malays formed the majority of the public sector and agricultural labour force, while the Chinese dominated the private sector in secondary and tertiary occupations. The New Economic Policy tried to restructure the economy and eliminate identification of race with economic activity, to urbanize the Malays and increase Malay participation in industry and commerce, so that within twenty years Malays would own 30 per cent of equity capital, other Malaysians 40 per cent and foreigners 30 per cent.

The New Economic Policy was incorporated in the Second Malaysia Development Plan (1971-75), which laid stress on modernizing and diversifying the economy, with special emphasis on encouraging rural industrialization in the form of agricultural processing. Whereas the First Malaysia Plan had depended primarily on private investment, the Second Plan entailed more direct state involvement, but also needed to attract private capital, since it projected total investments of 50 per cent more than its predecessor.

In the wake of the 1969 disturbances it was difficult initially to attract capital. Malays had little and other Malaysians were reluctant to invest in schemes which offered them no benefits. The state had to supply much of the funding and initiative: notably in the form of government corporations under Malay management: Pernas (national trading corporation); the Bank Bumiputra; and an Urban Development Authority, to promote the urbanization of Malays and smooth the participation of *bumiputra* businessmen.

For the first year or so the prospects for the Second Malaysia Plan looked gloomy, as trade fell and the price of rubber dropped. The Singapore government, realizing the island's prosperity depended on the well-being of its major trade partner, encouraged private Singaporean investment, and by the end of 1973 Singapore was the largest investor in Malaysia. By that time confidence was returning and the Second Malaysia Plan began to pick up steam with investment also coming from Britain, the United States, Japan and Hong Kong. In 1973 Malaysia offered further incentives to foreign investment and to export industries processing local raw materials.

The international oil crisis of 1973–4, which hit Singapore hard, also created problems for Malaysia but brought some side benefits since it coincided with the discovery of oil off the east coast of the peninsula and important oil strikes off the Sabah coast. At the same time the rise in world oil prices increased synthetic rubber production costs, giving a competitive edge to Malaysia's natural rubber industry.

Many Chinese shared the belief held by Tun Abdul Razak and the other moderate Malays that ultimately the only hope for national unity and security for minorities lay in bringing Malays up to the level of the other communities, so that ethnic origin would become irrelevant. But it was not possible to enhance the position of the Malays solely by creating new wealth. Equality in the short term entailed discrimination against non-*bumiputras,* specifically the Chinese. It often meant breaking down exclusive Chinese business links, since Nanyang Chinese business was traditionally organized on a family or clan basis. It was still difficult for outsiders to break in, and everywhere in the region the Chinese network constituted a barrier to the growth of multi-racial national economies.

Unlike Singapore, Malaysia had sufficient natural wealth to permit sacrifice of some efficiency in the interests of nation building, but at a risk. Non-Malays of ability emigrated and there was a dearth of foreign and local Chinese capital needed to finance economic development. Opposition political parties pointed to the creation of a new disunity by turning non-Malays into second-class citizens.

It became largely a race against time. How long would it take to bring the rural Malay masses into the mainstream of economic life? How long would non-Malays be willing to accept economic and educational discrimination in the interests of creating a stable and just society? How long would Malaysia be left to work out its own solutions, untroubled by internal communist subversion, external foreign pressures, or an international economic recession?

Education

Education policy played an important role in supporting the Second Malaysia Plan and the New Economic Policy. It aimed to improve rural schooling, upgrade technical education, to speed up the process of making *Bahasa Malaysia* the main language of instruction in all institutions of learning, and to admit increasing numbers of *bumiputras* to tertiary education, particularly from the rural areas and less developed states.

By 1972 free primary education was available to all children in peninsular Malaysia, and the New Economic Policy in Sabah and Sarawak also provided for the promotion of national unity through increased education opportunities and the introduction of *Bahasa Malaysia* as the language of instruction in all schools.

Prior to 1969 educational policy was designed to integrate all Malaysians by gradually spreading the use of the national language. But from that time the promotion of *Bahasa Malaysia* was seen as primarily satisfying Malay aspirations. It did not provide the same bond which the English language had done between the upper and professional classes of all ethnic groups in the past.

Political Rapprochement

Meanwhile Tun Abdul Razak set out to achieve political harmony. By June 1970, when the postponed elections were held in Sabah and Sarawak, all the opposition in Sabah had been absorbed into Tun Mustapha's United Sabah National Organization, which supported the central government. In July 1970 Tun Razak formed a coalition with the main Sarawak party, the Sarawak United People's Party.

By the end of 1970 the Malaysian government felt that passions had cooled and that it had sufficient voting power to control the situation in a return to democratic forms of government.

Parliament was reconvened in February 1971, the National Consultative Council wound up and the National Operations Council converted into a National Security Council. Control of 102 out of the 144 seats in parliament gave the government the bare two-thirds majority it needed, leaving the rest of the seats in the hands of opposition parties: the Democratic Action Party, the Pan-Malayan Islamic Party, the Sarawak National Party, the *Gerakan* and the People's Progressive Party. Considerable restrictions were placed on democracy. Sensitive issues were banned from debate and policy was to be determined by negotiation and consensus among groups, rather than by the clash of parliamentary debate.

Tun Abdul Razak, by patronage and persuasion, and by threats of withholding development funds from non-cooperative states, intensified negotiations to rejuvenate the parties to the original Alliance and to absorb opposition parties into one multi-racial National Front on a grander scale than the Alliance.

He patched up differences within UMNO, wooing back former members, and attracted others from the Pan-Malayan Islamic Party, culminating in December 1972 in the formation of a coalition between the Alliance and the Pan-Malayan Islamic Party at state and federal levels.

Under Tan Siew Sin, the Malaysian Chinese Association recovered its morale and resumed its place as UMNO's partner. Resisting attempts to make the party more chauvinistic, the Association won back many moderate members from the *Gerakan*, which split in mid-1971 with the splintering off of *Pekamas*, or Social Justice Party, and the following year the *Gerakan* itself joined the Alliance.

In May 1972 the Alliance won over the People's Progressive Party, so that by the beginning of 1973 all Malaysian political parties were absorbed into one National Front, with the exception of the Democratic Action Party, remnants of Party Rakyat, and *Pekamas* in peninsular Malaysia, and the Sarawak National Party. The opposition parties were isolated, weak and divided.

Tun Abdul Razak's aim was harmony, 'paternal leadership and controlled policies', diverting political passions towards economic restructuring. In federal elections in 1974 the National Front swept the polls. The opposition Democratic Action Party won only nine seats, while the Party Rakyat contested twenty-six but won none.

Foreign Policy

This period also saw a change in Malaysian foreign policy, which had hitherto been firmly committed to the West, although Malaysia was never a partner to the Southeast Asia Treaty Organization.

At the time of Singapore's separation from Malaysia in 1965, both territories still sheltered under the British defence umbrella. But the escalation of British military spending and obligations overseas in the post-war period was out of keeping with the decline of British power, and an open-ended commitment to the defence of Singapore and Malaysia became increasingly unrealistic. Confrontation with Indonesia between 1963 and 1966 proved a drain for Britain, and an economic crisis at home induced it in 1968 to announce the accelerated closure of its bases east of Suez by 1971, whereas a 1966 British Defence White

Paper had provided for closure in the 'mid-1970s'. The main British pull-out was followed by a Five Power Commonwealth Defence Agreement (Singapore, Malaysia, Britain, Australia and New Zealand) but this was a small-scale, stop-gap arrangement with no definite commitment.

Britain's decision provoked a flurry, particularly in Singapore. It led to a rapid change of defence arrangements, but also to a re-assessment in Singapore and Malaysia of their relations with each other, with the region and the world beyond.

The immediate years after separation had been difficult for Malaysian–Singapore relations. In building up its separate national identity, Singapore stressed the differences between itself and its neighbours, accentuating, by comparison, pride in its achievements. It thus intensified its image as an arrogant Chinese city-state. But the accelerated British withdrawal brought realization that its safety and prosperity were bound up with that of Malaysia in particular and the rest of Southeast Asia in general. Thus it became the prime investor in the Second Malaysia Development Plan. The remaining formal links between the two countries were broken in the early-1970s with the split up of the joint airline in 1972, and the ending of joint currency control and stock market trading in 1973. These were, as often as not, causes for contention, and formal separation brought the opportunity for a more cordial relationsip between the two countries. Tan Siew Sin in announcing the end of the currency link compared the two states to 'Siamese twins whose future growth would be threatened unless they were separated'.

At the same time both countries realized their dependence on regional security and stability. The British military run-down in 1971, followed by the American withdrawal from Vietnam in 1972 and the fall of Indochina to the communists in 1975, underlined the need to build up regional co-operation, repair friendships and produce regional cohesion by making the Association of Southeast Asian Nations (ASEAN) work. Evolved in 1967 by Indonesia, Thailand, Malaysia, the Philippines and Singapore, ASEAN remained for some years disunited by competing economies and political friction, the Philippines persisting with its Sabah claim and Singapore resented by the other four members who saw the Republic as an economic parasite.

But from the early-1970s attitudes softened, Singapore adopting a more conciliatory and accommodating stance towards its neighbours, and by 1976 President Marcos of the Philippines was declaring that the Sabah claim was 'at a standstill'. The different countries co-operated in keeping communist subversion in check and the first ASEAN summit meeting of prime ministers at Bali in February 1976 saw an approach to economic co-operation.

In the broader field of international relations, both Singapore and

Malaysia were prepared to give strong support to ASEAN but had different views on ASEAN's role. While Singapore urged the need for the continuing presence of friendly big powers, Abdul Razak wanted to establish a zone of 'peace, freedom and neutrality' in Southeast Asia. In 1971 he induced ASEAN to adopt a Declaration of Neutralization of Southeast Asia, but because of Singapore's resistance this remained a paper resolution, even though none of the ASEAN countries wished to get caught in the Sino–Soviet dispute and the general tussle for super-power influence.

From his time of taking office Tun Abdul Razak shifted Malaysia from the pro-Western, anti-communist stand consistently adopted by his predecessor, in favour of a non-aligned stance. He took the lead in seeking a wider circle of friends by courting both Russia and China and creating links with North Korea, North Vietnam and East Germany.

He established formal relations with Russia in 1970 and himself visited Moscow in 1972. Malaysia was the first ASEAN country to seek out friendship with China. It sent a trade mission in 1971 and Tun Abdul Razak visited China in 1974 and established diplomatic relations. Thailand and the Philippines followed suit, and Lee Kuan Yew of Singapore visited China in 1976. But Singapore, wishing to play down its Chinese image resolved to be the last ASEAN country to forge diplomatic links with China.

After the communist victory in Indochina in 1975, Abdul Razak was in favour of inviting Vietnam and Cambodia to join ASEAN to help create a neutral zone, but Singapore advocated keeping American and other-power interest in the region. Tun Razak, not expecting the communist victory in Indochina to affect Malaysia, rejected any idea that ASEAN should confront a communist-dominated Indochina.

Communist Activity

The attitude of Singapore and Malaysia towards China was tied up with the question of communist subversion at home.

The Malayan Communist Party had never recognized the Federation of Malaysia nor the subsequent independence of Singapore and was committed in principle to overthrowing both governments. At the end of the communist Emergency in Malaya in 1960, the number of guerrillas was probably reduced to about 600, and they retreated to the jungles of southern Thailand. For the best part of a decade the Malayan Communist Party lay low, but, perhaps taking heart from the British announcement of military withdrawal in 1968, the party revived the armed struggle. They sent infiltrators from southern Thailand into the northern peninsular states, particularly in areas such as Perak where they had had strong bases during the Emergency. A Voice of the Malayan Revolution radio station, believed to be operating from southern China, started broadcasting in 1969, and the Malayan Communist Party used the racial disturbances in May that year to stir up ill-feeling towards the Malaysian government.

But the party was torn by bitter internal rivalries. About 1970 its central committee issued orders to kill all recruits who had joined the movement since 1962, on the grounds that they were untrustworthy and might be government agents. These orders were disobeyed and the recruits formed two rival organizations: the Malayan Communist Party Revolutionary Faction and the Malayan Communist Party Marxist-Leninist Faction. The latter, probably numbering only a few hundred men, formed a New People's Liberation Army, which came to blows with the Malayan Communist Party's National Liberation Army in southern Thailand.

Because of internal dissensions the communists made no concerted attacks in the peninsula in the early-1970s and there was a period of superficial calm, punctuated by sporadic attacks on security forces and installations by rival factions.

Violence centred at the time in Sarawak, which was a new area for communist activity. Unlike Sabah, where the Chinese community was affluent, in Sarawak there were many thousands of poverty stricken Chinese farmers and labourers open to communist influence. During Indonesian confrontation a North Kalimantan Communist Party, comprising ethnic Chinese from Kalimantan and left-wing extremists from Sarawak, was supported and equipped by President Sukarno. Communist Sarawak guerrillas fought with the Indonesians during confrontation, but after the collapse of the Indonesian Communist Party in 1965 ended the hope of setting up bases in Kalimantan, the communists changed tactics by setting up a communist party in Sarawak itself.

Indonesia crushed the guerrillas in Kalimantan and combined with the Malaysian army to drive the communists out of their Sarawak bases. All Chinese were cleared from the Indonesian Borneo border area, so that by 1978 probably only about sixty guerrillas of the North Kalimantan Communist Party remained in hiding and inoperative in the mountains around Kuching.

Meanwhile the Malayan Communist Party and its breakaway factions quietly recruited followers in peninsular Malaysia, where the period of comparative calm was broken in 1975, soon after Tun Abdul Razak's visit to China. In establishing diplomatic relations Abdul Razak hoped to get China to withdraw any support for the communist guerrillas. At the time a joint Peking-Kuala Lumpur communique stated that 'the social system of a country should only be chosen and decided by its own people', and Mao Tse-tung and Chou En-lai personally assured Tun Abdul Razak that China would not interfere in internal Malaysian affairs and regarded the communist menace as a domestic problem.

Despite this, insurgency in Malaysia flared up alarmingly soon after

Abdul Razak's return. From southern China the Voice of the Malayan Revolution continued to attack the Malaysian government, urging that the armed struggle should continue and that diplomatic relations between Malaysia and China 'cannot change the relationship of oppressors and oppressed' between the Malaysian government and 'the people of our country'. While other Southeast Asian countries wooed China, support still came from the Chinese Communist Party for communist subversive movements in Thailand, in Burma and the Philippines.

In April 1975, on the 45th anniversary of the founding of the Malayan Communist Party, Kuala Lumpur was alarmed when the New China News Agency publicised the Malayan Communist Party statement that 'we hold that the victory of our country's revolution cannot be achieved through the path of so-called "parliamentary democracy" or the path of armed uprisings in the cities' but 'can only be achieved through the path of surrounding the cities from the countryside and seizing political power through armed struggle', giving priority to Mao's methods.

The anniversary of the founding of the Malayan Communist Party coincided with the fall of Indochina to the communists, which gave a boost of confidence to communists in Malaysia. In the next few months they renewed attacks in Perak, in Kedah and on the Thai border, and also extended their operations to the urban areas, including Kuala Lumpur.

By 1976 the communists probably numbered about 3000 armed men: the Malayan Communist Party with about 2000 guerrillas, the Marxist–Leninist Faction numbering about 900 and the Revolutionary Faction about 200-300. They were supported by perhaps six times that number of *min yuen* or civilian underground supporters.

Most communist recruits were still Chinese, many of them coming from the new villages, where about 750,000 Chinese lived, often in squalid conditions. Despite measures to give some security of land tenure on long leases, most inhabitants were landless, many of them unemployed, unable to obtain citizenship and ripe for communist activity. In 1976 the Voice of the Malayan Revolution broadcast a seventeen point land reform programme promising to distribute land.

In order to develop a united front, the Malayan Communist Party set out also to extend its appeal to other communities, and in particular ordered the training of Malay revolutionaries to rouse the peasantry.

In the communist Emergency of 1948-60 in Malaya, victory was won largely because of the almost universal Malay rejection of communism. But by 1974 communists began to infiltrate the *bumiputras*. Many radical Malays were convinced after the communist victory in Indochina in 1975 that Malaysia was bound to be engulfed, and they accepted the Russian thesis that the Malays would do better to accept the Soviet brand of communism which would support Islam, Malay tradition and the monarchy, rather than succumb to Chinese communism.

The assumption that Marxism and Islam would never mix was shattered, when Malay journalists, including two senior Malaysian newspaper editors were arrested in June 1976 in Singapore and Malaysia, on accusations of stirring up anti-government feelings among the Malay minority in Singapore, as a prelude to penetrating the Malay majority in peninsular Malaysia. Later that year it was discovered that the communists had penetrated the inner ranks of UMNO itself, when a former Deputy Minister and five other ranking Malaysian politicians were detained on accusations of Soviet connections.

The Malayan Communist Party played upon the confused situation in the southern provinces of Thailand where Muslim dissidents sought freedom from Bangkok. While Thailand was suspicious of Malaysian support for its Muslim separatists, the prospect of a pro-communist Muslim state comprising south Thailand and northern Malaya alarmed the two governments far more, and co-operation on border operations was agreed to in 1965, permitting Malaysian troops to pursue guerrillas into Thailand. For a time in 1976, this co-operation broke down, but a change of regime in Bangkok in October that year permitted a new accord, and a full-scale combined Thai-Malaysia military operation brought relative quiet to the border area early in 1977.

By 1978, with co-operation between Malaysia, Singapore, Indonesia and Thailand, the emergency situation became stable.

While the authorities stepped up restrictions, refenced some new villages and revived many of the British Emergency measures, they recognized that the fight against communist insurrection could not rest on the force of arms alone but demanded social and economic development. 'The only defence against subversion is a socially just and united society'.[2] But the implementation of the New Economic Policy to benefit the *bumiputras* created racial tension, particularly among the poor Chinese, which the communists could exploit.

Peking's call early in 1978 for closer ties between the Chinese communist masses and the overseas Chinese 'to develop a deeper love for the country' worried Southeast Asian governments afresh. It seemed a return to the former Manchu-Kuomintang policy of tapping the great wealth and skills of the overseas Chinese.

Recovery in the 1970s

Within a few years after the 1969 riots Malaysia had recovered its equilibrium to a marked degree and the effect of the violence was to consolidate power in the hands of a moderate leadership. In benefiting the Malays the new policy stilled the demands of Malay extremists,

while non-Malays were shocked into accepting the long-term necessity
of redressing economic imbalance.

For a brief spell this new-found stability and moderation seemed
threatened by the sudden death of Tun Abdul Razak in January 1976.
His successor, Dato Hussein Onn, had been in the background of
Malaysian politics for more than twenty years, but was untried, virtually
unknown and had no political power base. Son of Dato Onn bin Ja'afar,
Hussein had been secretary-general of UMNO and leader of the party's
youth wing in the early days but resigned in 1951 with his father. After
that he became a lawyer, and rejoined UMNO only in 1968 at the
invitation of Tun Abdul Razak, his brother-in-law. He had thus taken
no direct part in the campaign for independence, and although he
became deputy prime minister in 1974, he had no strong following
within the party and played no active part in the 1974 elections.

Hussein, a compromise choice, was faced with immediate problems.
He came to office on the eve of the first ASEAN summit conference, at a
time of international uncertainty in the aftermath of the fall of Vietnam
to the communists. The Malaysian economy was in sharp decline with
the fall in price of primary products, so that domestic and foreign
investment fell away. A wave of communist insurgency plagued peninsular Malaysia, with rumours of secession plots in Sabah and Sarawak.
A liberal, using a laxer rein than his predecessor, Hussein's lack of
political experience encouraged factions to emerge. There was a danger
that the National Front which Tun Abdul Razak had built up might
crumble and that UMNO itself might lose its authority within the Malay
community.

The immediate crisis arose in the right wing of UMNO, with the
arrest on corruption charges, in November 1977, of Datuk Harun bin
Idris, *mentri besar* of Selangor and president of the youth wing of
UMNO, who had been prominent in the 1969 riots. Harun was convicted and the sentence upheld despite vociferous demonstrations from
his followers in favour of a pardon.

Hussein also had to keep political peace among the different parties
of the National Front. The Pan-Malayan Islamic Party was expelled
from the Front in December 1977, following its opposition to the
imposition of emergency rule in Kelantan after the dismissal of the
state's chief minister. The Front subsequently won a landslide victory in
Kelantan, regaining control of the state for the first time since 1959.

In Sabah at the time of Hussein taking office, Tun Mustapha was
rumoured to be plotting a challenge to UMNO. Until mid-1975 the
United Sabah National Organization held all the seats in the Sabah
Assembly in coalition with the Sabah Chinese Association. Sabah was
very prosperous, Mustapha exceedingly rich and powerful, but growing
criticism of his alleged corruption, high living and dictatorial rule led a
handful of United Sabah National Organization politicians in July 1975

to break away and form a new party, *Berjaya* (the United People's Party of Sabah), under the leadership of Datu Fuad Stephens,* head of state and one of Mustapha's oldest supporters. *Berjaya* accused Mustapha of plotting to get Sabah to secede from Malaysia, and there were suspicions that he planned to establish a Muslim state comprising Sabah and the southern Philippines. During his term of office he admitted thousands of Muslim refugees from the Philippines, and Kuala Lumpur had been embarrassed by Philippine accusations that the Sulu-born Mustapha was openly supporting Muslim rebels in Mindanao, supplying them with arms and money in the hope of creating a new Islamic nation.

In October 1975 Mustapha resigned as chief minister after long differences with Abdul Razak but continued as leader of the United Sabah National Organization to dominate Sabah through trusted followers who assumed office in his place. Tun Abdul Razak encouraged the new *Berjaya* party to challenge Mustapha but at the time of Razak's death *Berjaya* held only three seats in the Sabah state assembly.

Immediately after Razak's death, the Sabah government called a snap election, expecting to sweep the polls. It represented a challenge to Hussein and to Malaysia's hold over Sabah, but in a surprise result in April 1976 the *Berjaya* party was swept to power and Fuad Stephens formed a government. Two months later he was killed in an air crash, along with other senior *Berjaya* ministers, but his deputy, Datuk Harris bin Mohd.Salleh, took over, bringing Sabah much closer politically to peninsular Malaysia. The secession fears faded, and Sabah developed an independent yet friendly relationship with the Hussein government. Mustapha tried to win over *Berjaya* supporters and assemblymen in a bid to regain power in November 1977 but failed and was seemingly reduced to ineffective opposition.

Hussein came to office shortly before the Third Malaysia Plan was due to be launched, but modified the plan in order to give more emphasis to the battle against poverty. The communist upsurge in 1975-6 showed the urgent need to eradicate poverty among all races and to achieve a 7 per cent economic growth. Almost double the amount was allocated to rural development schemes compared with the Second Plan and the basic aim was still to enable Malays to catch up with others, but Hussein revised Abdul Razak's plan in order to give a more multi-racial approach, promising land for Chinese, more government jobs for Indians, and safeguards for foreign capital.

Within two years of Hussein's takeover he was firmly in the seat of power. He was fortunate in coming to office at a time when the economy was on the upturn, with rubber, tin and palm oil prices rising, and in 1977 Malaysia achieved a record surplus. Hussein had stood firm over Harun, tamed the right wing of UMNO and established UMNO's

---

* Formerly Datu Donald Stephens before his conversion to Islam.

Datuk Harris bin Mohd Salleh *(By courtesy of the Sabah Information Department).*

Mount Kinabalu *(By courtesy of the Sabah Information Department).*

Jesselton (later Kota Kinabalu) after Allied bombing in 1945 *(By courtesy of the Sabah Information Department).*

Kota Kinabalu in 1979 *(By courtesy of the Sabah Information Department).*

Bajau Horseman *(By courtesy of the Sabah Information Department)*.

authority in Kelantan. Communism was in check, with terrorism declining and communist guerrillas on the run on the Thai and Kalimantan borders. Sabah and Sarawak were firmly established within Malaysia, their governments working amicably with Kuala Lumpur.

Hussein himself grew in the post, commanding increasing respect, acting with firmness and standing for honest, straight-forward government.

1978 Election

From this position of strength, in July 1978 Hussein Onn called a general election in order to secure a clear mandate to push through the Third Malaysia Development Plan.

The National Front, comprising ten parties, including the Malaysian Chinese Association and Chinese-based *Gerakan,* the Malayan Indian Congress and largely Indian-based People's Progressive Party, threw their weight behind Hussein Onn as the only leader who could provide a workable multi-racial government.

The Front won a comfortable majority and UMNO triumphed, winning seventy out of the seventy-five seats it contested in peninsular Malaysia, at the expense of the Pan Malayan Islamic Party opposition. At the same time UMNO emerged even more dominant in the National Front, since the Malaysian Chinese Association and Malayan Indian Congress did not fare so well. Despite dissensions within the Democratic Action Party and a ban on public campaigning, the party attracted a strong backing, particularly from Chinese who, as in 1969, were disappointed with the Malaysian Chinese Association.

The election represented a triumph for the moderates, making Hussein the unchallenged leader of the Malays, with greater authority over the minority partners in the ruling National Front. It meant the eclipse of the Malay extremists who had been fighting for strict Muslim government and the application of Muslim laws. But it showed that while the *bumiputra* programme had succeeded to a large extent in improving the Malays' lot, it had aroused the discontent of other communities. While non-Malays were prepared to accept the need to raise the status of the Malays, they resented the implementation and degree of discrimination and disability caused by the new economic policy and education restrictions.

Brunei

Through all these years Brunei survived as a peaceful and prosperous but potentially dangerous anachronism. Its semi-colonial status was an embarrassment to Britain, a subject of criticism in the United Nations, but it was the voluntary choice of its sultan, who refused to consider granting representative government.

Under an agreement made with Britain in 1971 Brunei became independent, but the sultan insisted on Britain retaining responsibility for foreign affairs and supervision of defence, although he contributed to defence costs. While the sultan described Brunei as 'a sovereign nation and self-governing state', Malaysia, Indonesia and the sultan's political opponents among his subjects urged self determination and free elections, and the United Nations criticized Brunei's status. Malaysia sponsored a resolution adopted in the United Nations in December 1975 calling for the Brunei people to choose their own government, for lifting the ban on political parties and for the return of

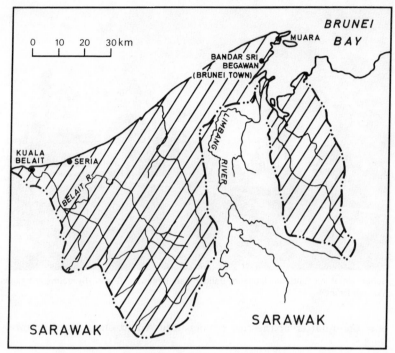

Brunei

all political exiles to Brunei. While the Labour Government in Britain would gladly have cut the links, the sultan saw the tie with Britain as giving the greatest freedom for himself and for his state, seeing the association as a protection against the possible encroachment of neighbouring governments, secessionists and political opponents within Brunei itself.

In June 1978 Sultan Sir Hassanal Bokiah and his father* flew to London in a final unsuccessful bid to resist the final break with Britain, but were compelled to sign an agreement by which Brunei was to become a sovereign independent state at the end of 1983.

Meanwhile the tiny state prospered, with oil revenues accounting for more than 90 per cent of its national income. But the oil industry did not furnish the basis for a permanent economy, and provided little employment. A National Development Plan for 1975–9 aimed to create 10 000 new jobs, to bring in industries and improve agriculture, but farming by tradition was despised and neglected in the state, producing

---

* Sultan Omar abdicated in favour of his son Sir Hassanal Bokiah in 1967 but retained his influence as adviser to the throne.

Sultan Omar Ali Saiffudin Mosque, Bandar Seri Begawan, Brunei *(By courtesy of the Muzium Brunei)*.

only one-quarter of the rice Brunei needed and one-fifth of its total food.

Conclusion

By the late 1970s Singapore and Malaysia were established as separate nations, with few prospects for future merger. Singapore had defied probability to become a viable, prosperous state with an individuality of its own. Energy and vigour, coupled with a decisive government prepared to exploit every opportunity for advancement, gave the momentum needed to survive and prosper despite its vulnerable economy.

Malaysia was fairly firmly set at its present boundaries and secession fears were waning. Both Sabah and Sarawak were concerned primarily with the process of modernization. While the two Borneo states were not fully assimilated, they were lightly ruled from Kuala Lumpur and profited materially from the union, particularly Sarawak whose progress had been held back during the long years of Brooke rule.

While Brunei continued to thrive in peace, a question mark hung over its long term future as an independent unit.

For Malaysia communalism was still a burning issue, and government policy was dominated by the need to weld one nation through a common Malay language, and to integrate the basically agrarian, rural

Malays into the commercial and industrial sector dominated by the Chinese and Indians, so that all Malaysians could live side by side, irrespective of ethnic origin. While Singapore had gone a long way towards its goal of creating a multi-racial society, it still needed to dispel its image as a Chinese city state in a Malayo–Muslim region.

Both Malaysia and Singapore had fairly stable political organization, a good administrative infrastructure and reasonably effective judicial systems. Both had a framework of parliamentary government but were somewhat authoritarian, retaining colonial emergency regulations which imposed restrictions on the individual. Malaysia was the more democratic, with a federal system of checks and balances, which acted as a challenge to the emergence of any powerful central leadership. Whereas the National Front government in Malaysia worked in effect through a consensus pattern of group bargaining, Singapore from 1968 was controlled by one party with a strong leadership, working through a framework of consultation devised and controlled by itself; although this situation arose largely by choice and the lack of a credible opposition.

Both countries had a mixed economy. Singapore developed its own brand of socialism after attaining independence, in favour of state participation in industry and commerce but with management in general in the hands of private enterprise. The state shared profits and used revenue for the betterment of the population, especially in providing housing, education and a sound infrastructure for the economy, rejecting the idea of a welfare state but trying to give equal opportunity for individuals to rise out of poverty. Malaysia moved from a free capitalist economy after 1969 to more state participation and control, in the interests of restructuring society. While Singapore aimed for maximum profit to remain competitive in a world of growing trade protectionism, Malaysia, enjoying good natural resources and a sizeable domestic market, had to follow a more complicated policy to raise prosperity with a more equal spread among ethnic communities yet sacrificing some efficiency in face of political and social considerations.

Thus both Singapore and Malaysia adapted the political and economic systems inherited from a colonial past to suit their individual needs. While they grew apart in character, they tended to live side by side more happily, both anxious for peace in the region, realizing that their interdependence for economic growth and stability meant co-operation with each other and support for ASEAN.

1. Hon, Sui Sen, Minister for Finance. Speech reported in *The Mirror* (Singapore), 11 April 1977, Vol 13, no. 15.

2. Government of Malaysia, Parliamentary White papers, on *Resurgence of Armed Communism in West Malaysia*, Government Printer, Kuala Lumpur 1971; *Threat of Armed Communism in Sarawak*, Government Printer, Kuala Lumpur, 1972.

Further Reading

In addition to the following recommended books, many useful articles are to be found in the *Journal of the Malaysian Branch, Royal Asiatic Society* and its predecessor, the *Journal of the Straits Branch, Royal Asiatic Society,* (1878-1922), in the *Journal of Southeast Asian History* (1960-69) and its successor the *Journal of Southeast Asian Studies.* Also in the *Journal of the Indian Archipelago and Eastern Asia,* (Singapore 1847-59) and reprinted Kraus Reprints, Liechtenstein, 1970.

GENERAL: SOUTHEAST ASIA

Bastin, J. S. & Benda, H. J. *A History of Modern Southeast Asia.* Prentice Hall, Englewood Cliffs, New Jersey, 1968.

Brimmell, J. D. *Communism in Southeast Asia.* Oxford University Press, London, 1959.

Cady, J. *Southeast Asia: its Historical Development.* McGraw Hill, New York, 1964.

Hall, D. G. E. *A History of South-East Asia.* 3rd edn., Macmillan, London, 1968.

Harrison, B. *South East Asia: a Short History.* 3rd edn., Macmillan, London and St Martin's Press, New York, 1966.

Kahin, G. McT. (ed.) *Governments and Politics of Southeast Asia.* 2nd edn., Cornell University Press, Ithaca, 1964.

Steinberg, D. J. (ed.) et al. *In Search of Southeast Asia.* Praeger, New York, 1971.

Tarling, N. *A Concise History of Southeast Asia.* Praeger, New York, 1966.

Wang Gungwu *A Short History of the Nanyang Chinese.* Eastern Universities Press, Singapore, 1959.

GENERAL: MALAYSIA, SINGAPORE, BRUNEI

Allen G. C. and Donnithorne, A. G. *Western Enterprise in Indonesia and Malaya.* Allen & Unwin, London, 1957. Reprinted Kelley, New York, 1968.

Bastin, J. S. and Roolvink, R. (eds.) *Malayan and Indonesian Studies: Essays presented to Sir Richard Winstedt.* Clarendon Press, Oxford, 1964.

Bastin, J. S. and Winks, R. W. *Malaysia: Selected Historical Readings.* Oxford University Press, Kuala Lumpur, 1966. 2nd edn.,Liechtenstein, 1978.

Carey, Iskander *Orang Asli: the Aboriginal Tribes of Peninsular Malaysia.* Oxford University Press, Kuala Lumpur, 1976.

Gullick, J. M. *Indigenous Political Systems of Western Malaya.* Athlone Press, London, 1965.

Jones, L. W. *The Population of Borneo: a study of the Peoples of Sarawak, Sabah and Brunei.* Athlone Press, London, 1966.

Lim Chong-Yah *Economic Development of Modern Malaya.* Oxford University Press, Kuala Lumpur, 1967.

Purcell, V. *The Chinese in Malaya.* Oxford University Press, London, 1948. Reprinted Oxford University Press, Kuala Lumpur, 1967.

Ryan, N. J. *The Cultural Heritage of Malaya.* 2nd edn., Longman, Kuala Lumpur, 1971.

Ryan, N. J. *A History of Malaysia and Singapore.* Oxford University Press, Kuala Lumpur, 1976.

Tregonning, K. G. (ed.) *Malaysian Historical Sources.* University of Singapore, 1962.

Tregonning, K. G. (ed.) *Papers on Malayan History,* Singapore, 1962.

Turnbull, C. M. *A History of Singapore, 1819-1975.* Oxford University Press, Kuala Lumpur, 1977.

Wang Gungwu (ed.) *Malaysia: a Survey.* Praeger, New York, 1964.

Wilkinson, R. J. *A History of the Peninsular Malays.* Singapore, 1923. Reprinted AMS Press, New York, 1975.

Wilkinson, R. J. *Papers on Malay Subjects.* Edited and selected by P. L. Burns. Oxford in Asia Reprints, Oxford University Press, Kuala Lumpur, 1971.

Winstedt, R. O. *A History of Malaya.* Luzac, London, 1935.

Winstedt, R. O., *Malaya and Its History.* 7th edn. Hutchinson, London, 1966.

Winstedt, R. O. *The Malays: a Cultural History.* 6th edn., Routledge & Kegan Paul, London, 1961

EARLY HISTORY

Devahuti, D. *India and Ancient Malaya.* Eastern Universities Press, Singapore, 1965.

Dunn, F. L. *Rain Forest Collectors and Traders: a Study of Resource Utilization in Modern and Ancient Malaya.* Malaysian Branch of the Royal Asiatic Society Monograph No. 5, Kuala Lumpur, 1975.

Harrisson, T. and B. *The Prehistory of Sabah.* Sabah Society, Kota Kinabalu, 1971.

Tweedie, M. W. F. *Prehistoric Malaya.* Donald Moore, Singapore, 1957.

Wheatley, P. *The Golden Khersonese: Studies in the Historical Geography of the Malay Peninsula before A.D. 1500.* University of Malaya Press, Kuala Lumpur, 1966.

Wheatley, P. *Impressions of the Malay Peninsula in Ancient Times.* Donald Moore, Singapore, 1964.

MELAKA SULTANATE

Brown, C. C. (trans.) *The Malay Annals,* Oxford University Press, Kuala Lumpur, 1970. This first appeared as *Journal of the Malayan Branch, Royal Asiatic Society,* XXV, parts 2 and 3, 1952.

Wolters, O. W. *The Fall of Srivijaya in Malay History,* Cornell University Press, Ithaca, 1970.

SIXTEENTH TO EIGHTEENTH CENTURIES

Andaya, L. Y. *The Kingdom of Johor, 1641-1728.* Oxford University Press, Kuala Lumpur, 1975.

Bassett, D. K. *British Trade and Policy in Indonesia and Malaysia in the Late 18th Century.* Zug, Switzerland, 1971.

Bonney, R. *Kedah, 1771-1821: the Search for Security and Independence.* Oxford University Press, Kuala Lumpur, 1971.

Boxer, C. R. *The Dutch Seaborne Empire, 1600-1800.* Hutchinson, London, 1965.

Cortesao, A. (ed.) *The 'Suma Oriental' of Tomé Pires.* 2 vols., Hakluyt Society. London, 1944.

Meilink-Roelofsz, M. A. P. *Asian Trade and European Influence in the Indonesian Archipelago between 1500 and about 1630.* Nijhoff, The Hague, 1962.

Sandin, Benedict *The Sea Dayaks of Borneo before White Rajah Rule.* Macmillan, London, 1967.

THE BRITISH COLONIAL PERIOD

Contemporary Nineteenth Century Works

Abdullah bin Abdul Kadir, Munshi *The Hikayat Abdullah* translated by A. H. Hill. Oxford University Press, Kuala Lumpur, 1970. This translation first appeared as *Journal of the Malayan Branch, Royal Asiatic Society,* XXVIII (3), 1955. The work was originally published in Malay in Singapore, 1849.

Begbie, P. J. *The Malayan Peninsula.* Vepery Mission Press, Madras, 1834. Reprinted Oxford University Press, Kuala Lumpur, 1967.

Birch, J. W. W. *The Journals of J. W. W. Birch, First British Resident of Perak, 1874-1875,* (P. L. Burns, ed.). Oxford University Press, Kuala Lumpur, 1976.

Bird (Bishop), I. L. *The Golden Chersonese and the Way Thither.* London, 1883. Reprinted, Oxford University Press, Kuala Lumpur, 1967.

Buckley, C. B. *An Anecdotal History of Singapore in Old Times.* 2 vols., Fraser & Neave, Singapore, 1902. Reprinted in one volume, University of Malaya Press, Kuala Lumpur, 1965.

Cameron, J. *Our Tropical Possessions in Malayan India.* Smith & Elder, London, 1865. Reprinted, Oxford University Press, Kuala Lumpur, 1965.

Earl, G. W. *The Eastern Seas.* Allen & Co., London, 1837. Reprinted, Oxford University Press, Kuala Lumpur, 1971.

Low, Hugh *Sarawak: its Inhabitants and Productions.* Richard Bentley, London, 1848. Reprinted Cass, London, 1968.

Low, James *A Dissertation on the Soil and Agriculture of the British Settlement of Penang or Prince of Wales Island.* Singapore, 1836. Reprinted as *The British Settlement of Penang.* Oxford University Press, Kuala Lumpur, 1972.

McNair, J. F. A. *Perak and the Malays.* London, 1878. Reprinted, Oxford University Press, Kuala Lumpur, 1972.

Newbold, T. J. *Political and Statistical Account of the British Settlements in the Straits of Malacca.* 2 vols., Murray, London, 1839. Reprinted Oxford University Press, Kuala Lumpur, 1971.

St John, Spenser *Life in the Forests of the Far East.* 2 vols., Elder, London, 1862. Reprinted Oxford University Press, Kuala Lumpur, 1974.

Swettenham, F. *British Malaya.* Lane, London, 1907. 3rd revised edition, Allen & Unwin, London, 1948.

Swettenham, F. *Sir Frank Swettenham's Malayan Journals, 1874-1876,* (P. L. Burns and C. D. Cowan, eds.). Oxford University Press, Kuala Lumpur, 1975.

Vaughan, J. D. *Manners and Customs of the Chinese of the Straits Settlements.* Mission Press, Singapore, 1879. Reprinted Oxford University Press, Kuala Lumpur, 1971.

Others

Blythe, W. L. *The Impact of Chinese Secret Societies in Malaya.* Oxford University Press, London, 1969.

Chai Hon-Chan. *The Development of British Malaya, 1896-1909.* 2nd edition, Oxford University Press, Kuala Lumpur, 1967.

Clodd, H. P. *Malaya's First British Pioneer: the Life of Francis Light.* Luzac, London, 1948.

Comber, L. *Chinese Secret Societies in Malaya: Survey of the Triad Society from 1800 to 1900.* Locust Valley, New York, 1959.

Cowan, C. D. *Nineteenth Century Malaya: the Origins of British Political Control.* Oxford University Press, London, 1961.

Drabble, J. *Rubber In Malaya, 1876-1922.* Oxford University Press, Kuala Lumpur, 1973.

Emerson, R. *Malaysia: a Study in Direct and Indirect Rule.* Macmillan, New York & London, 1937. Reprinted University of Malaya Press, Kuala Lumpur, 1964.

Hill, R. D. *Rice in Malaya: a Study in Historical Geography.* Oxford University Press, Kuala Lumpur, 1977.

Irwin, G. *Nineteenth Century Borneo: a Study in Diplomatic Rivalry.* Nijhoff, The Hague, 1955.

Jackson, J. C. *Planters and Speculators: Chinese and European Agricultural Enterprise in Malaya, 1786-1921.* University of Malaya Press, Kuala Lumpur, 1968.

Jackson, R. N. *Immigration, Labour and the Development of Malaya, 1786-1920.* Government Printer, Kuala Lumpur, 1961.

Jackson, R. N. *Pickering: Protector of Chinese.* Oxford University Press, Kuala Lumpur, 1966.

Khoo Kay Kim. *The Western Malay States, 1850-1873.* Oxford University Press, Kuala Lumpur, 1972.

Lee Poh Ping *Chinese Society in Nineteenth Century Singapore.* Oxford University Press, Kuala Lumpur, 1978.

Lim Teck Ghee *Peasants and their Agricultural Economy in Colonial Malaya, 1874-1941.* Oxford University Press, London, 1977.

Loh Fook Seng, P. *The Malay States: Political Change and Social Policy, 1877-1895.* Oxford University Press, Kuala Lumpur, 1969.

Mills, L. A. *British Malaya, 1824-67.* Oxford University Press, Kuala Lumpur, 1966. Reprint of *Journal of the Malayan Branch, Royal Asiatic Society,* XXXIII, part 3, 1960 (ed. C. M. Turnbull), which was a revised edition of the *Journal of the Malayan Branch, Royal Asiatic Society,* III, part 2, 1925.

Parkinson, C. N. *British Intervention in Malaya, 1867-77.* University of Malaya Press, Singapore, 1960.

Parmer, J. N. *Colonial Labor Policy and Administration: a History of Labor in the Rubber Plantation Industry in Malaya, c. 1910-1941.* J. J. Augustin, New York, 1960.

Pringle, R. *Rajas and Rebels: the Ibans of Sarawak under Brooke Rule, 1841-1941.* Macmillan, London, 1970.

Roff, W. R. *The Origins of Malay Nationalism.* Yale University Press, New Haven, and University of Malaya Press, Kuala Lumpur, 1967.

Runciman, S. *The White Rajas. A History of Sarawak from 1841 to 1946.* Cambridge University Press, London, 1960.

Sadka, E. *The Protected Malay States, 1874-1895.* University of Malaya Press, Kuala Lumpur, 1968.

Sandhu, Kernial Singh *Indians in Malaya: Immigration and Settlement, 1786-1957.* Cambridge University Press, London, 1969.

Song Ong Siang *One Hundred Years' History of the Chinese in Singapore.* Murray, London, 1923. Reprinted University of Malaya Press, Kuala Lumpur, 1967.

Stevenson, R. *Cultivators and Administrators: British Educational Policy towards the Malays, 1875-1906.* Oxford University Press, Kuala Lumpur, 1975.

Tarling, N. *Anglo–Dutch Rivalry in the Malay World, 1780-1824.* Cambridge University Press, London, and University of Queensland Press, St Lucia, 1962.

Tarling, N. *Britain, the Brookes and Brunei.* Oxford University Press, Kuala Lumpur, 1971.

Tarling, N. *British Policy in the Malay Peninsula and the Archipelago, 1824-1871.* Oxford University Press, Kuala Lumpur, 1969. Reprint of *Journal of the Malayan Branch, Royal Asiatic Society,* XXX, part 3, 1957.

Tarling, N. *Imperial Britain in Southeast Asia.* Oxford University Press, Kuala Lumpur, 1975.

Tarling, N. *Piracy and Politics in the Malay World.* F. W. Cheshire, Melbourne, 1963. Reprinted Kraus, Liechtenstein, 1978.

Tarling, N. *Sulu and Sabah: a Study of British Policy towards the Philippines and Northern Borneo from the late 18th Century.* Oxford University Press, Kuala Lumpur, 1978.

Thio, E. *British Policy in the Malay Peninsula, 1880-1910. Vol. I, the Southern and Central States.* University of Malaya Press, Kuala Lumpur, 1969.

Tregonning, K. G. *The British in Malaya: the First Forty Years, 1786-1826.* University of Arizona Press, Tucson, 1965.

Tregonning, K. G. *A History of Modern Sabah, 1881-1963.* University of Malaya Press, Kuala Lumpur, 1965. A revised edition of *Under Chartered Company Rule: North Borneo, 1881-1946.* University of Malaya Press, Singapore, 1958.

Tregonning, K. G. *Home Port Singapore: a History of Straits Steamship Company Limited, 1890-1965.* Oxford University Press, Singapore, 1967.

Trocki, C. *Prince of Pirates: the Temenggongs and the Development of Johor and Singapore, 1784-1885.* Singapore University Press, Singapore, 1978.

Turnbull, C. M. *The Straits Settlements, 1826-67.* Athlone Press, London, and Oxford University Press, Kuala Lumpur, 1972.

Wong Lin Ken *The Malayan Tin Industry to 1914.* University of Arizona Press, Tucson, 1965.

Wright, L. R. *The Origins of British Borneo.* Hong Kong University Press, Hong Kong, 1970.

Wurtzburg, C. E. *Raffles of the Eastern Isles.* Hodder & Stoughton, London, 1954.

Yen Ching Hwang *The Overseas Chinese and the 1911 Revolution, with Special Reference to Malaya and Singapore.* Oxford University Press, Kuala Lumpur, 1976.

THE PACIFIC WAR AND THE JAPANESE OCCUPATION

Allen, L. *Singapore, 1941-42.* Davis-Poynter, London, 1977.

Barber, N. *Sinister Twilight.* Collins, London, 1968.

Chin Kee Onn *Malaya Upside Down.* Jitts, Singapore, 1946.

Kirby, S. Woodburn *Singapore, the Chain of Disaster.* Cassell, London, 1971.

Percival, A. E. *The War in Malaya.* Eyre & Spottiswoode, London, 1949.

Shinozaki, M. *Syonan, my Story.* Singapore, 1975.

Tsuji, M. *Singapore: the Japanese Version.* Sydney, 1960.

Thompson, Virginia *Postmortem on Malaya.* Macmillan, New York, 1943.

POST-WAR AND INDEPENDENCE

Allen, J. De Vere *The Malayan Union.* Yale University Press, New Haven, 1967.

Allen, R. *Malaysia, Prospect and Retrospect.* Oxford University Press, London, 1968.

Baker, M. H. *North Borneo, the First Ten Years, 1946-56.* Malayan Publishing House, Singapore, 1962.

Clutterbuck, R. *The Long Long War. The Emergency in Malaya, 1948-1960.* Cassell, London, 1967.

Clutterbuck, R. *Riot and Revolution in Singapore and Malaya, 1945-63.* Faber & Faber, London, 1973.

Donnison, F. S. V. *British Military Administration in the Far East.* H.M.S.O., London, 1956.

Hanrahan, G. Z. *The Communist Struggle in Malaya.* Institute of Pacific Relations, New York, 1954. Reprinted University of Malaya Press, Kuala Lumpur, 1971.

Josey, A. *Lee Kuan Yew.* Singapore, 1968. 2nd revised edition, Donald Moore, Singapore, 1971.

Lee, Edwin *The Towkays of Sabah.* Singapore University Press, Singapore, 1976.

Means, G. *Malaysian Politics.* 2nd edition, Hodder & Stoughton, London, 1976.

Miller, Harry *Prince and Premier: a Biography of Tunku Abdul Rahman.* George C. Harrap, London, 1959.

Milne, R. S. *Government and Politics in Malaysia.* Houghton Mifflin, Boston, 1967.

Mills, L. A. *Malaya: a Political and Economic Appraisal.* University of Minnesota Press, Minneapolis, 1958.

Pye, L. W. *Guerrilla Communism in Malaya.* Princeton University Press, New Jersey, 1956.

Ratnam, K. J. *Communalism and the Political Process in Malaya.* Oxford University Press, Kuala Lumpur, 1965.

Roff, M. *The Politics of Belonging: Political Change in Sabah and Sarawak.* Oxford University Press, Kuala Lumpur, 1974.

Short, A. *The Communist Insurrection in Malaya, 1948-60.* Muller, London, 1975.

Sopiee, Mohamed Noordin. *From Malayan Union to Singapore Separation.* University of Malaya Press, Kuala Lumpur, 1974.

Stenson, M. *Industrial Conflict in Malaya: Prelude to the Communist Revolt of 1948.* Oxford University Press, London, 1970.

Tilman, R. O. *Bureaucratic Transition in Malaya.* Duke University Press, Durham, N.C., 1964.

Yeo Kim Wah *Political Development in Singapore, 1945-55.* Singapore University Press, Singapore, 1973.

Glossary

adat: Malay customary law
adat perpateh: indigenous Malay customary law
adat temenggong: Malay customary law modified by Indian practice
agar-agar: seaweed (for making jelly)
arrack: Asian distilled spirits
bahasa: language
Barisan Sosialis: Socialist Front
bendahara: chief minister
budak raja: raja's followers (literally raja's children)
bumiputra: Malays and other indigenous Malaysians
bunga mas: gold and silver flowers tribute (literally golden flowers)
daeng: Buginese title of nobility
dato, datuk: title of distinction for male, non-royal person (literally grandfather)
derhaka: treason against a Malay ruler
Dewan Bahasa dan Pustaka: Language and Literary Agency
Dewan Negara: Senate (Upper House, Malaysian parliament)
Dewan Rakyat: House of Representatives (Lower House, Malaysian parliament)
epposho: clubs for Chinese (Japanese occupation)
gunong: mountain
gutta percha: resin from the percha tree, precursor of modern rubber
haj: pilgrimage to Mecca
haji: one who has performed the pilgrimage to Mecca
hodosho: consultative committee (Japanese occupation)
imam: leading mosque official
Jawi-peranakan: local-born Muslim of mixed Malay/Indian ancestry
kampong: Malay village
kangany: Indian labour recruiter
kangchu: Chinese river headman (in Johor)
kapitan: community head
Kaum muda: Islamic reformists (literally young faction)
laksamana: admiral
linga: phallus
lombong: open cast (mining)
manora: Thai dance drama group

mantri: Malay official

mentri besar: chief official (of a state)

merantau: Minangkabau custom of 'wandering'

merdeka: independence

min yuen (min chung yuen thong): popular mass movement (underground civilian supporters of communists during the Emergency).

negri: state, country

orang besar: great chief(s) (literally big man)

orang kaya (and *orang kaya-kaya* in Perak): important chief(s) (literally rich man)

orang laut: sea people, sea nomads, coastal aborigines

pangiran: Brunei title of the lesser nobility

pantun: verse

penghulu: district headman

penghulu bendahari: treasurer

pulau: island

raja: prince, ruler

raja muda: heir apparent

rakyat: common people, peasantry

rial: Spanish silver coin

rukunegara: declaration of ideology

sejarah: history, chronicle

shahbandar: harbour master, trade official

sharif: Arab title

sinkheh: Chinese new immigrant

suku: clan

sungei: river

temenggong: Malay minister in charge of defence and justice

toddy: coconut palm wine, popular among the Indian community

tunku: Malay prince of royal blood

undang-undang: Minangkabau clan chiefs, laws

waris: Minangkabau headman

wayang kulit: shadow theatre

yamtuan muda (yang di-pertuan muda): under king

yang di-pertuan: he who is lord

yang di-pertuan agong: supreme head of state (Malaysia)

yang di-pertuan besar: head of state (Negri Sembilan)

Index